GARLAND STUDIES IN

AMERICAN POPULAR HISTORY AND CULTURE

edited by

JEROME NADELHAFT
UNIVERSITY OF MAINE

T0348035

A GARLAND SERIES

Garland Studies in American Popular History and Culture
Jerome Nadelhaft, series editor

THE LYRICS
OF CIVILITY

BIBLICAL IMAGES AND
POPULAR MUSIC LYRICS
IN AMERICAN CULTURE

KENNETH G. BIELEN

LONDON AND NEW YORK

Published in 1999 by
Garland Publishing Inc.

Published 2014 by Routledge

2 Park Square, Milton Park, Abingdon, Oxfordshire OX14 4RN

711 Third Avenue, New York, NY 10017

First issued in paperback 2014

Routledge is an imprint of the Taylor & Francis Group, an informa business

Library of Congress Cataloging-in-Publication Data
Bielen, Kenneth G.
    The lyrics of civility : Biblical images and popular music lyrics in American culture / Kenneth G. Bielen.
        p. cm. — (Garland studies in American popular history and culture)
    Discography: p.
    Includes bibliographical references.
    ISBN 978-0-8153-3193-3 (hbk)
    ISBN 978-1-1380-1207-3 (pbk)
    1. Popular music—United States—Texts—Religious aspects. I. Title.
II. Series.
ML3921.8.P67B54 1999
782.42164'0973—dc21   99-33782

Contents

Preface

In the early 1970s, I was a young graduate student at the University of Rhode Island in the Department of Geography. During my free time I was a disc jockey on the campus radio station WRIU-FM. Sunday afternoons I dedicated a segment of my time slot to music with religious images. I studied lyric sheets making notes of words that echoed the search for the sacred and for meaning in life. Shortly after I left the university I found myself living on an apple farm in the center of the Netherlands. The farm was part of a study community called L'Abri. An art history professor from the Free University of Amsterdam named Hans Rookmaaker (1922–1977) oversaw the community. Dr. Rookmaaker was a fan of American gospel music and jazz, and particularly, of Mahalia Jackson and Louis Armstrong. His thoughts on rock music in his book *Modern Art and the Death of a Culture* (1970) led me to the village of Eck en Wiel. He encouraged me to write about popular music. Thus, the study that culminates in this book began with thoughts and conversations in Kingston and the South County area of our smallest state and across the Atlantic in the orchard and fields surrounding an 18th Century farmhouse named Kortenhoeve.

I want to thank Professor Jerry Nadelhaft for seeing the promise in my original manuscript and offering the opportunity for publication. Also, thanks to Richard Koss, my editor at Garland, for pressing me to finish.

Portions of this work originated with my dissertation in the American Culture Studies program at Bowling Green State University. Thanks to Dr. Bruce L. Edwards (formerly of the English Department), Dr. Jack Nachbar (formerly of the Department of Popular Culture) and Professor William L. Schurk, Sound Recording Archivist, of the Music

Library and Sound Recording Archives at the university for their encouragement and suggestions.

I want to thank Mr. Joel Whitburn of Record Research of Menomonee Falls, Wisconsin. Mr. Whitburn has compiled a wonderful series of books that detail the performance of popular music singles and albums on the *Billboard* popularity charts. He has given permission to use the chart data in the text of the book.

My appreciation goes out to Professor William Edgar of Westminster Theological Seminary in Philadelphia for his enthusiastic response to an earlier version of the manuscript. Thanks to Ms. Rini Cobbey for closely reading the text and helping me to see the strengths and weaknesses. Thanks to my sisters, Judy and Joyce, for lots of music discussions and sharing concerts over the years.

This work could not have been completed without the support of my family and the strength they provide. Hugs and kisses to my children Kelly, Alex and Dylan who keep me young and let me know what youth are listening to these days. Words can not express my gratitude to my wife Mary. She has encouraged me to follow my dreams and I could not have done this without her.

I dedicate this work to my parents, Stan and Fran Bielen.

Ken Bielen
Bowling Green, Ohio
April 24, 1999

Introduction

Popular music is a forum for the discussion of God and religion in American culture. In 1999, hip hop artist Lauryn Hill received five Grammy Awards for her solo debut *The Miseducation of Lauryn Hill*, an album replete with Biblical images. Madonna sings a techno world-beat version of a prayer derived from the Yoga Taravali on her album *Ray of Light* (1998); Aretha Franklin closes the VH1 Divas Live 1998 concert proclaiming the name of Jesus over and over and announcing "we're going to have church here tonight"; country singer Faith Hill asks for God's help in "Somebody Stand By Me," a song penned by Sheryl Crow, a top artist of the late 1990s; and dance-pop debutante Jennifer Paige asks "Questions" of God about the purpose of her life. Whether the genre is contemporary hit radio, rap, new country, modern rock, rhythm and blues, adult contemporary or alternative, recording artists reveal their posture toward spiritual matters in their lyrics.

Several years earlier, in 1996, a number of popular recordings explored the character of God. Not since the Jesus rock of the late 1960s and early 1970s (the time of Norman Greenbaum's "Spirit in the Sky," the Five Man Electrical Band's "Signs," James Taylor's "Fire and Rain," and the Edwin Hawkins Singers's "Oh, Happy Day") was the presence of God so audible on the contemporary hit radio format. Dishwalla's "Counting Blue Cars," Jewel's "Who Will Save Your Soul," Dog's Eye View's "Everything Falls Apart," Jars of Clay's "Flood," and Joan Osborne's "One of Us" were all best-sellers in 1996.

The cover of the 1998 year-end issue of *Life* magazine asks, in big, bold, black letters on a stark white background, "When You Think of God, What Do You See?" Isolde Motley, Managing Editor of *Life*, ruminating on the December, 1998 cover story, wonders why faith, "the most important thing in life," is "exile[d] . . . from public discourse" (14). After all, according to the cover story, "Ninety-six percent of Americans believe in God" (McCourt 63). Certainly, on the radio and in CD changers, the dialogue about God is not missing.

The purpose of this analysis is to understand the presence in American culture of song lyrics with religious images. Through the twentieth century, and particularly in the latter third of the century, lyricists have employed Biblical and religious images in their songs. I am interested in the language of popular music and, in particular, the language that is used to represent religious images in bestselling recordings. Not only do I analyze the words of the songs, but I am also interested in why specific words are chosen. The role and status of religion in American society is revealed by the wording that is used to describe religious images; the way theological precepts are addressed; and the musical arrangements that accompany the recordings. Song lyrics also reveal changes in attitudes toward religion over time.

In the wide swath of songs that contain religious and, in particular, Biblical images, it is easy to recognize and conclude that the Biblical foundations of American society permeate much of American popular music throughout the twentieth century. The lyrics of these songs are rooted, in part, in values gleaned from the Biblical underpinnings of the nation. Lyrical images not only reflect the connection between American culture and the Biblical religion, but also act as shapers of culture. The words of popular songs have the power to influence the listener and, in the case of the songs analyzed here, have a role in informing the religious decisions of the popular music audience. The study focuses primarily on images associated with the religion of the Biblical tradition.

In the universe of popular songs that express an adherence to the Biblical sacred order, most images are couched in an inoffensive and civil content-less language. The mainstream listener supplies her or his own meaning to the words. The term "Lord" (a conventional reference to God in popular music lyrics) is a connotation word. It lacks a clear interpretation or an absolute meaning. Thus, lyrics with vague references reduce the meaning of the Biblical sacred order because of their nebulous connotations. It is ironic that those who opposed rock and roll music, because of its perceived attack on values derived from religious beliefs, embraced songs that dealt with religious ideas in contentless terms even though these songs watered down the teachings of the Biblical order. I label the inoffensive words of popular songs that embrace the Biblical tradition as *lyrics of civility*.

It is most important to keep the idea of choice in mind in thinking about lyrics of civility. Civil or inoffensive lyrics afford the opportunity of meaning choice by the listener. A choice can be made by the receptor as to the meaning of the words sung. Civil lyrics connote rather than denote. Connotation words are invested with whatever meaning the listener desires, whether or not it agrees with the meaning originally invested in them by the lyricist. The flexibility of meaning inherent in civil lyrics renders them contentless.

Use of offensive language by a lyricist has the potential to narrow one's audience. Thus, if an artist or record company desires to enjoy blockbuster sales, lyrics should not contain a meaningful philosophy or theology or cause the listener to think. One may argue that lyrics of civility simply are vague to garner the greater audience. However, unlike the lyrics of civility that embrace the Biblical sacred order, lyrics that reject the Biblical tradition use content-filled, offensive language. There are words used in the lyrics, e.g., the name "Jesus," that are not connotation words and have a clear meaning. These artists and their distributors desire just as much to release profitable recordings, yet they are not vague in their terminology. They target the same audience, Theodor Adorno's deconcentrated listeners (Negus 9), with the unfamiliar, yet they are successful. Thus, the receptors of songs that reject the Biblical tradition clearly get the message sent by the recording artist.

To the mainstream popular music audience, the recording artist becomes a victim of ridicule once she or he has found the answer *and* proclaims the life-change in clear, meaningful language. Whether the artist embraces Christianity (Bob Dylan at the time of the *Slow Train Coming* and *Saved* releases), a guru (Devadip Carlos Santana in the mid-1970s), or Hare Krishna (George Harrison in the early 1970s), the performer is the victim of a snickering market. In the mid-1980s, Paul Williams wrote, "Six years ago, when Bob Dylan embraced 'born-again' christianity (sic), the response of the rock audience was so hostile that he found himself unable to sell out 3000–seat theatres, when a year before he'd been playing very successfully in 15,000–seaters" (168). Searching is okay in the public square of rock and roll. Finding is not. Popular music critics or audiences are hesitant to embrace wholeheartedly an artist who expresses her or his theology in song because it may be perceived as an assent to the source of meaning expounded by the artist.

In Amy Grant's campaign to break out of the contemporary Christian music subculture and into the mainstream in the mid-1980s, she released an album (*Unguarded*) with lyrics that were more vague in their address of God than in previous albums. The presentation veiled the fact that she had found what she was looking for. There seems to be an unwritten rule in the mainstream purview of popular music that references to God or Jesus need to be vague or oblique. However, this precept only seems to hold in lyrics that indicate an embrace, rather than a refusal, of the Biblical sacred order.

Unlike lyricists who write songs that acknowledge the Biblical tradition, the English singer Sting has questioned belief in the God of the Bible in clear, meaningful language. In "All This Time," Sting's narrator sings, "Father, if Jesus exists, then how come he never lived here." The English band Genesis had a bestselling single titled "Jesus He Knows Me," a scathing attack on televangelists. The name "Jesus" is up front in a song that attacks a part of the Christian subculture.

If Amy Grant sang a song titled "Jesus He Knows Me," (and presuming it was not an attack on Christianity or part of its subculture), the composition would not be released as a single targeted to the mainstream, because its lyric would be considered too specific and offensive. If by chance a track with the name "Jesus" in the song lyric was included on a Grant album targeted to the mainstream, it would be buried at the end of the album's song order. Such was the case in Grant's 1991 release, *Heart in Motion*, the breakout album that brought her to national prominence in the mainstream market. Though the album contained a natural closing song—a song titled "I Will Remember You" which she used to close her concerts on the tour in support of the album—instead, the song placed at the end of the album was the one that specifically mentioned "Jesus," a track titled "Hope Set High."

A key sentence in the *Life* essay on faith is the first sentence of an introduction to the article. The author simply writes, "America's God is *vaguely* defined" (McCourt 63) (emphasis added). This vagueness is the key to the discussion of God in American culture. Song lyrics present a key to understanding the dynamic of how the dilution of the meaning of a sacred order, through the use of vague terms, creates an environment in which adherents turn to other possibilities for meaning.

Adherents to a traditional order may not loosen themselves from the precepts of the order altogether. In fact, they may consider themselves still members of the order. However, they find more meaningful substitutes to replace those precepts of the order which do not provide meaning in their lives. Religious or spiritual adherents, even if nominally associated with a sacred order, have developed personal customized sacred orders to make sense of their lives. The new precepts that seekers enjoin to themselves to create an individual core of meaning may be garnered from either the sacred or the secular realm.

The resulting maxims that become the ingredients of the individual's personal sacred order are defined in a clear manner so that the seeker understands that the principles that she or he chooses will provide meaning in the areas of life that need sensible resolution. The individual will not accept principles that are vaguely defined and do not present the opportunity to make sense of her or his life. An ambiguous precept can be re-defined by an individual so that it will have meaning for the person. By the act of remolding the precept, though, the individual is removing herself or himself from the order in which the precept originated. The analysis of lyrics unfolds the role of one component of popular culture, popular music, in transforming the religious element of a society.

The emergence of lyrics of civility is related to the dichotomy between the sacred and the secular in mainstream American culture. The integration of faith with the daily earthly walk was central to African-American culture and the corresponding music tradition. In the mainstream market, however, the same mingling of the spiritual and the natural did not fit with the mainstream construction of reality. A thread in this study is the integration by a number of artists of the sacred and the profane, Sunday morning and Saturday night, in their artistry.

I have reviewed the history of twentieth-century popular music (both sheet music and recordings) that reached the bestseller charts. I wanted to know if there was a time when there was a noticeable change in the manner of expressing Biblical images in popular music, a time when popular songs that suggested an acceptance of the Biblical sacred order declared their concerns in offensive, content-filled language. Further, I was interested in examining the history of popular songs that refuse the Biblical sacred order. I wondered if songs that express the dismissal of the Biblical sacred order with clear, meaningful lyrics were present prior to the candid lyrics associated with the rock music of the late 1960s.

I have undertaken a broad survey for the answers to my questions within the first half century of recorded music (from approximately the turn of the century to 1950) and more closely within the period since the birth of the rock music era (from approximately 1955 to the present). The popularity of recorded music has been charted on *Billboard*'s bestseller lists since the early years of the twentieth century. I focused on contemporary narratives, that is, songs that told stories that were of their time. I examined songs with Biblical images that unfolded tales of unrequited love or love separated by geography, or addressed the death of a teen idol or dealt with contemporary crises at home or abroad. It was not my intent to carefully analyze bestsellers that were not indigenously authentic, that is, not rooted in their time, e.g., Sister Janet Mead's "The Lord's Prayer" (no. 4, 1974).

Songs from film and theater soundtracks were excluded from the study because their appearance in media other than the radio adds a layer of exposure which may differentiate their popularity from that of songs only exposed via radio and the record market. The appearance of these songs in relation to other media may alter their meanings for the listener who can also attach a pre-described visual image to the lyric. Therefore, popular recordings associated with films, such as Perry Como's "Somebody Up There Likes Me" (1956), or songs from the play *Jesus Christ Superstar*, such as Yvonne Elliman's "I Don't Know How to Love Him" (1971) and Murray Head's "Superstar" (1971) were omitted.

I acknowledge that the contribution by popular music to American culture is based on more than the words to popular songs. One observer of the popular music scene speaks convincingly of the "dangerous and ultimately futile business of interpreting rock 'n' roll, with its abstract blend of image, sound and performance art" (Dunphy 154). The music that accompanies the words, the encompassing rock music culture, the image of the artist, the relationship between the artist and the audience and the sign value of popular music all contribute to the message of popular music. The focus, however, of this study is the lyrics of popular music.

The order of the first part of the lyrical analysis is primarily chronological. I begin by surveying popular songs from the first half of the twentieth century. This section unfolds the historical roots of much of the substance of later popular music with Biblical images. The utilization of particular motifs to signify religious concepts, e.g., bells or the chapel in a bucolic setting, began in the first years of the century. I demonstrate the use of vague terminology to refer to the God of the Bible. Further, I note that the aesthetic of civility was not limited to the language used to verbalize Biblical images. The aesthetic carried over into the theological precepts in the tales told in these songs. This is noticeable in songs that deal with sin, forgiveness and a non-exclusionary heaven.

The impact of the two world wars that occurred during this period is clear in the number of songs in which Biblical images are drafted into the narratives. Wartime offers the opportunity for lyricists to present more explicit lyrics that hold to the Biblical sacred order because the nation moves into a spiritual huddle to face the insecurities associated with a lack of world peace.

The aesthetic of civility carries over into the narratives in songs that adhere to the Biblical sacred order. A lyrical focus on a region noted for strong religious convictions or on the theology of a specific denomination tends to compartmentalize religious belief. By putting belief in a box of one's own making, the mainstream audience reads the resulting text in the same way that lyrics of civility are read. The words may be content-filled, but the narrative situation can be read through a filter of civility, because the religious content applies to a marginalized group, e.g., the population of a particular region, adherents to Roman Catholicism, or innocent children.

The inoffensive, easy listening instrumental accompaniment associated with songs that embrace the Biblical sacred order is also an extension of the aesthetic of civility. This further reduces the impact of the Biblical images in songs. Other songs that contain content-filled lyrics are minimalized through the novelty character of the song. The message is clear and content-filled, but because the record is viewed as a novelty, its meaning is minimized. The song is not considered to be indigenously authentic.

Next I follow more of a thematic approach as I investigate images of prayer and heaven, the two dominant themes in popular songs that include Biblical images. The records examined in this section were released primarily between 1953 and 1971. I also consider the meaning of heaven in the lyrics of African-American popular music and country and western music.

Following this, I focus on lyrics that reject the Biblical sacred order. Songs included attack the Biblical sacred order in content-filled language, rather than casting elements of the order in a meaningless light. There are songs that reject the Biblical sacred order that were not perceived as such in their time by the casual listener. Popular songs of this nature can be traced back to the 1930s, but the primary period of investigation here is between the years 1966 and 1971.

In the ensuing sections, I consider popular music beyond 1971 to view the impact of earlier music on more recent songs with Biblical images. The music of the artists who embraced Eastern sacred orders is discussed. I also review the music of the revival rock era which spanned the years 1968 to 1971. The birth of the contemporary Christian music and heavy metal music formats (which occurred at approximately the same time and perhaps not coincidentally) is viewed in relation to the discussion. I examine the romantic love as substitute for divine love phenomenon in the lyrics of the mid-1970s and beyond. The impact of Bob Dylan's conversion to Christianity is revealed in the lyrical interests of the singer-songwriters of the early 1980s. The songs of the 1990s clearly reveal the development of individual sacred orders. There is no common focus among lyricists regarding the concept of God at the end of the millennium as there was at the beginning of the twentieth century.

DEFINITIONS

A religion is a sacred or holy order of life that holds authority over and frames a person's and a society's presuppositions or system of beliefs. For a period of time in a culture, its influence holds sway and it allows for a level of communication in society through common attitudes toward the order prescribed by the religion. Its influence aids the adherent in the ascribing of meaning in areas of ultimate significance. Both Peter L. Berger and Frank D. Schubert add the idea of an order, a sacred order, to the definition of religion. Berger defines religion as "a human attitude that conceives of the cosmos (including the supernatural) as a sacred order" (40). Schubert defines religion as "a sacred order within which life makes sense" (6).

Though a religion provides an order that helps make sense of reality, this does not mean that the religion is an ordinary reality. Berger notes that religious experiences "breach" or "rupture" the "paramount" reality of ordinary, everyday life (35, 43). For a religion to be accepted by its adherents, it has to be sanctioned by a higher authority, one with the power to rent everyday life. Thus, traditional religions incorporate a spiritual or supernatural dimension to sanction the sacredness of the order. For Berger, the experience of the supernatural is of the "overwhelmingly other" (39).

The supernatural dimension, the overwhelmingly other, the unexplainable, that which must be embraced by faith, provides the authority that undergirds the religion's doctrines. Schubert asserts, "Such an order is designated sacred . . . to the extent that one considers the order itself to be inviolate and . . . holy—that is, worthy of one's deep reverence, awe and utmost respect" (7). There is no submitting or bowing unless there is a capacity for reverence or awe inherent in some object or element of the religion.

The religious tradition that this analysis deals with is the Biblical tradition. The order of life prescribed in the Biblical religion of Christianity has influenced American culture to varying degrees through history. Recent surveys indicate that 85 percent of Americans identify themselves as Christians (S. Carter 85). The term Biblical tradition is used to refer to the tenets of faith found in both the Old and New Testaments of the Christian Bible. These principles are those that are held in common by the majority of the Protestant and Catholic denominations in the United State. Members of the Jewish faith would hold in common with the Protestant and Catholic Churches the doctrines found in what Christians term the Old Testament of the Bible. Adherents to Judaism refer to these books of the Old Testament as the Holy Scriptures. Since this study primarily deals with the Christian tradition, the terms Old Testament and New Testament are used. These tenets from all 66 books of the Bible, that is, those included in both the Old and New Testaments, make up the sacred order of the Biblical tradition. When I reference the Biblical sacred order then, I am also referring to the Biblical tradition.

The basic tenets of the Christian faith are found in the Apostle's Creed:

> I believe in God the Father Almighty, Maker of heaven and earth. And in Jesus Christ His only Son our Lord, who was conceived by the Holy Ghost, Born of the Virgin Mary, Suffered under Pontius Pilate, Was Crucified, died and buried; He descended into hell; The third day He rose again from the dead; He ascended into heaven, and sitteth on the right hand of God the Father Almighty; From thence he shall come to judge the quick and the dead.

I believe in the Holy Ghost; the holy catholic (or universal)
Church; the communion of Saints; the Forgiveness of sins; the
Resurrection of the body; and the Life everlasting. (Bruce 15)

Steven M. Tipton observes, "biblical religion traditionally
conceives reality in terms of an absolute objective God who is the
Creator and Father of all human beings. God reveals his will to them in
sacred scripture and he commands them to obey him" (3). A key focus
of the lyric analysis that follows is the identification of the character of
this Creator God in song. Most of the songs included in the study were
rooted in the idea of Christianity presented in the Apostle's Creed even
if all the precepts were not embraced wholeheartedly during the study
period. In particular, the idea of God as a gender-specific being (Father
Almighty) and the idea of Jesus as "His . . . Son" were elements of
Christianity that were relatively more adhered to during the first half of
the twentieth century in American Christianity and, therefore, were also
found in the lyrics of American popular music. Steve Bruce suggests
that "mainstream Christianity" has changed its view of God and Jesus:
"God is rarely thought of as an actual person but as some sort of *vague*
power or our own consciences" and "Christ is no longer the Son of God
but an exemplary prophet and teacher" (16) (emphasis added). At the
end of the twentieth century, sermons, hymnbooks and popular song
lyrics express references to both God and Jesus in more gender-
inclusive forms. All scripture quotations in the text are from the King
James Version unless otherwise noted.

Popular music can be simply defined as music mass-produced for
an intended mass consumption. Its definition becomes less simple when
the idea of popular is considered. Whether or not a recording becomes
popular popular music, i.e., music which reaches a specific level of
popularity on bestselling record charts, the music is still popular music.
The number of records released to the market at the same time, the
artist's relationship with her or his record company and other factors
relating to the economics of the industry preclude all recording artists
from getting a fair shot at entering the bestseller chart.

Richard Middleton argues that *all* music is popular with someone
(3). This makes sense because musicians have audiences. Someone is
paying attention to the artist. And these audiences pique the interest of
record company personnel. Before a record label contracts an artist,
there is an implicit assumption that the artist is going to make popular
popular music, that is, music that will garner profits for the company.

Most popular culture critics differentiate popular music and all other popular arts as well from the arts of folk enclaves or classical, i.e., high art, audiences. This is not to say that folk or classical arts are not popular. However, they are not targeted to a mass market. In summary, popular music is best defined by defining its intended audience. This audience is the popular mass. In the present study, this mass is often referred to as the mainstream or the mainstream audience.

The Lyrics of Civility

CHAPTER ONE

Lawd, You Made the Night Too Long: Biblical Images in Popular Music, 1900–1945

From the time that the popularity of songs was first monitored via bestseller charts in the United States, there have been popular recordings of songs with lyrics which contain religious images. In the early part of the twentieth century, many of these songs were derived from traditional sources. In 1907, Harry MacDonough recorded a popular version of "Every Valley Shall Be Exalted" from Handel's *Messiah*. Several church hymns became popular in recorded versions. Richard Jose popularized "Nearer My God to Thee" in 1906. The traditional hymn "Abide with Me" was popularized by Elizabeth Wheeler in 1910 and, again, by Alma Gluck and Louise Homer in a duet in 1913. In the next two years, the Gluck and Homer duo charted again with traditional hymns: "Rock of Ages" (1914) and "Jesus, Lover of My Soul" (1915). The Fisk University Jubilee Quartet recorded a popular version of the spiritual "Swing Low, Sweet Chariot" in 1910. "The Battle Hymn of the Republic" was popularized in 1918 in a version by Charles Harrison with the Columbia Stellar Quartet and in another version by Thomas Chalmers. Enrico Caruso and Marcel Journet popularized a Latin-language version of Jean-Baptiste Faure's "The Crucifix" in 1912. Again in 1917, John McCormack and Reinald Werrenrath charted with a version of Faure's composition.

All of these songs were among the ten most popular in sheet music sales or in their recorded versions during the year they were released. The popularity of songs with meaningful and offensive lyrics is apparently indicative of a greater approbation of the Biblical sacred order at the beginning of the twentieth century. The success of these songs may reflect the existence of what John F. Wilson describes as the "cultural hegemony of republican Protestantism" during the period (14). At the least, the popularity of traditional hymns in the overall market suggests a significant embrace of the church worship service in American culture. However, songs derived from traditional sources do not present the whole picture of the relationship between American society and its traditional religious beliefs. This is because of the traditional roots and the cultural images carried in these songs. Their ownership is contained within a past era. Though there would continue to be popular recordings of religious songs from similar traditional sources for the next seventy years (though not with the frequency present in the first two decades of the twentieth century), e.g., Perry Como's two-sided hit of "Ave Maria" with "The Lord's Prayer" (1949); the "Make a Joyful Noise unto the Lord" medley by Jane Russell, Connie Haines, Beryl Davis and Della Russell (1954); and, as late as 1974, Sister Janet Mead's Roman Catholic folk-music-mass reading of "The Lord's Prayer," contemporary narratives, e.g., songs of romance with religious images, are more revealing of the culture's view of the Biblical tradition. That is why the focus of the present study is contemporary narratives that integrate Biblical images within the lyrics.

The First World War inspired several popular compositions with religious images. As with much of popular music and particularly popular music with religious, and especially prayer, images, the lyrical narratives of these songs were founded in the pain of separation. In this case, the separation was that due to American troops being sent overseas. John McCormack petitioned "God Be with Our Boys Tonight" (no. 3, 1918). In the same year, both Henry Burr and Charles Hart recorded popular versions of "Just a Baby's Prayer at Twilight (For Her Daddy Over There)" (Burr, no. 1; Hart, no. 10). Also in 1918, the Peerless Quartet charted with the request, "Say a Prayer for the Boys Out There" (no. 6).

In these three songs, there is a range of references to the God of the Bible. "God Be with Our Boys Tonight," the McCormack recording, specifically addresses "God." In the Peerless Quartet's patriotic plea to the American public, "Say a Prayer for the Boys Out There," they urge, "Let's call to the one upon high." In the narrative about a daughter's prayer for her father, "Just a Baby's Prayer at Twilight," there is only mention made of "Golden Gates." So, in the early decades of the century, within narratives that were of their time, there was a use of vague references to God in the lyrics of mainstream popular music. There was a particular protocol for describing religious images in the lyrics of contemporary narratives.

In Wilson's examination of "The Religious Language of American Presidents," he asserts that "most presidents have been relatively guarded in their religious references" (45). The language of civility in religious or Biblical pronouncements is not a phenomenon exclusive to the twentieth century. Wilson provides evidence that even in the first inaugural address by a president, the words chosen by Washington to refer to the God of the Bible were "Almighty Being," "Great Author," "Invisible Hand," and "Parent of the human Race" (49).

The World War I-era songs suggested an extra-Biblical theology of prayer. The lyrics of "Just a Baby's Prayer at Twilight" suggest that the prayer of a daughter for her father at war overseas has a higher priority than other petitions: "Some pray'rs may be neglected beyond the Golden Gates, but when they're all collected here's one that never waits." In the same song, the lyricist suggests a prayer that is not as important: "The gold that some folks pray for brings nothing but regrets, some day this gold won't pay for their many lifelong debts." This is in line with the Scriptural admonition: "For what is a man advantaged, if he gain the whole world, and lose himself . . . ?" (Luke 9:25). Although there is no specific reference to the divine, the target of the daughter's prayer, the song does contain a unity that centers on the Biblical sacred order. Though the Bible does not suggest that there exists a priority among legitimate prayers, a point argued in the lyrics, the song does embrace a Biblical principle in its lyrical notation of a prayer that is out of order, i.e., one related to the quest for wealth.

In the lyrics of "Say a Prayer for the Boys Out There," there is the suggestion that prayer makes a difference in space-time history: "A nation's prayers will help the weaker ones along and will strengthen them when everything goes wrong." In the same song, there is a clear suggestion of approval for American involvement in the war. The United States is described as a "mighty nation that hears a ringing call to arm." The boys are "out there" so that "the rest of us forever may be free." Though there is a nod to the idea that the American military is blessed by God, there is still presented the Scriptural idea that prayer can make a difference in history.

The popularity of songs with religious images during the World War I era is related to the stamp of insecurity of war on the national consciousness. In reference to the 1950s and the Korean War, Paul Carter observes a tendency to "huddle" at the time of war (138). The popularity of war-related songs with Biblical images during a time when there is a threat of impending war or during wartime itself is evidence of the spiritual "huddle" that encompasses a populace unsure of its future. There is a turning to the Biblical sacred order to grasp a life-order that makes sense. Wilson notes the same proclivity. He states, "Religious language about the public realm is occasioned by national crisis" (56).

Other popular songs in the first two decades of the twentieth century contained images that became part of the lyrical language or vocabulary of religious images in popular music. These early recordings set the standard for songs with Biblical images through the 1960s. Bells, either expressly noted in the lyrics or as part of the instrumental accompaniment, came to signify a church or chapel, a wedding ceremony, or a divine presence. Byron G. Harlan sang of the "Message of the Old Church Bell" (no. 4, 1905). In Harry MacDonough's "The Tale the Church Bells Tolled" (no. 3, 1907), the image of the bells is used to signify both a marriage ceremony and a funeral service: "one told of a wedding, the other was spreading the news of a soul that had flown." The juxtaposition of the wedding and the funeral tied together by the church bell is a motif that was borrowed for the lyric of the Browns's bestseller "The Three Bells" fifty years later.

Composer Teresa Del Riego's "Thank God for a Garden," written in 1915 and recorded with great success five years later by John McCormack (no. 8, 1920), contained the idea of God as creator. The lyrics thank God for sunshine, flowers, rain, dew and corn fields. But, most of all, the lyricist thanks God "for summer that brings me you." Though the lyricist may be referring to her father (who the song is dedicated to in its sheet music form), the thanking of God for another person, particularly a romantic love interest, became a popular motif in the lyrics of later popular music.

The language and motifs used to incorporate Biblical images in the lyrics of American popular songs were set in place by the first two decades of the twentieth century. Many of the images that were used in the popular songs of the 1950s and 1960s (both in the nascent recordings of rock and roll and in the works of the era's pop stylists) find their foundation in the early years of charted popular music. The use of a prayer theme, found in the World War I era songs, became a popular form of incorporating a Biblical image into a contemporary lyrical narrative. The use of Biblical images in songs related to the war was evidence of the spiritual huddling that takes place during the time of war. The language of Biblical imagery in pop lyrics was being cast in this era. The use of the image of bells to signify God or the holy place, cited in 1907's "The Tale the Church Bell Tolled," was used extensively in later popular music. In Mark Silk's analysis of journalism and religion, he introduces the concept of "topoi," or moral formulas whose substance is the values of the religious foundations of the United States. These "topoi" are the fabric from which religious news coverage is born (xii). The topoi (the word is part of a Greek phrase meaning "commonplaces") are used by reporters to endow their articles with a "familiar [social] context of meaning" (50). Similarly, lyricists invoke the image of the church bell or the chapel in the pines to construct a familiar meaning.

The examination of the lyrics of these early recordings also uncovers the use of the vague, contentless language in reference to God. In "Say a Prayer for the Boys Out There," God is referred to as the "one upon high." The use of language without meaning in the lyrics of popular music was present when song popularity was first charted. Though such usage may have been more prevalent later—the first decades of the century witnessed the co-existence of songs with vague references and traditional hymns, e.g., "Jesus, Lover of My Soul," on the popularity charts—there was still the notion of being civil in lyrical creation. Silk states that "topoi represent a series of moral least common denominators" (53). He notes that it is not the place of journalists on the religion beat to draw a line between allowable and intolerable religions. Similarly, lyrics of civility target the least common denominator among the acceptable sacred orders in American society.

In the period between the end of World War I and the end of the Second World War, popular songs contained images of prayer and heaven as the threat of war rose and became a reality again for the United States in the early 1940s. Before turning to those songs that resulted from the nation's spiritual nestling, I want to focus on a different image of prayer than was witnessed earlier, an image introduced in a song made popular by the Ink Spots. Their rendition of "My Prayer" (no. 3, 1939) is not specifically addressed to God or any other heavenly body or creature. Rather than petitioning God to work in space and time to see the narrator's dream become a reality, there is no sense of any call by the narrator for assistance from someone other than his romantic interest. The outcome of his prayer balances on his love's "answer": "My prayer and the answer you give, may they still be the same for as long as we live." He does not specifically pray to her, she is not his "overwhelmingly other," but she does control the outcome of his prayer.

His prayer "is to linger with [his love] at the end of each day in a dream that's divine." The description of his dream as "divine" ties into the idea of prayer as a sacred activity. This was an early, if not the first, example of a narrative which revealed the substitution for God in an individual's sacred order by another being or object of devotion. In this case, it is the narrator's romantic interest. The lyrics of "My Prayer" do not present a specific abandonment of traditional faith. The rejection of the tenets of the Biblical sacred order in mainstream popular music began with oblique lyric turns that did not attack the Biblical sacred order head on, but were still indicative of the place of the Biblical sacred order in American culture. The Biblical tradition was not a sacred cow that had to be revered. Rather than being held in awe, the lyricist transfers the focus of a prayer from God to a human love interest, who now controls the outcome of the life of the song's narrator. The lyrics of Tin Pan Alley have meaning and are authentic.

Turning to a song that more closely adheres to the Biblical sacred order, in the lyrics of Sam Lewis's "Lawd, You Made the Night Too Long," popularly recorded by Louis Armstrong (no. 15, 1932), God, addressed as "Lawd," is recognized as the author of creation, for he is the maker of the night. But the loneliness of the narrator causes him to complain about God's handiwork. Rather than praying for a romantic love to assuage his loneliness, the narrator not only suggests in his petition that the night is just too long for the lonely heart, but wonders what the purpose of creating man was if he is alone: "What good's a heart . . . if nobody lives inside." The narrator does not renounce the Biblical sacred order, but he questions the purpose of creation.

The narrator is not attesting to a lack of faith in God. The Armstrong recording opens with him singing repeatedly the word "Hallelujah," a Hebrew expression that means "Praise the Lord." By opening with repetitions of the "Hallelujah" phrase in his recording of the song, Armstrong personalizes the acknowledgment of the Biblical sacred order contained in the sheet music version of Sam Lewis's original lyrics which read: "You gave me lips to sing your praise and I'll be singin' 'Hallelujah, Hallelujah' to Ya the rest of my days . . . ."

The lyrics go on to say that the narrator is still "believin' in You," but he longs for less of a reminder of his loneliness.

Armstrong's recording is located within the meeting of the sacred and the secular, or grace and nature, in African-American popular music. The influence of the black church in African-American music culture is evident in the mingling of Christian images with lyrics that focus on a romantic love. Ronald Scott describes the African-American religious tradition as one in which:

> religion is depicted not simply as a set of beliefs that one should separate from his or her objective living conditions and only believe in or follow in an abstract, ideal manner; rather, it is represented as a tangible tool that can be utilized to structure and guide one's everyday existence and to empower individuals by providing them with direct control over their own lives. (Schwichtenberg 72)

There is a melding or fusion of the spiritual and the secular, the sacred and the profane, such as in Louis Armstrong's "Lawd, You Made the Night Too Long." The blending of the sacred and the secular is a dominant motif in African-American popular music. A similar mingling in the pre-rock era of grace and nature is found in Percy Mayfield's 1950 bestseller "Please Send Me Someone to Love."

Blues recordings that were contemporary with the Armstrong work evidence the integration of the sacred with the whole of life. At a recording date in New York during 1933 of songs primarily secular in nature, Blind Willie McTell recorded two tracks centered in the Biblical sacred order, "Lord Have Mercy if You Please" and "Don't You See How This World Made a Change." In the former track, McTell stresses the need when making a supplication for mercy to fall on one's knees before the Lord. In the latter composition, he paints a picture of believers "marching round the throne with Peter, James and John." An extensive treatment of the theology of the blues is found in Jon Michael Spencer's *Blues and Evil.*

African-American popular music did not secularize the Biblical tradition. Rather, it reflected the melding of the sacred and the secular in African-American culture. The music did not replace the overwhelmingly other of the Biblical sacred order with an alternate center, but placed the concerns of daily existence on the foundation of the Biblical tradition. No dichotomy existed between nature and grace.

There was no dilution of meaning of Biblical concepts in African-American music.

In "I Believe in Miracles" (1935), popularized by both "Fats" Waller (no. 10) and by the Dorsey Brothers Orchestra with vocalist Bob Crosby (no. 3), the narrator recognizes that someone or something outside of the tangible world brought his romantic love to him. The singer celebrates his love. Though there is a recognition of an outside other or force working in the narrator's life, there are vague allusions to this force. In the second verse, the lyric reads, "Long before we knew each other, long before that well-remembered kiss, something made us look for one another, someone must have planned all this." The narrator acknowledges that it was not his power or that of his mate, that brought the "miracle" about which he gets "lyrical." Rather, it was "something" or "someone" or "some magical power." He does make reference to "an angel" that "walk[ed] right up to [him] from out the skies" on the day he and his love interest met. It is not clear if the narrator is referring to her or is making an allusion to the source of the miracle in his life. The words of this song are evidence of lyrics of civility in early popular recordings. The deity is "someone." There is no specific reference to some "overwhelmingly other."

Bing Crosby's "Just a Prayer Away" (no. 4, 1945) recognizes that prayer can bring one to a place where she or he will be more content: "There's a happy land somewhere and it's just a prayer away. All I've dreamed and planned is there . . . ." The words sound as if they are an allusion to heaven, but as the song continues, the focus seems to be contentment in the present life. In this happy land, "the skies look down on a friendly town filled with laughing children at play." Written in 1944, the lyrics appear to be sung from the viewpoint of an American serviceman overseas looking forward to repatriation. He longs for the "somewhere," a place where his "heart will sing for it means one thing, I'll be home at the close of each day." It seems ironic that the song is vague about the location of the "happy land," considering the narrator's probable viewpoint and the galvanized support for the "good war." A clear patriotic meaning would have made sense given the timing of the song's release. If the narrator was alluding to heaven, it would then make more sense for the lyricist to use a nebulous reference for the mainstream audience.

Such a nebulous image of heaven is found in "There's a Gold Mine in the Sky" (no. 5, 1937), recorded by Horace Heidt and His Orchestra with vocalist Larry Cotton. The song is about heaven ("we'll say

'Hello' to friends who said 'Goodbye'"). But it is not until the vocalist is sixteen bars into the song that the listener realizes that the narrator is talking to his mule. Suddenly, the allegorical suggestion of the line about "clover just for you down the line" disappears. Heaven is a place where the old prospector and his "lame" mule will find what they have been searching for on earth—a claim to strike. The lyrics suggest that heaven is a reward for all who are tired and weary. There are no other requirements to "strike that claim." This is an early example in popular music of the theological notion that heaven is not exclusionary. That is, one does not have to live a life of a certain moral character to enter heaven. Rather, heaven is for all, no matter what the constitution of one's earthly activity. This theological view is just as civil as using vague references to the deity in popular lyrics. So, the civility of lyrics with Biblical images is not limited to descriptives. The aesthetic of civility also overlays Biblical views of heaven and prayer.

It was mentioned earlier in regard to the World War I time period that the popularity of songs with religious images was connected to an insecurity brought about by the uncertainties of war. This stamp on the national consciousness was again evident during the time of World War II. On the twentieth anniversary of the armistice ending the First World War, Kate Smith introduced Irving Berlin's composition, "God Bless America" (no. 10, 1939). The impetus for the song was the threat of another war in Europe. The song opens with the line, "While the storm clouds gather far across the sea." As uncertainty grew over the possibility of widespread conflict, there was a spiritual huddling. "God Bless America" was a prayer to the overwhelmingly other of the Biblical sacred order to "Stand beside [America] and guide her thru the night [the impending war] with a light from above." Because of the clustering atmosphere, a clear, offensive reference naming "God" was palatable in the mainstream market. Marshall Fishwick sees the spiritual huddle or clustering as one part of the cycle of revival. He states that revivals "peak during a national crisis" and "subside when the crisis passes" (6).

According to the "Story Behind This Song" included in the sheet music to "Praise the Lord and Pass the Ammunition!" (1942), songwriter Frank Loesser was inspired by an incident that took place at the Japanese attack of Pearl Harbor. Apparently, a Navy ship chaplain took the station of a gunner who had been killed and the newly-appointed gunner-chaplain uttered the words that became the title of Loesser's composition. The song was popularized by both the vocal group the Merry Macs (no. 8, 1942) and by band leader Kay Kyser, who, with vocals by the Glee Club, took the song to number one in 1943, as the war effort was in full gear.

Unlike other songs with religious images that deal with war themes, the song places the Biblical sacred order on a different plane in relation to the war effort. Rather than looking to the deity as a means of bringing order in the midst of uncertainty, God, or at least his representative on earth, in this case the chaplain (or "sky pilot," as the lyric refers to him), is an ally walking shoulder to shoulder on the front lines in the battle against the enemy. The sky pilot leaves his post—"he laid aside the Book"—to take up arms with the servicemen. In the lyrics, the chaplain warns "Can't afford to sit around a'wishin'" and, later, "We're not a'goin' fishin'." These may be references to prayer and evangelism, respectively. More important than the Great Commission or the power of prayer is victory. There is a clear assumption that the United States is on the God-ordained side of the battle. By praising the Lord and passing the ammunition, "we'll all stay free." The United States is portrayed as a God-ordained nation. The key proposal by this song is the place of God in relation to the American nation-state. He is no longer an overwhelmingly other; rather, he has been enlisted to fight in the "good war."

The theme of "Light a Candle in the Chapel" (no. 21, 1942) is the same as that of the World War I songs urging prayer for American troops overseas. The Tommy Dorsey recording, with vocal by Frank Sinatra, recommends that the listener pray for the protection of the "one who went away," the one the listener is "yearning" for. In this prayer song, the address is not to God, but to angels: "Say a pray'r and ask the angels." This type of song set the foundation for songs with inoffensive religious images and, in particular, for the prayer songs of the 1950s and 1960s which were rarely directed specifically to God. The reference to an image of a chapel also suggests an inoffensive way of portraying the Biblical sacred order. Chapels are usually non-denominational in nature. Though there is a turning to the Biblical sacred order to embrace a common sense order of life in a period of turmoil, the manner in which it is accomplished is through vague, inoffensive language.

The lyrics use the image of bells to open the song: "The bells are ringing in the steeple, ding, dong, ding." As noted earlier, the reference to bells became a common manner of introducing a religious text into popular music lyrics. In this era, there were several other images used in popular songs that would become part of the vocabulary of lyrical religious images.

One of these lyrical images is found in "Cathedral in the Pines" (1938), a number one song for Shep Fields and His Rippling Rhythm Orchestra with vocalist Jerry Stewart. The lyric presents the image of the church or chapel in a bucolic setting. The narrator's "cathedral" is described as "little," "quaint," and "old fashioned." It is a "church where ivy twines." For the narrator it is a cathedral because it is the site of his parents's marriage, the site of his baptism and the place where he, today, kneels "before the altar" about to marry his bride. In several ways the song parallels the Browns's "The Three Bells," a popular recording released two decades later. The Browns's recording is set in a similar setting. Also, the only instances of church attendance recorded are ritual events. Both texts include marriage and baptism rituals.

A little, quaint, old-fashioned church is an inoffensive place of worship. The locale of "Cathedral in the Pines" is rural, where traditional values still have some import. The song, then, reflects the idea of the regionalization or marginalization of traditional religious belief. The implication is that such belief is not plausible in more urban (or pluralized) areas. This narrative situation of the chapel in a pristine setting appears in the 1950s and 1960s in the Browns's "The Three Bells," the Dixie Cups's "Chapel of Love," and Lou Christie's "Lightnin' Strikes."

The identification of ritual events as the only noted periods of church attendance in "Cathedral in the Pines" (composed by Charles and Nick Kenny, who also wrote "There's a Gold Mine in the Sky") suggests that religious beliefs are only invoked at the time of these rituals. Here is another form in which lyrics reveal the place of the Biblical tradition in mainstream American popular culture. Unlike the commingling of the sacred and the secular, as is found in African-American popular music, in this song and others that follow, religion is not fully-integrated into the life of the adherent. Rather, faith is compartmentalized and the deity is only called upon in certain times of need, e.g., the war-time convergence.

"Jericho," recorded by Fred Waring's Pennsylvanians (no. 12, 1929), is an early example of the use of a Biblical story as the foundation for a lyrical narrative. The song, birthed in the Jazz Age, places a different spin on the tale of the walls of Jericho that came tumbling down. Though "there was no craze for jazz" in the Old Testament times, according to the lyric, "Still [Joshua and the

Israelites] knew when they went to war what a kick the cornet has."
The inhabitants of Jericho "liked [their] music low down" so when the
"trumpets blew," the city "Fell the same as we do."

The lyric secularizes the Bible story. Rather than the hand of God
participating in the victory of the Israelites, it is the inhabitants's
weakness for good music that brings about their demise. The song's
argument is that in the 1920s, the Jazz Age, the music of the period had
an overwhelmingly other character to it. Its power was equal to that of
the Hebrew God at Jericho. This relates to the idea of a popular
entertainment as a religion, or cultural religion. The analysis of this
song shows, again, fissures in the adherence to the Biblical sacred order
in the lyrics of popular music. Even in the 1920s, the power of jazz is a
substitute for the power of God.

In the period between the two world wars, several themes were
popular that would have a large impact on the popular music of the
1950s and 1960s. The idea of praying to some other being in the
heavens, i.e., angels, rather than God, was introduced in "Light a
Candle in the Chapel." The Ink Spots's "My Prayer" introduced the
notion of praying to another person rather than to God, or angels, or
some other heavenly being or object. A love interest substitutes for God
as the one who controls the outcome of the prayer.

The use of vague references to God continued, as was seen in the
reference to "someone" in "Fats" Waller's "I Believe in Miracles." A
vague theology of heaven was introduced in "There's a Gold Mine in
the Sky." This inoffensive view of heaven as a reward for all without
any moral considerations was embraced wholly in the teenage heaven
songs of the late 1950s and early 1960s.

The idea of religious belief being regionalized and located in a
harmless, inoffensive rural setting was introduced in "Cathedral in the
Pines." The image of the quaint, old-fashioned chapel aided in
marginalizing belief. Faith became an element of nostalgia. Even Fred
Waring's Pennsylvanians's "Jericho" anticipated the idea of popular
music as a religion. Jazz had the power to make the walls come
tumbling down.

The inoffensive conventions used to present the images of the
Biblical tradition during the period between the two World Wars was
consistent with the imagery present in the first two decades of the
twentieth century. The popular music from the first half of the twentieth
century introduced many of the themes and motifs and images that
became the vernacular of lyrics of civility in the 1950s and 1960s.

CHAPTER TWO

Crying in the Chapel: Post-World War II Popular Music, 1948–1966

The greatest upheaval in popular music history, the emergence of rock and roll music, occurred during the period examined in this chapter. At the beginning of this era the music of Tin Pan Alley was still dominant, but by its close, rock and roll music came to rule the popularity charts. Most of the songs surveyed are from genres other than rock music including ballad-style, rhythm and blues and folk music. Some songs that anticipated the rise of the new genre are songs that contain Biblical images, e.g., Percy Mayfield's "Please Send Me Someone to Love" and the Orioles's "Crying in the Chapel." The focus is not primarily on a particular theme, e.g., heaven or prayer, but on songs that were critical to the development of lyrics of civility as the expression of the Biblical tradition in American culture.

Not all of the songs examined contain lyrics of civility. Some are offensive and meaningful and are included to provide a fuller understanding of the presence of lyrical Biblical imagery in the mainstream marketplace. The song mentioned in the chapter heading is one of those with meaningful lyrics.

In the Orioles's "Crying in the Chapel" (no. 11, 1953), the chapel is depicted as a sanctuary, a place of rest. It is a holy place where one may communicate with God. It is a location where one may find peace. And, in the middle measures, the lyrics declare that there is no other way to find peace: "You'll search and you'll search but you'll never find no way on earth to find peace of mind." Peace does not come from a romantic love, according to the narrator, but from agape love, the divine, freely-offered love of God. Nor is peace necessarily found in ornate cathedrals. The chapel is physically described as "plain and simple."

The song is a statement of faith in the Christian sacred order. The narrator has found his peace. The tears he is crying in the chapel are "tears of joy." He witnesses to the positive effects of his spiritual experience in the chapel: "I know the meaning of contentment, I am happy with the Lord." He persuades the listener to share in the wonder of prayer. In the last verse, lead vocalist Sonny Til proselytizes, "Take your troubles to the chapel, get down on your knees and pray. Then your burdens will be lighter and you'll surely find a way."

The recorded performance by the Orioles belies the origin of the song. The song was written by country and western vocalist Darrell Glenn. Music issuing from the country and western subculture, that is, a marginalized group whose religious beliefs were perceived as different from the mainstream, caused the songs, and particularly the lyrics, to be heard and understood in a different way by the mainstream audience. The mainstream listeners heard the lyrics through a filter of civility. There was not the same response in terms of meaning as would be the response by members of the marginalized group. The cluster at the margins would most likely respond in a manner intended by the writer of the song, a member of the same group.

However, "Crying in the Chapel," broke out of its country and western setting and crossed over into different forms of music. In addition to Darrell Glenn's country and western-flavored recording, which peaked at number six on *Billboard*'s popularity charts, there were a number of other versions that were popular, all in the year 1953. The most successful version was by a big band singer, June Valli, whose recording peaked at number four. The Arizona cowboy, Rex Allen, carried a western version of the song to number eight on the popularity charts. Each of these three recordings outperformed the Orioles, whose recorded version peaked at number eleven. (Ironically, the 1995 Rock and Roll Hall of Fame inductees's version is the most recalled today.) Additionally, Ella Fitzgerald, a singer who, as Clarke says, "transcends category" (416), took a version of "Crying in the Chapel" to number fifteen. One other version, by big band singer Art Lund, also cracked *Billboard*'s Top 25 in 1953. As can be seen by the different types of recording artists who achieved popularity with the song, "Crying in the Chapel" transcended category. The mainstream listener does not view the religious images as emanating from a cultural tradition where religion is clearly tied with other aspects of life. The embrace of this song across a number of categories could be related to the Korean War huddle.

It is difficult to categorize the production of the song by the Baltimore vocal group, the Orioles. Their version would have been the one most popular with the younger segment of the radio listening audience. The Orioles's performance is not a gospel workout. Sonny Til and the Orioles were a secular vocal group who came to prominence in the late 1940s at Harlem's Apollo Theater. Charlie Gillett notes Sonny Til did not sound "black" in his vocals (42). Though the Orioles, African-American recording artists, were, like the country and western composer of the song, from a marginalized group, the lyrics are not foregrounded in the mind of the listener by the song's cultural origins. The significance of the widespread popularity of this song through a number of different markets testifies to the openness of the mainstream audience at this time period to an offensive message issuing from the Christian tradition. The song sounds a meaningful note.

The lyrics of "Crying in the Chapel" add up to a message with content. The message is offensive. There is a place, and only one place, to find peace. Elvis Presley's version of the song, recorded seven years later in 1960, though not a hit until 1965, is even more specific. In the last line of the song, as a result of prayer, he intones, "you'll surely find *the* way" (emphasis added). The Orioles sang a slightly vaguer version: "you'll surely find a way."

The song is unique because it unfolds a clear element of the Biblical sacred order, yet it is not a novelty, or a traditional hymn. It uses a contemporary narrative and a contemporary vocal and instrumental production to express its point. With one or two exceptions, this type of song would not be popular again until the revival rock era at the end of the 1960s.

"Crying in the Chapel," however, is not completely devoid of the conventions of lyrics of civility. Though "Lord" is even used in the Bible as a form to address God, the vagueness of the word made it an attractive way to refer to the deity in popular songs with Biblical images. Also, the chapel signifies a non-denominational place of worship. It is specifically a Christian holy site, but it encompasses all forms of Christianity.

Lyrically, "Crying in the Chapel" focuses on the prayer element of the Christian tradition. As will be shown in subsequent songs with Christian images, the act of petitioning God is one of the most popular images utilized by lyricists who bring an element of the Christian sacred order to popular music lyrics.

The only gospel song by an African-American singer to chart on the *Billboard* national bestseller charts in the pre-rock era was Mahalia Jackson's "Move on Up a Little Higher" (no. 21, 1948). The lyrics specifically relate to the Christian sacred order. The narrator is going to drink the "ol' healing water" from the "Christian fountain" located "on high." One interpretation of the song is as a look forward to heaven. The narrator, again invoking a specific Christian image, is "gonna lay down my cross, get me a crown." In this longed-for place "way back in glory," where she will "Walk and never tire, fly and never falter," the narrator plans to "meet old man Daniel," the "Hebrew children," and the "Lily of the Valley" (that is, the Christ).

In viewing popular music that originated in musical subcultures that have strong ties to Biblical tradition, it should be noted that songs with meaningful lyrics such as "Move on Up a Little Higher" are heard differently by the mainstream popular music audience than the popular songs that contain lyrics of civility. Faced with offensive phrases such as "Christian fountain" or "Zion" in recordings by artists from Biblically-influenced musical subcultures, the mainstream audience uses a filter to translate these meaningful lyrics to those of civility. This filter of civility compartmentalizes or marginalizes the intended meaning. The audience hears the recorded work as part of the American folk culture tradition rather than as an embrace of a real space-time Biblical sacred order. The content of the lyrics is removed to the mainstream listener who is outside the source culture. Charles H. Lippy notes the observation of Joseph R. Washington, Jr. that the form of Christianity practiced by African-Americans is a folk religion, in the manner that it has been molded by the "experiences of the common people" (46). It has been freed from the limits of the boundaries of the sanctuary. This helps to explain why there is no dichotomy between the sacred and the secular in the music of African-American culture.

Also, listeners who are members of the musical source subculture hear meaningful lyrics differently than the mainstream audience. The subculture audience has a clear contract of understanding with its musicians. Though there is this agreement, this does not mean that the lyrics are limited to only one meaning. The music of the African-American subculture can be understood on more than one level by the subculture audience. The image in "Move on Up a Little Higher" of the "beautiful golden gate" is not only a reference to the Biblical concept of heaven. It refers to a higher place in the earthly walk for African-Americans than what was being experienced in the United States in 1948. The "heavy burden" that Mahalia Jackson sings of "laying down" is not only a reference to the toil of earthly living, but also to the weight of oppression on African-Americans and other minority ethnic and racial groups living under the shadow of prejudice and misunderstanding. Bernice Johnson Reagon notes that the "troubled waters" referenced in the spiritual "Wade in the Water" personally denoted the struggle to obtain voting rights for African-Americans in southern states in the 1960s (21).

"Stars Are the Windows of Heaven" (no. 17, 1950) by the Ames Brothers displays a clear use of the inoffensive language used to express Biblical images in American culture. Rather than the Father or the Son watching over God's children, or "kids" in this case, it is celestial bodies that look over humanity and disapprove or affirm people's actions: "They keep an eye on kids like me and you." According to the lyric's theology, the stars "cry each time we are naughty" which results in rain. On the other hand, "when we're good they are smiling and they shine again." In addition to the language being inoffensive, the theological content is civil. There is a differentiation between correct and incorrect actions, but there is no statement as to the implications of moral trespass other than a change in the weather. The closest reference to a spiritual being in heaven is to angels: "stars are the windows . . . where angels peak through." In the teenage prayer songs which became popular later in the 1950s, stars and angels were frequently used as substitute images for God. So, in addition to the deity being identified through nondescript terms, there was a substitution of other heavenly beings for God in making references to the central character of the Biblical faith. Stars and angels provide less offensive references to the overwhelmingly other of the Christian sacred order.

My use of the terms "Father" and "Son" reflects part of the Christian tradition that has been more traditionally accepted in the past, but is now under fire in some denominational circles. I refer here to the debates regarding the gender of God and the idea of anthropomorphizing the persons of the Godhead. Traditionally, in American culture, in the Christian religion, God has been referred to as a father and as Our Father in the Lord's Prayer and Jesus Christ has been identified as the son of God. Within the traditional doctrine of the Trinity, God the Father is the first person of the Trinity, Jesus Christ is the second person of the Trinity and the Holy Ghost, or Holy Spirit, is the third person of the Trinity. These tenets of faith have been accepted as part of the traditional sacred order of Christianity.

These references were accepted through most of the twentieth century by those who embraced the Biblical tradition. Thus, when a reference is made to the gender of God, or to the Father and Son, the purpose is to keep in line with the tradition of the period during which the songs in the study were popular, rather than to present a theological argument to add to the debate about the nature of God.

Frankie Laine's "I Believe" (1953), released to great success in the same year as "Crying in the Chapel," is an even stronger expression of the inoffensive language of the 1950s. "I Believe" can be labeled inspirational music. This type of song has no specific Biblical or religious image grounded in a spiritual or sacred order, but songs of this nature invoke that which is tangible to the listener, normally what is visible in the physical world, to inspire or uplift. They evoke what Berger may term the "plausible." Hope is found in what can be easily grasped by the mainstream audience, rather than in a supreme being. The hope articulated in "I Believe" is similar to that addressed in Rodgers and Hammerstein's "You'll Never Walk Alone." In their inspirational composition, not walking alone does not necessarily mean walking with God or some spiritual being, but rather it refers to walking with "hope in your heart." Hope is an emotion, a feeling that can be drawn up from within the self. Hope is a possible center of the order subscribed to by individuals. Similarly, in Gogi Grant's "Suddenly There's a Valley" (no. 9, 1955), the focus is on hope as the center of one's spiritual strength. The narrator closes the song with the words, "When you think there is no bright tomorrow and you feel you can't try again, suddenly there's a valley where *hope* and love begin" (emphasis added).

Laine's *Billboard* number two hit has two verses. Almost every line begins with the phrase, "I believe." It is a creed. In the first line, the singer announces, "I believe for every drop of rain that falls a flower grows." No listener is going to disagree with that whether she or he accepts or refuses the Christian sacred order. The same goes for the next line: "I believe that somewhere in the darkest night a candle glows." These are tangible illustrations that the listener can readily imagine. To be fair to the lyricist, these statements can be read allegorically. Even the Psalms of David use poetic terms to refer to God. One can argue that the wordsmith is not suggesting that on a dark night one can find a light in a window if one looks hard enough. Rather, the lyricist may be echoing the proverb about it being darkest before the dawn. Somewhere out there one can uncover hope. The question is, just what is the specific belief that issues from these credal pronouncements? In whom or what does one's hope rest?

In the second verse of the song, the element of prayer is introduced. Unlike the other lines of the song, the first two lines of this verse are closely connected. The first line reads "I believe above a storm the smallest prayer will still be heard." The second line follows: "I believe that someone in the great somewhere hears every word." These lines bring the song closest to flirting with the idea of accepting a sacred order in the universe. The general suggestion in both lines is that when a prayer is launched forth, it finds a target. But who is it that hears the petitions of the believer? The answer is "someone in the great somewhere." To say this is vague is understatement. "Someone" may or may not be God. Even the address "Lord" would be more specific. The "great somewhere" may be an allusion to heaven, or it may not. The term "heaven," like "Lord," had it been inserted in the lyric, would hardly have been considered offensive. The listener is left knowing why the singer believes, but is without a clue as to who or what the singer believes. So, in the same year of the offensive message of "Crying in the Chapel," there co-existed the ultimate inoffensive dogma of "I Believe." "I Believe" signaled the emergence of the dominant period of lyrics of civility on the mainstream popular music charts.

Silk has written that religion became "less controversial" during the "so-called Eisenhower revival of the 1950s" (28). Is it any wonder that with lyrics as inexplicit as those of "I Believe" there would be no controversy? In the same year that "I Believe" rose to popularity, Dwight Eisenhower moved into the White House. His much-quoted remark on the eve of his first inauguration promotes the same appearance of common accord: "Our government makes no sense unless it is founded in a deeply felt religious faith—and I don't care what it is" (P. Carter 124). The plurality of religious choices results in adopting the lowest common denominator from varied doctrines as the only possible public religious pronouncement. There is little that can articulate the lowest common denominator more than the identification of a national faith with no more detail than the description "deeply felt." Paul Nathanson points out that "presidential speeches never refer to specifically Christian notions of God. . . . They never mention Jesus. . . . [T]his indicates a vestigial place of religion in American life . . . the forms of religion are preserved but emptied of content" (268). This is exactly what is revealed in songs with lyrics of civility. They have the form of the Biblical faith, but do not have the substance. Three recorded versions of "I Believe" charted. All remain exactly faithful to the lyrics, suggesting that the inspirational creed is almost beheld as scripture. The words are sacred and inerrant. They are not lyrically tampered with by the individual recording artist who approaches them. Neither of the other versions were as successful as Laine's performance. Broadway singer Jane Froman introduced the song on her television show *USA Canteen* and used it for the show's theme. Her version peaked at number eleven on the *Billboard* popularity chart. Eleven years later, the Bachelors, a vocal group who, though it seems odd now, was considered part of the British invasion (they were Irish and it was 1964), cracked the *Billboard* Top 40 with their remake.

Les Paul and Mary Ford's "Vaya con Dios" (no. 1, 1953) tells the story of a couple in love who are separated. It is another separation narrative. The narrator evidences an acknowledgment of the Biblical sacred order. While her love is away, the narrator (Mary Ford sings all parts of the harmony) promises to pray every night for her beloved.

In several ways the embrace of the Biblical sacred order is made inoffensive in the lyrics. The mention of God's name is in Spanish rather than English. The phrase "Vaya con Dios" may be more melodic than "May God be with you" or the literal translation "Go with God," but even the sheet music suggests including both the Spanish and English phrases. The lyrics off the sheet music read, "Vaya con Dios, my darling, may God be with you, my love." Neither in this recording or the Drifters's remake (no. 43, 1964) is there a mention of God in English. This reduces the meaning of the reference to the deity in the hearing of the phrase by the mainstream market. Here is another form of how lyrics (again, lyrics emanating from Tin Pan Alley, which some have suggested were without meaning) use conventions of civility in presenting images of the Biblical tradition. In Spanish, "Dios" is a clear identification of God, but in the English-speaking popular music marketplace, it is a vague melodic sound.

Not only does the use of a foreign language reference to God render the name inoffensive, but the lyrical acceptance of the Biblical tradition in "Vaya con Dios" is also perceived as something connected to a marginalized group. The setting of the narration is in a rural area of Hispanic influence. There are images of an "hacienda" or ranch and of "village mission bells . . . softly ringing." Thus the embrace of a Biblical sacred order by the song's narrator is perceived as being part of the cultural heritage of a narrow segment of society, rather than something that encompasses all of American culture.

Similar to the type of landscape that surrounds Shep Fields's "Cathedral in the Pines," the locale of "Vaya con Dios" is rural, where traditional values still have import. The lyrics suggest the idea of the regionalization of traditional religious belief. Such an adherence to the Biblical sacred order is not plausible in more urban (or pluralized) areas. A similar setting and suggestion of the marginalization of belief is evoked later in the decade in the Browns's "The Three Bells."

The year 1953 also brought to the bestseller charts "God Bless Us All" (no. 18), recorded by five-year-old Brucie Weil. The song is a snapshot of a child's bedtime prayers. The recording opens with a mother reminding her son to say his prayers. She notes that "someone's listening up above," and tells the boy that it is "time to ask the Lord to bless everyone you love." As in "I Believe," there is a reference to "someone," but in this case the next line notes that the someone is the "Lord." The five-year-old goes on to bless everyone from the "postman" to "cowboys" to "servicemen" and the "spaceman on my TV set." The blessing is not specific other than in a couple of cases where his prayer appears to be for protection, such as for the servicemen (the song was released in the same year that the war ended in Korea) and for "circus acrobats, never let them fall."

Though the offensive title "God" is used to refer to the Christian deity in this production, the recording was embraced by the mainstream marketplace for several reasons. As songs that regionalize faith suggest that adherence to a traditional sacred order belongs to marginalized groups, so the image of a child with faith can be viewed as the embrace of religion by a marginalized group, the little children who Jesus loves. The adherence to the Biblical sacred order can be seen as something found in the innocent child but not as something to be realistically appraised by the entire mainstream audience.

"God Bless Us All" has a novelty character to it which compartmentalizes the message, much as the offensive messages of artists rooted in marginalized groups find their lyrics compartmentalized by the mainstream audience. The novelty character distances religion even further from the listener. A novelty song does not have the indigenous authenticity to give its message currency within the context of contemporary music culture and contemporary society. Thus, there is no meaning to "God bless." If the song is unauthentic, so is its suggestion that God can make a difference in space-time history. For the no-longer-innocent majority, the idea of praying for the protection of someone is not plausible. Rather, that act belongs in the province of a marginalized group outside the mainstream.

Don Cornell's reading of Dale Evans's "The Bible Tells Me So" (no. 7, 1955) expresses a clear message about the Christian sacred order. However, like Brucie Weil's bestseller, the song has a novelty character which compartmentalizes the message. The narrator sings of Biblical truth. The lyrics proclaim the importance of "faith, hope and charity" and of doing "good to your enemies." The words of the song do not go against the grain of the teachings of the New Testament. But the song comes off as a Sunday School chorus, something to be forgotten once the bell rings signifying the end of class. Its Sunday School chorus character is evidenced by the repetition of verses in the recording. The first verse is repeated three times during the course of the production.

The song is a reminder of the Christian tradition in American society, but it does not authentically call on the listener to take hold of the message. A radical idea, "do good to your enemies," is couched in a singalong context. An offensive message is transformed into an inoffensive statement not only through the mainstream audience's interpretation of the lyrics but also through the musical arrangement that complements the words of the song.

At some point in the mid-1950s, songs that accepted the idea of the existence of a Biblical sacred order became associated with a popular music aesthetic, rather than a rock music aesthetic. This was a carry over from the aesthetic of civility in song lyrics and in the theology presented in songs that supported the Biblical tradition. Cornell's recording is an early example of this process. Charlie Gillett identifies three types of songs that were popular before the rock era. He labels them sentimental, melodramatic and novelty (4). "The Bible Tells Me So" is both sentimental and novelty. Though on the cusp of the rock era, like other songs in the pre-rock era, Cornell's recording has an instrumental backing track that would now be identified as easy listening or middle-of-the-road (M-O-R). (When the Cornell recording was released, the terms "easy listening" and "middle-of-the-road" were not used to identify types or genres of music. The Cornell record would have been described at the time of its release as "ballad-style.") This form of instrumental arrangement is the norm for a sentimental song. In the pre-rock era, all lyrics in mainstream popular music, whether they incorporated religious images or not, had common instrumental tracks, in terms of their easy listening character. But, there was a separation during the early years of the rock era. The inoffensive character of the pre-rock music form became the musical support for lyrics of the Biblical tradition. This further promoted the notion that songs of this genre should be inoffensive and unmeddling, even if the lyrics, on the surface, had content.

The easy listening instrumental character sapped meaning from the lyrics because as rock music began to dominate the charts, songs with inoffensive instrumentation were perceived as less authentic. This is why, even today, popular music scholars, e.g., Simon Frith, are oblivious to the significance of Tin Pan Alley lyrics. Their analysis is colored by middle-of-the-road instrumental arrangements. Song arrangements, thus, were also part of the package of ways in which religious images in popular songs were couched in an aesthetic of civility.

The combination of sentimentality and novelty in Cornell's song suggests several ideas about the place of the Christian tradition in American culture. The sentimental character of the song suggests that the place of religion is limited to the emotions. It is not something to utilize in living everyday life. The novelty character separates the currency of the Biblical tradition from the perceived reality of the listener. The song does not possess indigenous authenticity.

When former Ellington vocalist Al Hibbler sings of "He" (no. 4, 1955), rather than of, say, an infinite-personal God, he is reflecting the notion of defining God through the least common denominator among an array of doctrines, at least among the various offshoots of Biblical doctrine. Though most, if not all, listeners would understand that "He" refers to the Biblical God at this juncture in history, the word "God" was too content-filled to be prevalent in the public marketplace of popular music. For the same reason, Laurie London sings, "*He*'s got the whole world in His hands" (emphasis added). Extending Francis Schaeffer's thought on "contentless faith" (64), the use of the word "He" can be seen as contentless as well.

The God of "He" is all-forgiving. The lyric expresses a centralizing of the doctrine of forgiveness. There is no need to confess wrongdoing because forgiveness will be provided no matter what. However, although there is an all-encompassing forgiveness, there is still the idea that there is something that needs to be forgiven, that is, sin. The sinner, according to the lyricist, actually has the capacity to sadden God. This parallels the Ames Brothers's pronouncement that "stars cry each time we are naughty" in "Stars Are the Windows of Heaven." In "He," there is an acknowledgment, one rooted in a conservative tradition, that a person can indeed turn away from God. However, there is no indication that there needs to be repentance or a turning back in order to restore fellowship with God. The implication is that God will wipe clean the slates of everyone.

A song that held the number one spot for four weeks on *Billboard*'s "Most Played by Jockeys" in the spring of 1958 also referred to God only as "He." However, this song reveals even less about the character of God, though ostensibly its entire lyric revolves around God. Recorded by thirteen-year-old English boy Laurie London, "He's Got the Whole World (In His Hands)" says little more than what is included in the song's title about God. Aside from detailing who is in God's hands, e.g., "little bitty babies," no other information is offered. Similar to the God sung about by Al Hibbler, thoughts of London's God are surely to warm the heart and cater to the emotions, but to do little more. Meaning is vacant. Certainly, there is not the faintest notion in this singalong that God is also described as a God of judgment in the tenets of the Christian tradition.

Though somewhat older than five-year-old Brucie Weil who recorded "God Bless Us All," London's vague, though affirming, faith in the Biblical tradition is also perceived in the market as the faith of a child, a member of a marginalized faith group. The embrace of the Biblical sacred order is not viewed as something that necessarily should be spiritually involving of the more "mature" segments of the mainstream audience. London's rendering of the song is as that of a young child. His voice sounds younger on record than his thirteen years of age.

There were a number of popular recordings in the early 1950s that revolved around the theme of sin and romantic attraction. The theme of Nat "King" Cole's "My One Sin (In Life)" (no. 24, 1955) is, as in Louis Armstrong's "Lawd, You Made the Night Too Long" and Percy Mayfield's "Please Send Me Someone to Love," in line with the African-American building of secular concerns on a spiritual foundation. The narrator recognizes the existence of a moral universe. He acknowledges that committing a sin is something wrong. The song is about the narrator's passion for his love interest. If it is wrong for him to be as smitten with her as he is, then his "one sin in life is loving

[her]." In an interesting juxtaposition, the narrator describes his love as both his "temptation" and his "heaven" in the same breath.

However, the narrator in all actuality does not view himself as a sinner. If his passion for her is not the right thing to do, he admits that this is his *one* sin in life. He can number no other transgressions in his conscience. There is little evidence of the Biblical suggestion of a sin nature in humanity. The lyrics only note that temptation leads to sin and that sin is wrong.

And there is no reason to believe that the narrator's passion for his love is sinful. Unlike popular recordings of the late 1960s and early 1970s which detailed the entanglements of adulterous relationships, e.g., the Brooklyn Bridge's "Your Husband-My Wife" (1969), Luther Ingram's "(If Loving You Is Wrong) I Don't Want to Be Right" (1972) and Billy Paul's "Me and Mrs. Jones" (1972), there is no hint in the Cole recording that the relationship is anything but pure. So, the end result is that the narrator is not a sinner. He can not control his passion for his love—"wanting [her] heart and soul as [he does]"—but there is no evidence that his desire is wrong. Though the Biblical sacred order is not excluded, the lyric still presents a vague theology in regard to the notion of sin. The individual narrator decides what is sin for himself and he concludes that he has no sin. Though he does not say he has no need of God, he suggests that he alone is the judge of his moral actions.

"(It's No) Sin" (1951), a number one bestseller for Eddy Howard and His Orchestra, asserts that there is nothing wrong with the narrator's love for his romantic interest. Though the two are parting, he promises to "keep loving [her] forever, for it's no sin." Again, the narrator is the judge of whether or not an activity is a failing in his life.

In the theological universe of the narrator of Frankie Laine's "Answer Me, O Lord" (no. 24, 1953), loneliness is viewed as a retribution for unconfessed sin in one's life. He asks God, "Just what sin have I been guilty of, tell me how I came to lose her love?" Here again is the application of an extra-Biblical principle. The narrator recognizes that there is sin and that it has negative consequences, but he also adds to the Biblical instruction. He asserts that his loneliness is the punishment he has been given for what he has done (though he is unsure of the nature of his sinful act). The lyrics also include a prayer to God to return the narrator's love to him: "Let her know I've been true, send her back so we can start anew." This follows the idea of praying for a romance following the theme of Percy Mayfield's "Please Send Me Someone to Love" (1950).

Johnnie Ray labels himself a sinner for being in love. But his definition of sin is not the same as that suggested in the Scriptures. The narrator of "A Sinner Am I" (no. 20, 1952) confesses that he is a sinner "for falling in love with [her]." Though he describes himself as a sinner, the narrator goes on to say "I can never be blamed 'cause I'm not ashamed." Theologically, the lyrics suggest that if one is not conscience-stricken from an action, there will be no retribution. If a Biblical definition of sin is a break of fellowship with God, the suggestion in the Ray recording is that there is no need for the restoration of fellowship with the Christian deity. There is no condemnation because the narrator (sinner) does not have any sense of remorse or guilt—"I'm not ashamed." The narrator sets his own absolutes. There may be sin, but sin is self-defined. Morals are relative. The popular conception of the notion of sin as expressed in these songs falls within the conventions of civility because the meaning of the Biblical concept is reduced to whatever the individual decides its connotation should be.

Before a Las Vegas showroom, Johnnie Ray introduced "I'm Gonna Walk and Talk with My Lord" (no. 24, 1953) as a "jubilee song." Known for his emotional delivery, as expressed in his biggest hit "Cry" two years earlier, Ray brought a rhythm and blues influence to the floor that was rare among contemporary popular music vocalists (Clarke 962). The impetus for recording "I'm Gonna Walk and Talk with My Lord" was most likely due to his affinity for rhythm and blues. The popularity of Ray's "jubilee song" may have been due in part to the spiritual huddling of the nation during the Korean War, which ended in July of the same year as the record's release.

Ray's song uses clear, offensive terminology drawn from the Bible. In the opening measures, he tells the listener, "I'm gonna save your souls from hell." Ray sings of a "thunderin' voice in heaven" who invites him, "Come unto me." The voice tells him that he will be "happy . . . if you just abide with me." He goes on to specifically sing of "an introduction, come to the Father and the Son." He preaches to the listener: "if we stand as He planned upon His promises, well, soon, I'll hear Him say, 'Well done.'" Certainly, the song is not vague in its lyrical intent. Released in the same year as the various successful versions of "Crying in the Chapel," the popularity of Ray's recording may have reflected a climate that was open to more meaningful images rooted in the Christian tradition.

Pat Boone, who had established his career by singing what Langdon Winner refers to as "pale cleaned-up imitations" of rhythm and blues market hits (39), was also known for his religious faith. His beliefs supplemented his clean-cut, white-buck shoes image (Clarke 138). Record industry leaders, who feared the reaction of parents of white teenagers drawn to the music of rhythm and blues recording artists such as Fats Domino, Little Richard Penniman, the El Dorados and Ivory Joe Hunter (all of whom recorded songs that were successfully covered by Boone), viewed Boone (and several other artists, e.g., Georgia Gibbs) as what Greg Shaw labels a "safe alternative to Elvis" (100), though as can be seen from the above list of rhythm and blues performers, it was not only the product of Elvis that the record companies were concerned about entering white homes.

The success of recordings by Boone that de-racialized rhythm and blues songs, combined with the knowledge of his religious beliefs, aided in maintaining the perception in the music industry that pop music lyrics reflecting the Biblical tradition should only be supported with the easy listening arrangements of the pre-rock era, as opposed to the arrangements associated with the increasingly prominent rock and roll recordings. This is the case with Boone's remake of "There's a Gold Mine in the Sky" (no. 20, 1957). The recording underlines the contemporary view that the Bible and rock and roll did not mix. As rock music evolved, most songs with Biblical images remained static in terms of their instrumental arrangements. These civil arrangements nullified the message presented in the lyrics of the songs.

Dorsey Burnette's "(There Was A) Tall Oak Tree" (no. 23, 1960) is an exception to the idea that lyrics with religious images need to be accompanied with middle-of-the-road instrumentation. Burnette had a rock and roll music history, having recorded with his brother Johnny Burnette as a duo and in a trio. So singing a rock song was not a novelty for him, as it would be for Pat Boone. "(There Was A) Tall Oak Tree" is a rock production.

It is also an early musical example of environmental consciousness. The lyric is a complaint against those who destroy the handiwork of the Creator: "along came man to burn the oak tree down and now the babbling brook is solid ground . . . and there's a cloud of smoke that covers up the clear blue sky." From the point of view of the narrator, the destruction of the environment is due to the sin nature of humanity. In this song, God is identified as the "Creator." The lyrics go back to the Garden of Eden story to locate the origin of sin. The lyrics of Burnette's recording present a meaningful, offensive message. There are consequences of sin. The song does not even leave open a possibility for forgiveness.

Wink Martindale's spoken "Deck of Cards" (no. 7, 1959), penned by T. Texas Tyler and a country and western bestseller in 1948, combines ideas of the Biblical sacred order and a World War II scene. In addition to stimulating religious emotions, the song draws up patriotic emotions relating to a war fought victoriously less than fifteen years earlier. The story is about a soldier who has to defend himself before a Provost Marshal because he pulled out a deck of cards in church. He is acquitted because his cards act as "a Bible, an almanac and a prayer book."

The words of the narrative are specific and offensive. In going through the cards before the court, the soldier narrator notes "there is but one God." He mentions "the Father, the Son and the Holy Ghost" as who he thinks of when he sees the "trey." The king invokes the image of "one king in heaven, God Almighty."

The lyrics bring up specific stories of the Bible that detail the Biblical religion as having absolutes and God as a judge. There is the story of the ten virgins and their lamps. Only five were saved because they were prepared. In other words, heaven is not open to all as is suggested in earlier records, such as "He." The eight reminds the narrator of the number of "righteous persons God saved when He destroyed the earth." The words reprove those who turn their back on the Christian sacred order. For the narrator, the nine brings to mind the nine of the ten lepers healed by "Our Savior" who "didn't even thank Him."

This song not only mentions "God Almighty" but it makes reference to "Our Savior" which was rare in this era. Except for an occasional indirect reference, such as in Patti Page's "Croce di Oro" (1955), the Christ or His work on the cross was lyrically out-of-bounds. The image of Jesus Christ is viewed as much more offensive than God, because it more narrowly focuses the deity to the Christian tradition. Certainly, the name God is more specific than "someone up above," but God can still be used as a connotation word, unlike the name Jesus Christ. Despite the large percentage of persons who described themselves as Christian, the references to the deity of the Christian sacred order were almost universally to the first person of the trinity, as "Lord" or "He," rather than to the Son.

Though "Deck of Cards" was written shortly after the end of World War II, the song achieved its greatest popularity over a decade after its creation. It became popular during a period when the United States was not actively involved in a conflict of the magnitude of a World War I or World War II. The songs's lyrical content, however, is reminiscent of the recordings that were popular when the nation drew together in a spiritual cluster during the two World War periods. The "God words" in the lyric of the song can be conjured up during the heat of battle, but would not be appropriate at other times. The success of the song suggests an uncertainty in American society in the late 1950s perhaps due to the Cold War tensions between the United States and the U.S.S.R. and the Communist bloc and the increasing number of American military advisers shipping out to southeast Asia.

LaVern Baker's "Saved" (no. 37, 1961) sounds as though it was drawn from an evangelistic service. The narrator sings of how she has been saved from a life of sin—she used to "smoke, drink and dance the hoochie-coo"; "cuss, fuss and boogie all night long"; and "lie and cheat and step on people's feet." But she has turned her back on sin: "I know right from wrong." She testifies of a new way: "I'm steppin' on to glory, salvation is my beat." Billie Holiday may cover the waterfront, but for the narrator of the Baker recording, her beat is salvation. She has been enlisted in "that soul-saving army."

The lyrics of the recording by Baker, like the lyrics of Mahalia Jackson's "Move on Up a Little Higher," are not given the same currency by the mainstream audience that would be invested by the subculture in which "Saved" is rooted. The Biblical call for repentance found in the words of "Saved" does not tug at the heart of the mainstream. Also, unlike Mahalia Jackson, LaVern Baker's reputation was made not in gospel music, but in rhythm and blues. Baker's earlier bestsellers included "Tweedle Dee," "Jim Dandy," and "I Cried a Tear." This may further assign the song to a novelty spot in the minds of the mainstream audience, as may another aspect of this song. "Saved" was composed by two Jewish-Americans, Mike Leiber and Jerry Stoller, who were hired by her record label (Atlantic) to produce Baker's recordings.

Gene McDaniels's "A Hundred Pounds of Clay" (no. 3, 1961) speaks of God as a creator, though it again, only refers to God as "He." The production is another rare example of the accompaniment of Biblical images with authentic rock music rather than an inoffensive middle-of-the-road instrumental arrangement. The lyrics primarily celebrate the love between the male narrator and his woman, though the song has incurred the wrath of feminists who are angered by the line "He created a woman and lots of lovin' for a man." The lyrics follow the Biblical order of creation by suggesting that God created the woman after He created the man. Like the God of the Book of Genesis who remarks, "It is not good for the man to be alone. I will make a helper suitable for him" (Gen. 2:18, New International Version [NIV]), the God of McDaniels's hit says, "I'm gonna fix this world today because I know what's missing."

The important theme of the song is missed by those who focus on the order of gender in creation and the interpretation of the woman's reason for being. In the second verse, the narrator vows, "I will thank Him everyday for every kiss you're giving." The thanksgiving of the narrator underlines the celebratory character of the song. The narrator acknowledges that the romantic love he experiences with his life partner was brought about by the actions of God's hand in history. The narrator is not asserting a higher place for the male. Rather, he acknowledges the existence of a Biblical sacred order that has brought him to his happy state. For the narrator, God is the author of creation and of romantic love. As the Orioles accomplished in their version of "Crying in the Chapel," McDaniels presents a Biblical message within a production founded in the contemporary record production aesthetic.

The blending of the sacred and the secular, e.g., McDaniels's melding of the creation with romance, is a dominant motif in African-American popular music. In the 1960s, the composers of Marvin Gaye's "Can I Get a Witness" incorporated the language of the testimony portion of a church service in his hit single. In Ray Charles's "Hallelujah I Love Her So," he combined signals from eros and agape love. Charles took gospel songs and spirituals and changed the lyrics to express secular concerns. Thus, "This Little Girl of Mine," "Talkin' 'Bout You," and "Lonely Avenue" were drawn from "This Little Light of Mine," "Talkin' 'Bout Jesus," and "How Jesus Died" respectively (Clarke 225). In "(Your Love Keeps Lifting Me) Higher and Higher," Jackie Wilson sang of a transcendent love that could equally be about the Divine or a significant other. Later, in the mid-1970s, Al Green sang to "Belle" of the tensions between the sacred and the spiritual: "it's you that I want but it's Him that I need." In each of these songs there is a commingling of divine and human love. Romantic love (eros) and divine love (agape) are two powerful dynamics in the universe and the wielding of these two dynamics in close context results in a highly-charged energy in recorded performances.

These songs do not represent a turning away from traditional presuppositions. They are not de-spiritualizing religious images. Rather, these songs engage the religious heritage in a dialogue with human day-to-day concerns. Each of these artists understood the fusion of the sacred and the spiritual. Some struggled with it. On the liner notes of *Midnight Love* (1982), his last album release before he died, Marvin Gaye told friends and family not to worry, he still loved Jesus. Mikal Gilmore writes of the album, "the singer clearly pursued physical and spiritual notions of fulfillment . . . as if they were mutually inseparable ends" (359). Little Richard Penniman ebbs and flows from the pompadour to the pulpit.

The combination of the secular and the spiritual was not limited to lyrical content. Dave Marsh writes of Aretha Franklin's first session for Atlantic Records: "Franklin's inspiration on 'Respect' is to use gospel chords from her own piano as a base for both the band's arrangement and for her own feints toward improvisation. . . . Had Aretha not been trained in church, she'd never have known what to do here" (*Heart* 11). The call-and-response between Ray Charles and his backup singers, the Raelets, evident in "What'd I Say," "Hit the Road, Jack," and "The Night Time is the Right Time," demonstrate the musical influence of the African-American church service. When Clyde McPhatter was brought into the Dominoes as the group's lead singer, he brought a gospel singing style to secular tunes. On their first single, "Do Something For Me" (1951), McPhatter "opened a courtship with magical incantations previously reserved for the good Lord" (Hansen 16).

Country and western recording artist Ferlin Husky invokes a symbol of peace, the dove, in "Wings of a Dove" (no. 12, 1960). Husky makes reference to an event in the New Testament that involves Christ. In the first verse, he sings, "He sends His pure sweet love, a sign from above, on the wings of a dove." This alludes to the baptism of Jesus Christ by John the Baptist (Matt. 3:13–17), as well as to the Father sending the Son. In the following verse, Husky reminds the listener that God is available "when troubles surround us, when evils come." The narrator has a trust in the God of the Biblical sacred order. This trust is not embraced by the mainstream audience because, again, the song is foregrounded by the mainstream audience's perception of the country and western music subculture.

Like the African-American recording artist, the country and western artist who sings lyrics that embrace the Biblical sacred order is read as reflecting the religious tradition of a subculture rather than as a personal, meaningful conviction that demands a response from the mainstream audience. Southern U.S. European-American gospel music emanates from the same subculture as country and western music. Southern gospel may not have the same layers of meaning found in African-American gospel, but the response of the outside mainstream audience is the same to Southern gospel as it is to African-American gospel. The mainstream market minimizes the meaning of the content-filled, offensive lyrics of popular songs that are rooted in the Southern gospel and country and western traditions.

Parallel to African-American gospel music, Southern gospel is not only about the God of the Bible. Jim Curtis writes:

> For to be Southern is to be an evangelical Protestant, just as to be Irish is to be Catholic—even if one does not go to church. . . . In most Southern towns, the neighborhood church . . . served . . . as a social and cultural, as well as a religious, center. In a region which had very few theaters, dance halls, and bars, gospel singing was one form of truly popular music which people enjoyed, and which the preachers couldn't denounce as immoral. (29)

Southern gospel was a unifier of the secular culture, in addition to having a spiritual meaning. It firmed up the insider status of the members of the subculture. But the mainstream audience responded to content-filled Biblical images emanating from the songs of the region as the voice of a marginalized distant group not relevant to the mainstream.

In a small village, surrounded by pine and nestled in a rural valley somewhere in country-pop America, baby Jimmy Brown was christened on a sunny morn, as chapel bells rung. Two decades later, the bells again pealed, this time celebrating Jimmy Brown's marriage. Sometime thereafter, on a rainy morn, a single chapel bell tolled, as "good, old" Jimmy Brown passed on from this life. So goes the story of country-pop trio the Browns's "The Three Bells" (no. 1, 1959). The song evokes images of peace in the valley, of a simple faith and of an uncomplicated, rural lifestyle. The faith in the Biblical sacred order unfolded in the song can be read by the outside mainstream audience as emanating from a musical subculture for which traditional values still have some import. The Biblical images in the song are regionalized and, therefore, distanced, from the "real world" of the outside, surrounding mainstream culture.

There are two primary ways that folk songs with Biblical images interact with the mainstream audience. The first is as a presentation of America's (and the world's) folk music heritage in a celebratory manner to an audience that, though not unaware of this heritage, was becoming increasingly interested during the mid-to-late 1950s and the early 1960s. As the new folksinger movement emerged, recording artists turned to native folk compositions from around the globe and often presented these songs accompanied with simple, acoustic instrumentation similar to what would have accompanied the original renditions.

Another way that songs of the new folksinger movement interacted with the mainstream audience was as an allegory for issues emanating from a rising social consciousness. These songs played a similar role to those with religious images that rose from African-American popular music. As portions of the mainstream audience became more aware and supportive of the need for all peoples in the United States to have the same civil rights, songs that spoke of liberation from the present existence, including spirituals and gospel songs, became part of the folksinger's repertoire.

Thus, Harry Belafonte included "In That Great Gettin' Up Mornin'" on his second album *Belafonte* (no. 1, 1956). Joan Baez performed "Gospel Ship" and "Kumbaya" for her recording *Joan Baez in Concert* (no. 10, 1962). Bob Dylan recorded "Gospel Plow" for his debut album, *Bob Dylan* (1962). These songs presented a hope for freedom from the chains of oppression.

The theme of the Highwaymen's "Michael" (no. 1, 1961), the idea of crossing over to a promised land, had several meanings in the African-American song tradition, including passing to the free states to the north and the Dominion of Canada, as well as to the Biblical kingdom of heaven. According to Fred Bronson, "Michael" was sung "by slaves who lived on the islands off the coast of Georgia and traveled to work on the mainland each day by boat" (96).

The popularity of "Michael" was related to the fact that its lyrics resonated with the rising consciousness among African-Americans and other supportive segments of the nation's populace regarding the hope of an extension of civil rights to all peoples, particularly in the optimistic, heady, early months of the Kennedy administration. The "milk and honey on the other side" was perceived as close to becoming a reality in the country. "Michael" worked on several levels. It addressed a contemporary social issue and it celebrated the American folk music heritage.

Though the lyrics of "Michael" mention the "River Jordan" and the land of "milk and honey," the song does not focus on the Biblical tradition from which its allusions are borrowed. Though folk songs such as this and other tracks sung by the folk artists identified above may have incivil, meaningful language rooted in the Bible, such as the name "Jesus," one level that the mainstream audience did not interact on with the message was as a celebration of Biblical religion. These songs were responded to as part of a native music tradition, or as an allegory for freedom for the oppressed. Thus, the lyrics also acted as lyrics of civility, when it came to reading them as lyrics that approved the Biblical sacred order.

Simon and Garfunkel provide an example of folk artists who do not sing gospel songs to honor or celebrate the Biblical sacred order nor to convey their personal religious convictions. On the duo's first album, *Wednesday Morning, 3 A.M.* (published 1964, no. 30, 1966), they included two songs that proclaim Christ as savior, "You Can Tell the World" and the traditional "Go Tell It on the Mountain." The lyricist of Gibson and Camp's "You Can Tell the World" proclaims that "the gospel has come," the "victory's been won," and, as a result, "He brought joy . . . into my heart." "Go Tell It on the Mountain" contains an explicit message about Christ and redemption: "the humble Christ was born and God sent salvation that blessed Christmas morn." The lyrics of these two songs are a far cry from the tracks on the folk-rock duo's follow-up longplayers, including the immediate follow-up, *The Sounds of Silence* (published 1965, no. 21, 1966), in which songwriter Simon explores, among other things, the empty blessings of the Beatitudes.

Peter, Paul and Mary's "Tell It on the Mountain" (no. 33, 1964) is revealing in its reworking of the lyrics of the traditional ballad. In their version, they eliminate any reference to Christ or his birth. For the line in the refrain, "Jesus Christ is born," they substitute "Let my people go." The theme is salvation, but not that brought by Christ.

The folk trio fuse paraphrases of verses from the spiritual "Wade in the Water" with the chorus of "Go Tell It on the Mountain" to produce a proclamation of deliverance for African-Americans. They transform one verse of the spiritual, "See those children dressed in white, the leader looks like that Israelite" to "Whose that yonder dressed in white, must be the children of the Israelite." Peter, Paul and Mary's recording is a clear example of the use of songs with Biblical images for purposes other than unfolding an acceptance of the Biblical sacred order. Their lyrical transformation clearly secularizes the redemptive message of the song.

There were songs in folk music circles at this time that incorporated meaningful terms. These songs were not part of the above two identified classes of folk songs with religious images. The use of incivil religious language would not be acceptable to a mainstream audience, particularly in the early 1960s, but it was acceptable in a folk music context. In "Masters of War," Bob Dylan's protest against the burgeoning defense industry, he evokes the name of Jesus. In his condemnation of industrialists who profit from military conflicts, he suggests that their actions are unpardonable crimes: "even Jesus would never forgive what you do." He compares the enterprise of profiteers from war to that of Judas. Judy Collins popularized the Leonard Cohen art-folk composition "Suzanne" (1966). The middle verse fixes its gaze on the Jesus of the cross. Cohen writes of "Jesus . . . watching from his lonely wooden tower." Cohen describes the Incarnate God as "forsaken, almost human" on the hill of Calvary.

CHAPTER THREE

I Say a Little Prayer: Images of Supplication in Popular Music

Anyone who analyzes popular songs that incorporate Biblical images will conclude that there are two fundamental themes that were used in the 1950s and 1960s to invoke the Biblical tradition. These themes are prayer and heaven. In this chapter and the next, the focus is on these themes during the period 1953 to 1971. As in the prior half century of popular music recording, the lyrics of the 1950s and 1960s served up vague religious images to the popular music marketplace.

One may consider prayer as a supplication or petition to God for divine assistance in attaining a certain outcome in the life of the one who prays. Secular popular songs of the 1950s and early 1960s with religious content deal with the ultimate concerns of the teenager: winning someone's love, marriage and death. It is no surprise that there is an invocation to a deity at the time of marriage and death. It was a customary practice and still is in most segments of American society. However, the petition for divine assistance in capturing the love of another is a more unusual theme, though as I have shown, it is not unique to this era. It becomes more prevalent, however, in the early 1950s than in earlier popular music history.

The prayer theme is used in several types of lyrical narration. There is the idea of supplication to win the love of a romantic interest, or to protect the health and welfare of the same. There is the prayer for peace on the planet. And there is a prayer for peace within the individual.

The lyricists of this form suggest that no petition addressed to the divine is too trite, or unimportant, including one related to a teenage infatuation. In a sense, these songs do acknowledge the existence of a sacred and supernatural order. God, or someone or something, is capable of hearing petitions and acting upon them. But in a number of songs considered below, the language of the lyrics used to express the Biblical imagery hints at a shallow endorsement of the tradition. There was no unanimity among the era's lyricists regarding to whom or what the prayer should be directed. In some songs the prayer is made to heaven or angels or to stars above rather than to God. Angels or stars are even less offensive references to God than "He." This usage dilutes the Biblical message.

Percy Mayfield's "Please Send Me Someone to Love" (no. 26, 1950) is one of the first bestselling narratives that unfold the story of going to God for help in finding romance. Mayfield fuses the spiritual with the secular. Mayfield combines a concern for humanity with his personal desire for companionship. Before he asks for "someone to love," he first asks for a divine hand to heal world strife. He places a higher priority on community than on his personal interests. The lyric starts, "Heaven, please send to all mankind understanding and peace of mind, but if it's not asking too much, please send me someone to love." His concern reflects the atmosphere of the Cold War era and the beginning of the war in Korea. In the middle measures, he describes the "world troubles" as "this damnable sin" which has the potential (under the shadow of nuclear weapons) to "put the world in a flame." Reflecting the care to employ a lyrically inoffensive address to God in the circle of the mainstream market, the narrator's prayer, as verse one begins, is to "Heaven."

The Canadian quartet the Crew-Cuts's "Angels in the Sky" (no. 11, 1955) provides instructions for what the listener should do if she or he is lonely. Though the lyrics recommend petitioning angels for aid in romantic considerations, the lyrics still point to God as the source of divine assistance. The lyrics assure the listener that there is a promise or contract: the "Lord will always hear you." The lesson to be learned from the lyric is that prayer does make a difference for the lonely teenager.

In the teenage invocation to God for assistance in winning the love of a member of the opposite sex, the address to God is revealing of how God was perceived by the lyricists. As in "He," released in the same year as the Crew-Cuts recording, the word God is not used. "God" was too meaningful and, therefore, controversial.

The narrator of "Teenage Prayer" (no. 6, 1956) follows the suggestion of the Crew-Cuts to direct her petition to angels. Gale Storm's supplication is "whispered to angels." Again there is the inoffensive focus to whom the prayer is addressed. But this song also establishes the ordinariness of prayer. Prayer does not have to be liturgical. It can be a confidence, as illustrated in the narrator's "whispered" petition. It can also be part of a teenager's life. The supplication is not just a prayer from a lonely heart, but a prayer from a *teenage* lonely heart. "Teenage Prayer" is one of the earliest popular music statements that defined romance as the significant element in the world of the teenager. The term "teenager" is prominent in the title and lyric.

The ballad form emphasizes the seriousness of the narrator's "Teenage Prayer." The opening instrumental bars define the song as a slow dance number, a popular form for a narrative about unrequited love. The slow dance was a way for the Boy and the Girl to manifest their interest in one another. Unlike the fast dance, the couple touched in the slow dance. They were close enough to talk to each other, if conversation was in order. At the Junior High Sock Hop in the gymnasium, as the opening notes of the slow dance record reached their ears from loud, blasting speakers of the school's P.A. system, the girls, lined up along the painted cinder block walls on one side of the cavernous facility, wished and hoped that their special guy, lined up with the other boys across the great divide on the other side of the basketball court cum dance floor would cross over the line and ask for this dance. If, after an eternity of waiting, they did in fact meet, they would dance close, real close.

In "Teenage Prayer," the narrator's heartthrob is the answer to her prayer. Had the object of her desire noticed her, the song could not have been written as a slow song. The difference is illustrated in the next discussed song, a testimony to prayer. Unlike the melancholy pace of the Gale Storm recording or Gloria Mann's even more melancholy version of "Teenage Prayer," the peppy and upbeat rhythm of "The Angels Listened In" suggests that it is not a cry for help.

Paralleling "Angels in the Sky" and "Teenage Prayer," the idea of angels as the receptors of prayers is evident in the Crests's "The Angels Listened In" (no. 22, 1959). But this song is the antithesis to Gale Storm's prayer. The Girl now belongs to the Boy. The narrator celebrates the result of divine intervention in a manner akin to a witness to the power of prayer at a midweek worship service. But, again, the angels, not God or "He," worked in history to bring the Girl to the Boy: "They came down to interrupt just as I had given up." There is the acknowledgment of a sacred order (the narrator confesses that what transpired was the work of a divine hand in history), but there is an inoffensive attribution of romantic success to the action of angels.

In addition to angels, some of these songs propose the petition for divine intervention be directed to stars above. In the Elegants's "Little Star" (no. 1, 1958), a reworking of the "Twinkle Twinkle Little Star" nursery rhyme, it appears in the early portion of the lyric that the narrator is making his petition to a star above. Within the first verses, there is the notion the narrator is asking a star to send him the "one [he's] thinking of" so that they can "share" love. And the casual listener may come away with the interpretation that the stars in the heavens listen and act on petitions from below. Certainly this is an inoffensive interpretation of the work of the divine in space and time.

But in the midst of the song, the Boy prays specifically to God "high above," the same God who is "lighting up the sky," to send him a love to share. This is one of the few songs of this genre to actually name "God" in the lyric. I suggest that either because of the lack of clarity in the invocation of "God" as sung by lead vocalist Vito Picone in the bridge of the recording, or because of the innocuous context of the song's roots (a nursery rhyme), the naming of God as "God" was able to make it past the record company decision makers and broadcasting executives to the radio airwaves. The casual listener may easily miss the Boy praying to God "high above." The unthreatening character of little stars and nursery rhymes combine to make the religious image palatable to the mainstream. And palatable it was. "Little Star" was number one for one week on *Billboard*'s "Hot 100" chart.

(As late as 1966, the word God in the lyrics of a song could prevent it from receiving airplay in some of the nation's major radio markets. The Beach Boys's "God Only Knows," half of the two-sided hit single with "Wouldn't It Be Nice," received heavy airplay at Pittsburgh's powerful Top 40 station KDKA but received no airplay in the New York area and other large markets. Therefore, the record stalled at number 39 on the *Billboard* Hot 100 chart.)

In the Chantels's "Maybe" (no. 15, 1958), the Girl narrator prays every night not to angels or stars but "to the Lord" hoping that her supplications will "send back [her] love." Like Gale Storm's "Teenage Prayer," this is a slow (dance) song of unrequited love. After the opening reverberating piano chords, lead vocalist Arlene Smith offers her anguished cry of youthful passion. The Girl had the Boy but now he's gone.

The Chantels's followup single "Every Night (I Pray)" (no. 39, 1958) is both musically and lyrically a continuation of "Maybe." The opening piano chords are similar and the title inverts the lyric of "Maybe" which opened, "Maybe if I pray every night." Continuing her storyline, the narrator explains why she has been praying for this boy since the last song. She treated him "like a toy" and then wanted to "run away." To win back his love she "falls" on her knees and prays. She asks the Lord to "keep him safe for me," even though "he doesn't love me." Throughout the recording, the background singers emphasize the need for divine intercession. At the beginning, they repeat "Dear Lord" behind the lead vocal line in the opening bars of the song and, at the end, they repeat "I pray" a number of times. Perhaps, the word "Dear" is more of an adjective expressing a characteristic of the God to whom the narrator prays than it is salutatory, but, again, the word God is not used. The address "Lord" by this time was the most prevalent form of directly addressing God in popular music lyrics when the narrator was not addressing "stars" or "angels" or "heaven." Though the address is rooted in the Bible, it was viewed as a less offensive reference for the mainstream market. The address "Lord" is used in both of these *Billboard* Top 40 singles to refer to God.

The clearest address to God in a teenage prayer song in this era is found in Annette's "O Dio Mio" (no. 10, 1960). Annette sings, "O Dio Mio, please hear my prayer." The difference between this song and other teenage prayer songs is that the address is in a foreign tongue and specifically, in this case, Italian. This reduces the meaning of the phrase, similar to the cases of Patti Page's "Croce di Oro," Les Paul and Mary Ford's "Vaya con Dios," Perry Como's "Ave Maria," and Caruso and Journet's "The Crucifix." Even though Annette Funicello was an American sweetheart through her association with Disney's *Mickey Mouse Club*, she would have received little airplay if she had sung the English translation ("Oh, My God") of the recording's title.

Not only does the use of a foreign language reference to God or some element of the Biblical sacred order render the term inoffensive, but the lyrical embrace of the Biblical tradition is also perceived by the mainstream market as something connected to a marginalized group. "O Dio Mio" reflects the Roman Catholic beliefs that are part of Annette's Italian-American heritage.

Similarly, Toni Arden's "Padre" (no. 13, 1958) focuses on the Roman Catholic aspects of the Biblical tradition. In this story, the narrator is not a teenager praying for romance. The narrator and her husband were married in a church wedding ceremony by the Padre, but another woman took her spouse away (a radical narrative for this time in popular music history), so she "kneel[s] and pray[s] . . . counting [her] beads alone." Reflecting the idea of an earthly mediator between humanity and the Godhead as espoused in Roman Catholic theology, the narrator asks the Padre to "pray for my love and me." The reference to her priest in Spanish makes her address to him less offensive than the word "Father" to the mainstream marketplace.

The Roman Catholic notion of a mediator between humanity and God is more pronounced in Vic Dana's "Little Altar Boy" (no. 45, 1961). The narrator confesses that he is a sinner—"I have gone astray"—so he looks to a "holy" mediator or go-between to restore his fellowship with God. He differentiates himself from those with priestly stations in the Roman Catholic Church. He asks the altar boy to pray to the Lord to "take my sins away." Rather than speaking directly to God himself, the narrator asks the altar boy, "What must I do to be holy like you?"

The narrator is not specific about his sin. It is not clear whether he is longing for release from a loneliness due to some unspecified sin, as the narrator of Frankie Laine's "Answer Me, O Lord," or if there is some other offense of which he is aware. The latter may be the case as Dana's narrator appears ready to reform: "Tell Our Lord I'm gonna change today."

The use of the image of a little altar boy rather than a Roman Catholic priest or even the Padre of Toni Arden's recording can be viewed as an inoffensive manner of laying out an important tenet of Roman Catholic belief. Also, the image of a child with faith can be viewed as the embrace of religion by a marginalized group, as in the case of five-year-old Brucie Weil's "God Bless Us All" or thirteen-year-old Laurie London's "He's Got the Whole World in His Hands." As noted earlier, the acceptance of the Biblical sacred order can be seen as something found in the innocence of a child but not as something to be realistically appraised by the entire mainstream market.

At the "Altar of Love," the sacred focal point of God's dwelling place on earth, the narrator of the Channels's recording and his girl made a vow (in church) that they "would be two." But, this is a song of unrequited love as well. Though she said "someday [they'd] marry . . .

she took someone new." The Boy has not given up though. He returns and, on his knees, he petitions the "Dear One Up Above" for assistance. (Though the prayer is not directed specifically to the "Lord," it is not directed to angels or stars either.) The teenage prayer songs, though acknowledging the presence of a sacred order in addressing God, reflect the nature of the religious environment of the late 1950s in the use of the unobjectionable vernacular.

In the lyric of the Channels's recording, though the Girl broke her promise, the Boy's love, like marriage which is vowed to at the same altar, is forever: "the torch will be burning for her love eternally." In this song there is an added dimension to praying, that is, there is the idea of traveling to a sacred location from which the person praying sends forth a petition. The prayer is not from a lonely bedroom.

The narrator of Dionne Warwick's "I Say a Little Prayer" (no. 4, 1967) prays not only from her bedroom, but from wherever she happens to be at the moment. She prays while running to the bus stop, riding on the bus, at her desk and during her coffee break. Though the narrator suffers from an unrequited love, her condition is not as implicit in Hal David's lyrics as in other songs of the genre. This may be so because of several factors: the upbeat rhythm of the tune; the terms of endearment that she voices, e.g., "Dear" and "Darling;" or, and I think primarily, because within the four verses of the song and the chorus as well, the nature of the relationship is ambiguous. She vows in the chorus that he will stay in her heart forever and that they will never part. This could be a marriage vow. Her prayer could be for his well-being. The subject of the narrator's prayer can easily be interpreted as ranging from her spouse to someone who does not even know she exists.

The clues that detail the nature of the relationship appear in the closing phrases of the song, when Warwick departs from the verse and chorus structure and breaks into ad lib phrases. The heartbreak she alluded to earlier in the chorus is revealed to be real and is the impetus for her prayer. After singing "My Darling, believe me, for me there is no one but you," words that continue the ambiguity of what the bulk of the lyrics have revealed about the relationship to this point, the narrator sings the following phrases: "Please love me, too. I'm in love with you. Answer my prayer. Say you love me, too. Why don't you answer my prayer?" So, as the song fades, the listener learns that the subject of the narrator's affection does not yet love her. There is no relationship.

These closing phrases bring to question the receptor to whom the narrator's petition is directed. Until the end, just as one may easily assume that the narrator and her "Dear" are a couple, one can just as readily suppose that the prayer is to God. Similar to the theme of the Ink Spots's "My Prayer," Warwick asks her hoped-for love to answer her prayer rather than the Lord, or angels, or the stars above. Not only is he the answer to her prayer, but he is the one who has the power to answer her prayer. In earlier teenage prayer songs, though the references to God may have been vague, there was the idea that prayer was to someone or thing in heaven, an element of the Biblical sacred order. But in this Bacharach-David collaboration, there is no need for a Biblical tradition. It does not matter whether God speaks or is silent. The petitioner turns to the object of her desire with her prayer. Twice she asks him to answer her prayer. He can do that by telling her that he loves her as much as she loves him.

The last successful recording with the theme of petitioning God for the purpose of gaining the attention of one whom the narrator admires, and possibly the best performance of the genre, was the third *Billboard* number one hit by Motown's Temptations, "Just My Imagination (Running Away with Me)" (1971). Sung by lead vocalist Eddie Kendricks, the lyrics speak again of an unrequited love. The narrator daydreams of his romantic interest's "heavenly" love "when her arms enfold [him]," but it is "just [his] imagination." His prayer follows the same theme. Though, like the narrator of "Maybe," he goes down on his knees to make a supplication and prays to the Lord—"Every night on my knees I pray, Dear Lord, hear my plea"—his prayer is imaginary. He asks, "Don't let another take her away from me or I will surely die." The Lord cannot act on this request, because the petitioner does not have what he asks not to lose. This song adds another dimension to the theme of prayer for an unrequited love. The narrator offers a supplication that can not be answered. This song closed the era of the prayer of the lonely heart genre.

Not all teenage prayer songs were voiced by unrequited or spurned lovers. Sometimes, the petition for divine assistance expressed a concern for the well-being of the Boy or the Girl by one of the two. This notion was present in the Chantels's "Every Night." Though the impetus of the narrator's prayer is the fact that "he doesn't love me," the narrator of "Every Night" unselfishly asks the Lord to "keep him safe for me." In the songs that follow, the couple is already an item. The prayer motive is not to capture the love of the other.

Lead singer Jackie Wilson voices a supplication for guidance and protection for his "sweetheart" and himself before their nuptials in Billy Ward and the Dominoes's "St. Therese of the Roses" (no. 13, 1956). Following the Roman Catholic tradition, the narrator prays to a saint rather than to God or another member of the trinity. Like the narrator of Vic Dana's "Little Altar Boy," the narrator of the Dominoes's song prays through a mediator, though not an earthly one. He vows to pray to the canonized woman daily: "Near the altar in the chapel, I will come by candlelight." Oddly, though the lyric is very specific in its Roman Catholic theology, reference is made to the inoffensive "chapel," rather than to a church. Paralleling the Roman Catholic images of the Vic Dana recording, as well as Perry Como's "Ave Maria," and the Toni Arden and Annette recordings noted above, the desire of the couple to have their love encompassed by a Christian sacred order can be viewed in the mainstream marketplace as something distinctly different from normal lived reality. The activities of the couple in the song are those of a distinctive subculture, the Roman Catholic community.

Though not songs of unrequited love, there are other popular lyrical narratives of separation. Lovers are separated by vast distances due to work, or military service or summer vacation. In Patti Page's "Croce di Oro" (no. 16, 1955), the narrator and her darling are separated by the sea, so she vows to "pray . . . 'til you return." The stars, or, actually in this case, a specific "star in the blue," though not representing heaven or God, does take on characteristics beyond that of inanimate celestial objects. The narrator tells her love: "Each night I will give it [the star] a message and the star will give it to you."

The song does make reference to the "Good Lord," but overall the lyric is experienced aurally by the mainstream market in the same way that Toni Arden's "Padre" or Annette's "O Dio Mio" are. In English, the title of Page's recording is even more offensive than "O My God." The "croce di oro" that the narrator sends along with her love is a cross, a cross of gold. The cross is a specific reference to the Christian tradition and to the crucifixion of Christ. The reference to the cross in a foreign language transforms the term into one more musical than meaningful. The cross becomes inoffensive and insignificant. Also, as in the Arden and Annette recordings, the carried cross, as well as the use of the Italian language, allude to the Roman Catholic tradition. So, the embrace of the Biblical tradition by the narrator is read as the embrace of Christian faith by a group with a distinctive religious tradition and not something that is applicable to the mainstream audience.

The plea for the well-being of one member of a romantic couple by the other is the central motif of the Shirelles's "Dedicated to the One I Love." A *Billboard* number three hit in 1961, the recording originally cracked the Top 100 in 1959. The production's more successful showing its second time around was due in part to the momentum created by the girl group's previous single, the number one "Will You Love Me Tomorrow." Through the narrative of "Dedicated to the One I Love," the listener learns that the Girl and the Boy are separated. Atypical of separation songs, the lyrics imply that the female rather than the male has left the couple's native area. Lead vocalist Shirley Alston sings, "While I'm far away from you . . . I know it's hard for you . . . because it's hard for me. . . ." The lyrics indicate that there is a mutual affection. The separation is difficult for both of them. This idea is also underlined later in the middle measures, when she sings, "I can be satisfied just knowing you love me."

Though the couple is separated, there is hope. Similar to an idea presented in the inspirational "I Believe," the narrator closes the first verse with the line, "And the darkest hour is just before the dawn." The hope is unfolded in the second verse. The narrator requests prayer from her beau. This is where the assurance of their continued relationship lies (and also firms up the notion that she is the one who has left the area). She asks him to "whisper a little prayer" on a daily basis for her, the one he loves.

Like the prayer receptor in the Elegants's "Little Star," the narrator of "Dedicated to the One I Love" asks her beau who is far away to "tell all the stars above." Again, though a central theme of the song is a petition to God, there is the inoffensive reference to stars, signifying heaven and the maker of heaven.

A similar idea, that is, a prayer for the welfare of a separated beau, is found in the Shangri-Las' last appearance in the *Billboard* Top 40. The girl group of two sets of sisters from the Borough of Queens in New York City had an image of street-wise toughness. They were an early model of sisters with attitudes. Often the female protagonist in the lyrics of their songs was named "Mary," the given name of the lead singer of the group, Mary Weiss. This gave credence to their image. The protagonists in the bestselling records of these four young women ("Remember [Walkin' in the Sand]," "Leader of the Pack," "I Can Never Go Home Anymore," "Give Us Your Blessing") lived close to the edge of earthly existence. They were rebels. For true love, they would stand up to their parents. If they did not receive a desired parental blessing, they might just take fate into their own hands.

"Long Live Our Love" (no. 33, 1966) was atypical of the Shangri-Las's recorded output. Though it did have elements that were characteristic of their spoken-sung mini-soap operas, it was an upbeat and patriotic song. The production opens with melodramatic, almost brooding background voices singing "When Johnny Comes Marching Home Again" in a slow tempo and in a lower register than normal. Several measures into the patriotic hymn, the rhythm section makes its entrance, the song's tempo changes to a faster, march-like rock music form and the lead vocalist breaks into the song's chorus. The lyrics of the chorus are a "toast" to happiness and love.

The first verse follows and the narrative unfolds. The narrator and her "childhood sweetheart" made a vow "to love each other" and she knows this vow will not be broken. The second verse explains the reason she affirms the vow: "Something's come between us and it's not another girl." The two are separated but not because of changing affections. This signifies that the lyric is not just another story of teenage unrequited love. The narrator continues to sing, "A lot of people need you, there is trouble in the world." Their separation is due to a higher calling. Something is more important than teenage romance. This idea was quite a departure from the themes of previous Shangri-Las's records.

After the second verse, there is a spoken section which details the higher calling that has brought about the separation of the Girl and Boy. (The spoken section was a characteristic of a number of Shangri-Las' productions including their biggest hits, "Remember [Walkin' in the Sand]" and "Leader of the Pack." On one Shangri-Las's single release, "Past, Present and Future," the lead vocal was entirely spoken word.) The military has separated the couple. The "fighting" has taken him "far, far away." The "fighting" was a reference to the military activity in southeast Asia occurring in late 1965 and early 1966, the period of the record's issue.

As U.S. military commitment to the Vietnam conflict escalated and protests against American involvement commenced, the lyrics of the song provided a response to the situation. They were an affirmation of faith in the American servicemen sent overseas, though not an assent to America's participation. The Girl was sending a message to the Boy. She understood that military duty was more important than the Boy and the Girl being together. And the Girl's support was further evidenced by her vow to wait for him to return. The narrator tells her sweetheart not to worry: "But please don't wonder if I'll be faithful, you're in my heart both night and day."

After another refrain, the song returns to the slow-tempoed "When Johnny Comes Marching Home Again" section. Over the almost mournful voices of the background singers, whose tone underlines the seriousness of the Girl's next words, the narrator speaks a prayer to the "Lord" to not "let anything happen" to her sweetheart, her Johnny. Earlier in the spoken section, the narrator had made a reference to God, actually using the offensive name "God." She spoke, "I know one day if we are lucky, God will send you back to me." On one hand, this can be interpreted as a form of civil religion-type invocation. That is, the song may be extending the idea that America's military involvement is divinely sanctioned. However, her prayer gives greater focus to the earlier statement. She is not saying God will protect him because the American involvement is blessed by the Lord. Rather she is petitioning God, whose hand works in history according to Biblical tradition, to protect her beau. The hope of the narrator is not in her Johnny or her country, but rather in God. God is the one who has the power to answer the narrator's prayer. This hope is underlined as the tempo speeds up to a rocking march and the group repeats the refrain twice, before the song fades.

"Long Live Our Love" did not perform as well on the charts as the girl group's less politically-fueled songs, though it did crack the Top 40. It was a patriotic song like "Deck of Cards," but unlike "Deck of Cards," it did not work as a remembrance of victory in combat. The use of the word "God" was abnormal in the context of contemporary popular music, but because of the patriotic theme, its use was not seen as offensive as it may have been. The use of the incivil "God" may be related to the notion of huddling in time of crisis, in this case the Vietnam conflict. Later in the same year, the Beach Boys released "God Only Knows," which though it offered no information about the character of God other than the fact that God only knew what the Boy would be without the Girl, the actual use of "God" in the lyrics restricted the song's exposure on AM Top 40 radio stations.

In the songs considered above, in which God is the third member of the romantic triangle, there is an acknowledgment of a Christian sacred order. There are some elements revealed about prayer that parallel the tenets of Biblical teaching about prayer, e.g., the idea that prayer makes a difference in one's life and changes history; the idea of falling on one's knees to submit a prayer to God; and the idea of making a pilgrimage to the altar to pray. However, in the unfolding of these narratives centering on the Boy, the Girl and God, there is more often than not a descriptive or a lyrical turn that reduces any meaning implied by the embrace of the Biblical sacred order.

One may wonder what can be incorporated in the lyrics of these songs that would make the songs offensive to one who does not embrace the teachings of the Biblical tradition. Aside from including the name of Jesus, or proselytizing the listener, there may not be a way that the lyrics of these songs could be threatening or uncomfortable to one who had the capacity to be threatened by the details of Biblical doctrine regarding prayer. Though a song like "Teenage Prayer" illustrates the commonness of prayer, its availability to anyone and the idea that one does not have to go to a sacred site to pray, Gale Storm's recording or any of the other examples above are certainly not evangelizing the listener. The songs remain in the mainstream and, therefore, fit into the milieu of lyrics of civility and do not threaten the non-believer.

On the other hand, one may question why there was a need for songs in the mainstream to contain inoffensive lyrics since such a large percentage of the population professed the Christian faith. If 85 percent or more of all Americans identified themselves as Christians, one could assume that Christianity was the religion of the mainstream. Therefore, one would think that the name Jesus Christ, for example, would not be offensive. Certainly, in the 1950s, there was not a great sensitivity to the feelings of non-believers. Concern for non-Christians was not the cause of vague, meaningless lyrics. John F. Wilson suggests otherwise. He states that because American culture is "religiously plural in the extreme," the necessary outcome is that "religious language of the public realm is veiled, obscure, and shifting" (47). Nathanson sees this pluralism as the raison d'etre of the First Amendment of the United States Constitution (267). He argues that church and state were separated not to keep one from interfering with the other as much as to not hinder colonies with different established churches from uniting in one nation (267). So, perhaps, civil language is rooted in deep-seated traditions. Still, though many religions, and sects within each religion, existed in the 1950s and 1960s, the vast majority of Americans professed to being Christian.

One can only assume that the lyrics of civility of mainstream popular music in the 1950s and early 1960s were a response to the form of Christianity practiced by most Americans. It was a vague, civil form of religion that did not ask too much of the adherent.

All pop music songs that relied on prayer as a motif did not deal with romance. There were bestselling records with lyrics related to prayer that dealt with the issue of peace in the world and the peace of the individual. Though for the most part couched in civil terms, these songs indicated that there was a search for an order to turmoil caused by experiences other than an unrequited love.

Jackie DeShannon's "What the World Needs Now is Love" (no. 7, 1965) is a prayer for peace among nations. It was released at a time when American military involvement in southeast Asia was beginning to mark the national consciousness. The narrator implores God for world peace, an all-encompassing peace "not just for some but for everyone." No one nation or specific group of nations should be blessed with peace, but rather all should experience peace. The peace referred to in the lyrics is not the personal peace that may come from a right relationship with God as outlined in the Biblical tradition, but a freedom from war and strife, a peace among the peoples of the world.

Though the lyrics of the DeShannon recording use the customary popular music address of "Lord" in this supplication to God, there is the recognition by the lyricist of God as the author of creation. The praying narrator suggests "we don't need another mountain" or "ocean" or "cornfield" or "sunbeam." And she recognizes it is God who can make the difference in history. In this Hal David and Burt Bacharach composition, released several years before their song "I Say a Little Prayer," the narrator sought the Lord to answer her prayer rather than another person.

In the heat of the Vietnam conflict, Stevie Wonder appealed to the "Lord" in the Ron Miller-penned "Heaven Help Us All" (no. 9, 1970). Both "heaven" and "Lord" are meant to denote God. In this composition, the focus is not on the conflict in southeast Asia alone, though there is an allusion to the "bombs." The lyricist pans eastward across the Pacific to the strife on the streets of urban America. The narrator sings, "Heaven help the child who never had a home, Heaven help the girl who walks the streets alone." The narrator also focuses on race relations: "Heaven help the black man if he struggles one more day, Heaven help the white man if he turns the black away." In the bridge, an appeal is made for the oppressed: "Keep hatred from the mighty and the mighty from the small."

Gary Puckett and the Union Gap's "Let's Give Adam and Eve Another Chance" (no. 41, 1970) similarly makes a plea for peace among all peoples. The lyrics do not focus specifically on internal or external conflicts involving the United States and its population. Rather the narrator's petition is that "He" would "show us how to love one another" so that all will "be free." The premise of the lyric is that all peoples are related through Adam and Eve. The lyricist draws back to the Creation story to set up the narrative.

Though not a prayer song, the San Francisco band We Five's second Top 40 single, "Let's Get Together" (no. 31, 1965)—a song released several years later in a more popular version by the Youngbloods—expresses a parallel notion about all peoples being children of God. There is a need for urgency in bringing about peace for all because, as the narrator notes, "the One who left us here [will return] for us at last." Despite the vague reference to God as "the One," the lyric (written by Dino Valenti, who later became the lead singer of the Bay Area's Quicksilver Messenger Service) is revealing about the God of the Biblical tradition. The phrase about the One acknowledges the Biblical teaching of the Christ's promise to return.

Further, there is a recognition of the ephemeral character of human life. The narrator closes the second verse with the words, "We are but a moment's sunlight fading in the grass." The inclusion of the idea about the transitory nature of humanity in the same verse with the coming return of the Christ suggests a contrast with God, whose character is eternal according to the Bible. Further, the phrase "we must surely pass" in the same verse suggests that rather than life having an absolute close, there may be a transformation to another existence in a heavenly form.

The Beach Boys's "In My Room" (no. 23, 1963) focuses on the internal peace of the individual. Later revelations about the life and crises of Beach Boy leader Brian Wilson more than a decade removed from the time of the song's initial popularity have colored the interpretation of the song and cast the lyrics in a purely autobiographical light. The common interpretation of the narrator of the lyrics as a character insulated from the world of reality fits neatly with the factual picture of Wilson in a tent in a sandbox in the living room of his California mansion.

The lyrics of "In My Room," like most songs composed by Brian Wilson, were written by a collaborator. In the case of this work, Wilson's lyrical partner was Gary Usher. According to Beach Boys biographer Steven Gaines, the lyrics were prompted by Wilson's confidences in Usher (78). At the time of the song's composition, Wilson was still living at his parents's residence. Apparently, there was a great deal of tension between father (Murry Wilson) and son. The music room at home was the younger Wilson's only sanctuary. Not only did he compose there, but he slept there as well. Gaines quotes Usher as saying, "Brian was always saying that his room was his whole world" (78). In Brian Wilson's autobiography, *Wouldn't It Be Nice*, he writes, "Gary recognized that the music room served as a sanctuary to me. He never got over the fact that I slept there, right beside the piano" (58). Gaines asserts that the lyrics "were all based on Brian's sentiment" (78).

Without ignoring the biographical elements of the song, it can be argued that the lyrics go beyond the idea of closing the door on reality, or discovering a protective musical cocoon. Within the sanctuary world that the narrator opens up to the listener, he can whisper his secrets, "lock out" his worries and cares, do his "dreaming" and "scheming," and his "crying" and "sighing." This certainly correlates closely with the idea of the narrator's room as a sanctuary. But the cast of his meditation goes beyond the self. The narrator is not conversing alone. In the middle eight measures, he notes that he lies awake and prays. He may not be on his knees, but he is praying. In revealing his secrets, he is not talking to himself. He recognizes the existence of a sacred order, though, as is the usual case, there is no specific reference to God. There is someone outside the room who aids in bringing about the peace he finds in his quiet place or refuge, so he is empowered to "laugh at yesterday." Though the present understanding of the song does not discount what Ken Barnes labels the "room-as-sanctuary theme" or a "first glimpse at Brian Wilson's reclusive side" (13), there is more to the lyrics than the idea of an escape from reality.

The record was the B side of the Beach Boys's third Top Ten hit single, "Be True to Your School" (no. 6, 1963). "In My Room" rode the crest of that song's popularity to almost crack the *Billboard* Top Twenty.

John Lennon called on "Christ" for inner peace in a composition that he labeled a prayer. On April 14, 1969, Lennon and bandmate Paul McCartney swiftly collaborated on a musical slice of Lennon and wife

Yoko Ono's autobiography. Within an eight hour session at London's Abbey Road recording studios, without George Harrison and Ringo Starr in attendance, Lennon and McCartney started and finished, ready for 45 RPM single release, the Beatle song, "The Ballad of John and Yoko" (no. 8, 1969). The lyrics tell the story of Lennon and Ono's attempts to obtain a visa to travel to France or Holland to get married and describe the couple's first bed-in for peace at the Amsterdam Hilton, as well as other events in the early days of their marriage.

The significant and controversial element of the song was the refrain. Lennon sings, "Christ, you know it ain't easy, you know how hard it can be. The way things are going they're gonna crucify me." Not only does he invoke Christ's name, but he also incorporates the crucifixion event to tie the refrain together lyrically. This was too offensive for AM Top 40 stations. Broadcasters perceived the lyric as taking God's name in vain, so the record received limited airplay. In New York, neither of the two AM Top 40 stations added the song to its playlist. The perception of the song's offensiveness overrode the fact that "The Ballad of John and Yoko" was a Beatles record. Despite the refusal of the radio stations to touch the song, the single crept into the *Billboard* Top Ten.

Lennon argued that he had not taken God's name in vain. Murray "the K" Kaufman, a New York area disc jockey who had been closely identified with Beatlemania from the time the Beatles arrived in the States in 1964, conducted a telephone interview with Lennon over the Memorial Day, 1969 weekend. Regarding the controversial refrain, Lennon refuted radio programmers all over America by explaining that the song was a prayer. Rather than breaking the third commandment given to Moses, Lennon argued that he was actually addressing Christ. Extending his argument, it appears he was indicating that the trials and tribulations he was facing over his relationship with Yoko Ono, which were related to the fact that a Beatle celebrity was supposed to live a life of approval by his fans and he was presently under disapproval, were issues that Jesus Christ would understand. Lennon felt as though he were being persecuted by both the press and Beatlemaniacs.

Whether or not Lennon was sincere about his explanation is unclear. In the same interview, he asked Murray the K if he was playing the single on the air. So, in this context, Lennon was defending the single in his campaign to increase radio exposure of his recent record release. But several years earlier, in his defense of his 1966 remarks comparing the popularity of the Beatles to that of Jesus, Lennon

indicated that he believed there was an historical Jesus. He put forth
what amounted to a creed, one that was valid at least until the time he
imagined a world without religion. In an interview, he remarked:

> I'm not anti-God, anti-Christ or anti-religion. I was not saying we are
> greater or better. I believe in God, but not as one thing, not as an old
> man in the sky. I believe that what people would call God is
> something in all of us. I believe that what Jesus and Mohammed and
> Buddha and all the rest said was right. It's just that the translations
> have gone wrong. (Miles 28)

Certainly, his creed bore a strong Eastern influence and would not rest
well with Biblical tradition, but Lennon did say his song was a prayer.
And a prayer is a communication, which in the case of "The Ballad of
John and Yoko," was directed to Christ.

Lennon had accomplished what few other popular music lyricists
had attempted. He invoked an offensive word ("Christ") which had not
appeared in Biblical images in popular songs that either accepted or
declined the Biblical sacred order. And he defended his use of it by
pointing back to the Biblical tradition for support.

The lyrics of the Browns's "The Three Bells" (no. 1, 1959) focus
on three religious rituals in the life of Jimmy Brown: his baptism,
marriage ceremony and funeral. Because of its focus on ritual, it is
logical, then, that the petitions found in the song lyrics are liturgical in
nature. The lyrics focus on the ritual prayer of the Christian tradition.
After each ritual event (one per verse of the song), within the refrain,
the congregation asks for "guidance from above" and prays "Lead us
not into temptation." Though the word "temptation" alludes to the sin
nature of humanity, which can be viewed as an offensive notion in a
popular music song, the fact that the line echoes the Lord's Prayer
reduces its effect, because the petition taught by Jesus Christ to his
disciples is something that the audience knew by rote. Words recited
from memory suffer from a reduction in content due to their repetition.

Though the setting of the song is within the walls of a chapel, God
is addressed only once and in that instance as the standard (in the case
of popular music lyrics) "Lord." Even on this occasion, the framing of
the lyric suggests that the address is only a liturgical pronouncement, as
mentioned above in reference to the congregation's prayers. At the
marriage ceremony, the congregation sings: "Lead us not into
temptation, Bless, O Lord, this celebration, may their hearts be filled

with love." There is no sense of actually addressing God, but rather of playing back one's memory. This further reduces the meaning of the call to God as "Lord."

Further, for all the listener knows, Jimmy Brown may not have entered the church or chapel at any other time in his life. Religious beliefs may be only invoked at the time of these rituals. The song is an example of how religion is not fully-integrated into the life of the adherent but is compartmentalized. The deity is only called upon in harmless ways at certain inoffensive or common times of need. Gazing beyond American popular music culture to the encompassing national culture, there are similar ritualized "correct" times for prayer. Typically, the only time there is nationwide public prayer for the President is at his inauguration or after his death.

The prayer songs considered above primarily reflected a concurrence with the idea that humanity needed to look beyond itself for assistance with its greatest concerns: inner serenity, world peace and romance. Most of the lyrics peer outside the tangible for solutions to the problems of the present reality. There is the underlying notion that supplication to God has the potential of making a difference in space-time reality. Though these lyrics follow the vernacular of civil images in many cases, there is not a vague theology presented about the root dynamic of prayer. According to Biblical teaching, it is available and it can change the life of the individual. Though prayers are whispered to stars or angels, there is still an acknowledgment of a need for support from outside the self.

CHAPTER FOUR

There's a Place Called Heaven: Images of Heaven in Popular Music

From prayer, the focus turns to the other prevalent theme in popular songs with Biblical images in the 1950s and 1960s, the idea of heaven. There are two types of narratives that encompass most of the lyrics that incorporate the idea of heaven. One type finds its story line in the separation of two lovers, one of whom met an untimely demise and is now presumed to be in glory. The other type considers popular celebrities, particularly teen idols from the music scene, who in reality lost their earthly lives. The chapter closes with an investigation of other popular songs that incorporated the theme of heaven. Before considering the lyrics of mainstream popular songs, the discussion focuses on the way lyrics are heard differently by separate audiences. Subsequently, the analysis turns to an examination of the promised land of African-American popular music and the peace in the valley of country and western music.

MOVE ON UP A LITTLE HIGHER: MEANING IN POPULAR MUSIC LYRICS

In the world of popular music, there are recordings that, though initially targeted to a limited music subculture, such as gospel music or rhythm and blues or country and western, "crossed-over" and became hit records in the mainstream market, e.g., Mahalia Jackson's "Move on Up a Little Higher." These songs garnered popularity beyond the intended audience. Though the Biblical images in these songs are clear and offensive, the mainstream audience, the audience that may not have been the initially intended audience, hears the lyrics through a filter of civility. This softens the meaning of the words as intended by the artist from the musical subculture whose mythos contains a strong religious tradition in the perception of the encompassing mainstream culture. In this case, I am thinking of artists who issue forth from specific racial, regional and/or ethnic enclaves and particularly of African-American artists and country and western artists.

The filter of civility compartmentalizes or marginalizes the intended meaning of the original artist. The filter defuses the charge or energy tied to the words. One form that this takes is the popular expression "she (or he) learned to sing in church." The myths surrounding the origins of many African-American singers begin in the church choir. The implication is that the artist is presenting her or his heritage and not a personal conviction even if the artist is indeed sharing her or his personal belief. Irwin Stambler, influenced by this myth, notes of vocalist LaVern Baker: "She first sang gospel music in her childhood" (33). In an article about Patti LaBelle, Associated Press writer David Bauder notes she was "first noticed in a Baptist church choir" (10).

Similar historical roots are cited for Aretha Franklin. When she sings "Amazing Grace," a song that details the possibilities of Biblical redemption, the mainstream audience does not hear the words as a testimony of God's work or as an invitation to experience the same. Rather, the audience hears the recorded work as a thread in the tapestry of America's folk culture tradition. The content of the lyrics is removed. The mainstream audience "hears" Franklin as a disseminator of part of her cultural and familial heritage. Folk singer Judy Collins's motive for recording "Amazing Grace" was her interest in presenting the nation's folk music heritage rather than sharing a personal creed.

Mainstream listeners receive "Oh, Happy Day," another song about redemption, because, in their perception, lead vocalist Dorothy Morrison and the Edwin Hawkins Singers are celebrating the community of church and the gospel choir. The song's meaning is diminished to being another aspect of the varied cultural traditions that form American society as perceived by the mainstream audience. The larger audience disregards the proclamation that the day was happy because "Jesus . . . washed our sins away."

This is not to suggest that it is wrong to celebrate these songs as part of the American music tradition. However, the point is, though the lyrics of the two examples cited above are incivil and content-filled, there is a process that takes place which transforms them. The lyrics become as ineffective as vague and inoffensive words of civility used to create lyrical images of the Biblical tradition for the mainstream market. In a way, the content-filled songs of the musical subcultures, e.g., "Oh, Happy Day" and "Amazing Grace," are treated as novelties. They are not considered to be indigenously authentic. They are viewed (by the mainstream audience) as not being specifically entwined with the rituals and contemporary lyrical concerns of mainstream culture.

William Edgar uses the term "indigenous authenticity" in the context of explaining how a musician may communicate to an audience and defines it as "stylistic adaptation to the particular paradigmatic, moral and social context in which one is operating" (120). I would suggest that the idea of indigenous authenticity can be extended to mean more than an adaptation. Music of indigenous authenticity is birthed in a culture, but it is more than something that makes sense, more than something that fits in with the listener's construction of reality. It forces or stretches the listener to go beyond what she or he has already experienced, yet the recorded result is not a novelty. It rings true.

Although a song from a musical subculture may be considered indigenously authentic, in the mainstream construction of reality, such songs are viewed as aberrations. They are compartmentalized in such a way that they will not shape the beliefs and values of the mainstream culture. Whether it is LaVern Baker's "Saved," the Impressions's "Amen," or Elvis Presley's "(There'll Be) Peace in the Valley (For Me)," each of these works carries a certain cultural baggage (e.g., "she/he learned to sing in church"), that places a preconception on the lyrics. Andrae Crouch (an African-American) was one of the first contemporary Christian music artists to experience popularity outside of the Christian subculture. This was due, in part, because he fit in with the conventions of who was supposed to be singing music about the Lord (from the secular audience perspective).

The country and western artist is in a similar situation to the African-American artist because of the connection of southern gospel music to the country and western music subculture. The offensive lyrics of Ferlin Husky's "Wings of a Dove" are "read" or "heard" as issuing from a region with a mythos of strong moral fiber and deep faith in the Christian tradition. Through this process of hearing, then, the words become minimalized. The artist is read as reflecting the religious tradition of a culture rather than a personal, meaningful conviction.

It should be noted that listeners allied to the common ethnic or regional tradition from which their artists and their songs emanate do *not* also only hear these words through the filter of civility that the overall mainstream audience does. The meanings of words used in songs by artists in Biblical sub-traditions are more understood within the bounds of the source culture. As a result, there are less frequent instances of ambiguity. When a particular term is used, be it "God" or "Jesus" or "Christian fountain," for example, there is greater denotation and less connotation. A parallel can be drawn to Theodor Adorno's idea of popular music as "social cement" (Mohan 283). There is a more explicit contract of understanding between the songwriter and the listener because the values expressed in the lyrics are common to the members of the music subculture, but not necessarily to the mainstream audience. Mohan and Malone expand on the concept of "social cement":

> Following Adorno, we would expect that the feelings of identification created in the audiences of these musical styles are determined by the values inherent in the lyrical content of the songs. Thus, when pop music acts as a 'social cement,' it is working to communicate a value system to its audience. (284)

This "cement" or common embrace of values offers the opportunity to the subculture to use words and expressions that are not understood in the mainstream culture.

This contract of understanding does not limit the lyrics of the song to only one meaning. Gospel songs including "Move on Up a Little Higher" are understood on several levels by the subculture to whom the music is initially directed. When Mahalia Jackson sings of the "beautiful golden gate," she is not only singing about the heaven described in the pages of the Bible. She is speaking of and hoping and praying for a better social position for her sister and brother African-Americans than what was being experienced in the United States in 1948. I continue with an extended consideration of the meaning of the lyrical image of heaven in African-American and country and western popular music.

PEOPLE GET READY: THE IMAGE OF HEAVEN IN
AFRICAN-AMERICAN POPULAR MUSIC

Mahalia Jackson's "Move on Up a Little Higher" was a proclamation for change. The theme of this and other gospel songs was picked up in the 1960s by Curtis Mayfield and the Impressions and by Sam Cooke. Curtis Mayfield encouraged African-Americans with "Keep on Pushing," "People Get Ready," "I'm So Proud," and "We're a Winner." Sam Cooke longed for and prophesied "A Change Is Gonna Come." Otis Redding's "Respect" was about more than the tensions between a man and woman in love; it, too, dealt with recognition of the human rights of the African-American. And, Aretha Franklin expanded the meaning of Redding's composition to encompass gender issues. Gospel songs were instrumental in opening the marketplace to songs that galvanized support for the concerns of African-Americans, e.g., James Brown's "Say It Loud-I'm Black and I'm Proud."

Curtis Mayfield, leader of the Impressions and the group's songwriter, focused on the "higher" place that was central to Mahalia Jackson's recording in a number of his compositions. In "Keep on Pushing" (no. 10, 1964), Mayfield encourages his sisters and brothers. He sings, "Maybe someday I'll reach that higher goal, I know I can make it with a little bit of soul." He spiritualizes the context by ending several verses with the phrase, "Hallelujah, Hallelujah," a statement of praise to the Lord. But the "higher goal" is not heaven alone. Mayfield notes "a great big wall . . . ahead of me." The wall represents the barriers to equality facing minority populations. He goes on to sing, "But I've got my pride and I'll move the wall aside." The song was a charge to African-Americans to not give up in the face of adversity and to find strength within their individual selves and their collective unity. "Meeting Over Yonder" (no. 48, 1965) continues the charge to keep on pushing toward the higher goal, which in this case is "yonder."

Mayfield's masterpiece, "People Get Ready" (no. 14, 1965), melds the Biblical and secular images of the promised land. He uses the image of the train which relates both to the chariot of the spiritual "Swing Low, Sweet Chariot" and the Underground Railroad that spirited escaped slaves to freedom. The destination of the train is "Jordan," which again evokes both earthly and heavenly images of the higher goal. This destination is exclusionary. The Impressions's sing, "There ain't no room for the hopeless sinner who would hurt all mankind just to save his own." In other words, there is no place for the oppressor, for the one who keeps people separated from freedom, be it earthly or heavenly.

There are clear references in the lyric to the heaven of the Biblical tradition. Before the last recital of the refrain, the lyric warns, "For there's no hiding place against the Kingdom's throne." The description of heaven in the lyric differs from contemporary inoffensive images of an all-encompassing heaven for all. Earlier, the lyric states, "All you need is faith to hear the diesel's hummin'." To reach the higher goal requires a spiritual preparedness. Mayfield is not secularizing the gospel.

Popular culture critic Greil Marcus oddly seems to miss Mayfield's message. In the same work that includes an insightful analysis of the effects of racism on Sylvester "Sly" Stewart of Sly and the Family Stone, Marcus describes Mayfield's work prior to the *Superfly* soundtrack (1972) as "a somewhat bland Martin Luther King-style progressivism . . . complete with sincere heart, boundless optimism, tortured lyrics, and brotherhood speeches to nightclub audiences" (242). I think Marcus's myopic view stems from his dismissal of the notion that an artist can hold on to an otherworldly faith—to a Biblical sacred order, in this case—in the face of oppression.

The policies of Nixon-era America harshly influenced Mayfield's vision of hope. In his first solo release after departing the Impressions, "(Don't Worry) If There's a Hell Below, We're All Gonna Go" (no. 29, 1971), a production undergirded by an instrumental arrangement that would influence Isaac Hayes's "Theme from *Shaft*," Mayfield presents a bleak vision. He does not anticipate a reconciliation between "blacks and the crackers."

The title of Mayfield's composition is easily misunderstood. He is not saying that all are damned and nothing can be done about it. Rather, he points an accusing finger at the "don't worry" attitude. This attitude, present in the White House—"Nixon talking 'bout don't worry"—and in the church—"Ev'rybody praying, and ev'rybody's saying, but when come time to do, ev'rybody's laying"—has eroded the hope Mayfield unfolded in "Keep on Pushing" and "People Get Ready." Marcus suggests that with the *Superfly* soundtrack, "Mayfield found a completely new voice" (242). This voice was already evident in his attack on the nation's complacent attitude toward minority issues.

Near the end of the song, Mayfield sings, "This ain't the way it ought to be." His accusations focus not only on the "crackers" and the judicial system. Something has been lost that felt real when Mayfield encouraged African-Americans to push toward a higher goal and get ready for a better place. A promotional piece titled "Nice Guys Don't Finish Last. They Just Finish Top Thirty" was sent along with Mayfield's single to radio station program directors urging them to play the provocative song. The piece underlined the notion that all were to blame for the current state of affairs. The piece reads, "Curtis is looking at all the hate between blacks and the crackers . . . each one thinks he and he alone is right. Curtis wants them to get it together and work together instead of working against each other."

Mayfield's earlier songs evidenced an embrace of a Biblical sacred order, but in this composition, Mayfield questions whether there is even a hell. This loss of faith in the Biblical sacred order further deepens the bleakness of his vision.

In Sam Cooke's elegiac "A Change Is Gonna Come" (no. 31, 1964), one of his concerns is the Biblical notion of heaven. In the second verse, he admits, "I'm afraid to die 'cause I don't know what's up there beyond the sky." In this line, he questions the notion of patiently suffering through the tribulations of an oppressive culture in order to attain the reward of glory in the afterlife. He is not refusing heaven or the Biblical sacred order (as evidenced in his address to the "Lord" in the last verse). Rather, he is renouncing a cultural sensibility that suggested the need to ignore the harsh toil of an oppressive existence by pointing to the thought that things would be better later in the bye and bye, that is, in the kingdom of heaven.

Cooke sensed a hope in the air for the African-American people following the March on Washington in August, 1963 and the passage of the Civil Rights Act of 1964. He knew a change was going to come, not in the hereafter, but in this generation. He also was aware it was not going to be easy for a restructuring of society to come to fruition, being cognizant of the violence brought upon marchers in Birmingham and participants in freedom rides. In his closing words, he articulates his hope: "Lord, there've been times that I thought I couldn't last for long, but now I think I'm able to carry on." He has witnessed enough to discern that reformation is possible.

The Rascals, a rock band comprised of three Italian-Americans and a Canadian, recorded an album that was a tribute to the sentiments of Cooke and Mayfield and to the sound of the Impressions. The main theme of *Freedom Suite* (no. 17, 1969) was the idea of heaven as an earthly freedom from oppression. At the close of the number one single, "People Got to Be Free" (1968), from the album, lead singer Felix

Cavaliere invokes the image of the "train to freedom . . . comin' right on through" as he ad libs to the fade. This mirrors Mayfield's "People Get Ready" and earlier images of the train or chariot to glory. The last song of the Rascals's "suite," "Heaven" (no. 39, 1969), combines phrases from both Mayfield and Cooke in one line as Cavaliere leaves the verse-chorus structure to bring the song to a close. He sings, "You know somebody said, 'Now, keep on pushin' 'cause there's a change that's got to come.'" Cavaliere goes on to proclaim, "And everyday, I thank you, Lord." He understands the interaction of the spiritual and the secular in African-American popular music.

The most popular of the recordings with a message that centered on the promised land was the Staple Singers's "I'll Take You There" (no. 1, 1972). Lead singer Mavis Staples invites the listener to a place where there is no "crying" or "worrying." The message is carried by a pop-funk gospel arrangement. The genesis of the group in the 1950s was in the gospel realm but by the time of their number one hit their repertoire was less specifically Biblical, though the music was still rooted in the Christian sacred order. The mainstream listener could interpret the track as a summons to the promised land of the Bible, or to peace on earth or to freedom for all peoples.

The image of the promised land has held a number of connotations among the people of the African Diaspora. The "Promised Land" of African-American spirituals was the land (Canaan) across the border from the land of bondage (Egypt), it was the free states to the north and the provinces of Canada, it was a better way of living the daily walk and it was the promise of a heavenly eternity for those who toiled in the present life. Citing the work of James Cone, Venise Berry notes, "words and phrases which seemed harmless were filled with latent meanings, such as, 'De promise land on the other side of Jordan,' which meant 'freedom north' and later 'Canada,' rather than 'heaven' as slave owners were led to believe" (167). The idea that these words "seemed harmless" fits in with the idea of the filter of civility applied by the mainstream audience to meaningful lyrics. The thought is the singer is only proclaiming her or his religious tradition. The listener is dulled to the expressions of faith emanating from the lyrics.

Even Chuck Berry, though focusing primarily on the concerns of emerging youthful record buyers, e.g., school and the car, employs the image of the "Promised Land" in his song of the same name (no. 41, 1965). For Berry, the Promised Land is the "Golden State" of California, far from where the St. Louis Tiger grew up. Berry writes about the car as a vehicle of redemption. It has the potential to take him to the promised land.

The multiple connotations of the promised land relate to the fact that in the African-American religious tradition there is no dichotomy between the secular and the sacred. The liberation that comes from the laying down of one's cross is not only something to experience in the afterlife. This meaning is not always received by the mainstream audience who may perceive the recording artist's work as a nod to a musical tradition, or even as an embrace of nostalgia.

PEACE IN THE VALLEY: THE IMAGE OF HEAVEN IN COUNTRY AND WESTERN MUSIC

In addition to quoting Curtis Mayfield and Sam Cooke in their *Freedom Suite*, Felix Cavaliere and the Rascals recognize the image of "peace in the valley" as an allegory for heaven. The band quotes the phrase in "People Got to Be Free." The image of peace in the valley is central to Elvis Presley's first gospel bestseller.

At a press conference in Vancouver early in his career, Elvis Presley was asked about his familiarity with gospel music. His response was, "I think I know every gospel song that's ever been written" (McGee 556). During his lifetime, Presley recorded three albums of southern gospel: *His Hand in Mine* (1961), *How Great Thou Art* (1967) and *He Touched Me* (1972). In the same year as the press conference, the year he held the number one spot on *Billboard*'s singles charts for 26 weeks, Presley released an EP (Extended Play, a 45 RPM record that typically contained four tracks) titled "Peace in the Valley" (1957).

On the title track, "(There'll Be) Peace in the Valley (For Me)" (no. 25, 1957), a remake of Red Foley's 1951 recording that had charted in the country and western market, Presley is accompanied by the gospel quartet the Jordanaires. The song contains one of the few allusions to Christ in popular music lyrics in the 1950s. Though it is an oblique reference, in the first verse Presley sings, "the lamb is the light." The singer anticipates a new heaven and a new earth. In the last verse, he notes, as the Scriptures read (Isa. 11:6), "the lion shall lay down with the lamb." He looks forward to a transformation in his existence: "I'll be changed, changed from the creature I am." Though the lyrics are specific in their reference to the Biblical sacred order, the popular music audience has the ability to shield itself from the offensive nature of the message by considering that the song issues from a region with a mythos of strong moral fiber and deep faith in the Christian tradition.

For the country and western music subculture adherent, the idea of peace in the valley also brings up images relating to the character of the landscape in which the culture rests and having an identity separate from the rest of the nation. The members of the subculture are interested in maintaining an insularity from outside forces which are perceived as less peaceful, such as government regulations which emanate from lawmakers who live in urban areas and violate the serenity of peace in the valley.

The lyrics reveal a difference between the culture that is home to southern gospel and country and western music and the culture in which African-American music is rooted. In the first line of "Peace in the Valley," the narrator sings, "I'm tired and so weary but I must go alone." In the Southern tradition, it is the individual who has to make his own peace in the world. In contrast, Curtis Mayfield calls to the community, "People, get ready." Similarly, in the lyrics of Percy Mayfield's "Please Send Me Someone to Love," the narrator places a priority on communal serenity ahead of his desire to be free from loneliness. There is, in the African-American image of heaven, a collective push to the higher ground.

TEENAGE HEAVEN: IMAGES OF HEAVEN IN MAINSTREAM POPULAR MUSIC

Returning to mainstream popular music, teenage death songs, songs in which the Boy or Girl experience the death of their beau, at their core submit to the idea that one goes to heaven after one dies. There is no attachment of a specific doctrine related to how one may pass through heaven's gate. During the late 1950s and early 1960s, there were a number of death songs that became popular. These fell into two groups. One group focused on the couple who was separated by a tragic accident. The other group dealt with non-fiction subjects, that is, the deaths of actual teen heroes.

The first group includes Mark Dinning's "Teen Angel" (no. 1, 1960), Ray Peterson's "Tell Laura I Love Her" (no. 7, 1960), the Everly Brothers's "Ebony Eyes" (no. 8, 1961) and J. Frank Wilson's "Last Kiss" (no. 2, 1964). Except for "Tell Laura I Love Her," in which Ray Peterson narrates the story of Laura and Tommy, the singers of these teenage death songs are first person narrators whose (female) beaus were killed in untimely accidents. (Peterson was the first to record "Give Us Your Blessing" [1964], the double-death song that was a hit for the Shangri-Las in 1965.)

The assumption of the narrators is that their "girls," as well as Tommy, the novice stock car racer who left the message to "Tell Laura I Love Her," are in heaven. The lonely mates hope to see their beaus if and when they get to heaven. The narrator of "Last Kiss" knows that he has to lead a life of good moral character if he is to see his "baby" again. Only Laura, girlfriend of the deceased Tommy, goes to the chapel where she hears his voice. Oddly enough, three of the victims were killed in what Chuck Berry had introduced as rock and roll's vehicle of redemption, the car.

"Ebony Eyes," the flip side of the Everly Brothers's "Walk Right Back," a two-sided Top Ten hit recorded shortly after the duo moved to Warner Brothers Records, introduces a religious aspect before the tragic accident. The narrator obtains permission from the chaplain to have his dark-eyed betrothed fly to the military base where he is stationed to recite their vows. (Later in 1961 the Everly Brothers were actually inducted into the Marine Corps.) The chaplain, who personifies the Biblical sacred order (a non-denominational order it should be noted), is an agent in the demise of the young woman for allowing her to travel to participate in the ceremony. Though the narrator is sure his beloved is in heaven, he is unsure if he will be there. He states, "if ever I get." He acknowledges a resentment for the chaplain and God which may lead to a disbarment from entering heaven. The death of the narrator's fiancee in a plane crash echoes the actual accident two years earlier (February, 1959) that killed Buddy Holly, Ritchie Valens and the Big Bopper (J.P. Richardson).

Tommy Dee's "Three Stars" (no. 11, 1959) addresses the death of the early rock and roll stars. The spoken recording (Carol Kay and the Teen-Aires sing the chorus), released several weeks after the tragedy, asserts, in the song's refrain, that all three are in heaven and have been transformed to stars that can be observed to the north. The spoken narrative suggests an ambivalent attitude toward rock and roll music and its audience of teenagers. The reason seventeen-year-old Ritchie Valens may have been called to heaven is that troubled teenagers (delinquents?) may benefit from his presence or counsel. The narrator suggests that Buddy Holly was misunderstood while he lived. The lyric submits that the sobering experience of the accident is to be viewed as a corrective to those seduced by the culture of 1950s rock and roll. The narration does not suggest that the three teen heroes are part of a heavenly band. Rather, they may be counselors. The juxtaposition of the notion of heaven with rock and roll and a tragic accident can be viewed as an offensive move to bring those who do not subscribe to a Biblical sacred order back into the fold.

Tex Ritter's "I Dreamed of a Hill-Billy Heaven" (no. 20, 1961), written and originally recorded by Eddie Dean in 1955, has a theologically less-stringent view of the relationship of country and western popular music and heaven. The song does not consider the notion that dabbling in music may lead to one's demise. This relates to the idea of country and western music emanating from a region that adheres to the Biblical tradition. This is a death song, but not a teenage death song. The musicians Ritter evokes are not teen idols, but rather those from a long-standing, deeply-rooted tradition. Thus, the music is more tolerable from a moral or religious point of view. This does not mean, however, that the narrator's view of heaven is associated with a more Biblically conservative view of salvation. The lyrics of the major portion of the heaven songs including "I Dreamed of a Hill-Billy Heaven," and unlike Pat Boone's "A Wonderful Time Up There," reflect the belief that there is no need to adhere to doctrines relating to forgiveness or the afterlife because everyone will experience the same. Heaven's gate is open to all.

In Ritter's vision, heaven has a "hall of fame with all the gold guitars and fiddles a-hangin' on the wall." God is identified as "the Big Boss of all the riders up here." Like Dee's song, Ritter's recording was released shortly after the death of a major recording artist, in this instance, Johnny Horton, who is found "standin' side by side" with Hank Williams.

After identifying those who have already entered hill-billy heaven, the narrator has the opportunity to glance at "the big tally book" and proceeds to list those who will enter over the course of the next century. This may be the closest that lyrics from this period came to paralleling the visions of the Old Testament prophets and the Apostle John in the last book of the Bible, the Book of Revelation.

Johnny Cymbal's "Teenage Heaven" (no. 58, 1963), though it addresses the 1959 plane crash and the death of other teen idols, particularly rock and roll recording artists, borrows its form from Ritter's recording. Cymbal sketches a similar vision of heaven where musicians continue to perform rock melodies for eternity. Cymbal's narrator envisions heaven not as a place where streets are paved with gold, but rather a site where singers approach a gold microphone to perform. Unlike the somber covering that shrouds Dee's song, Cymbal's heaven is the site of a rock and roll dance party—an *American Bandstand* in the clouds. The performance of rock music, it is suggested, is a path, a theologically-inoffensive one, to redemption.

Following the lead of Tex Ritter's recording, Cymbal also has the opportunity to see heaven one hundred years from now. He sees that everyone who was in the rock and roll pantheon at the time he recorded the song, including Little Eva and Duane Eddy, will be in that heavenly band. Again, the lyrics suggest, in opposition to Dee's "Three Stars," that rock and roll is one path to salvation. This may have been offensive to some who accepted a Biblical sacred order, but in the overall context of lyrics of civility, it fit well, because there were no doctrinal requirements that had to be met to enter the heavenly city. Unlike Dee's "Three Stars," "Teenage Heaven" was not a direct response to the 1959 plane crash, but was released in 1963 (the same year as Cymbal's one Top Twenty hit, "Mr. Bass Man") which may account for the record's limited success.

Almost all of the teenage death songs have a funereal character to them. They are dirges. Though they present the hope of a non-exclusionary heaven, the music that accompanies the lyrics more reflects the notion of separation and loss. There is no celebration over the musing that there is free and easy access to heaven. More importantly, for the teenager, the walking hand in hand on earth is over. There will be no more performances of "That'll Be the Day" by the Crickets with their lead singer. But "Last Kiss," by Texan J. Frank Wilson and his band the Cavaliers, almost exudes optimism in its shuffling rhythm. Unlike the saddened and in-need-of-redemption narrator of "Ebony Eyes" who does not know if he will ever get to heaven, the Boy narrator of "Last Kiss" knows how to get to heaven to "see his Baby again." He knows that he has to be good. As in the words of "The Three Bells," there is the notion of temptation and sin, but beyond the Browns's ballad, there is the idea that a choice can be made to live a life of a particular moral character. The optimistic beat of "Last Kiss" is attributable to the assurance that the narrator will get to heaven if he lives according to the Biblical code.

It is worthwhile to turn once again to the Browns's "The Three Bells" (1959) to examine the image of heaven in the song's lyrics. The little congregation's prayer makes reference to the Biblical doctrine of salvation. On the "dark and grey" morning on which Jimmy Brown's "soul had winged its way to heaven," after the congregation prays to not be tempted by sin, they petition the Lord: "May his soul find the salvation of thy great eternal love." Though the idea of heaven and the afterlife is present in a number of songs that acknowledge a Biblical sacred order, there is rarely the sense of a need to be saved as a requirement for entrance to heaven. Its exclusionary aspect is considered offensive.

The God of the little congregation in the valley is not exclusionary as well. He is not the God of judgment of Pat Boone's "A Wonderful Time Up There" but rather the same all-forgiving God found in Al Hibbler's "He." Though the last two lines of each chorus (after the group sings "lead us not into temptation") change with each of the three choruses, each chorus ends with the word "love." This highlights the idea of God as love. And God's love is described as everlasting. At the end of the first chorus, after Jimmy Brown's christening, the congregation asks that he be guided with "eternal love." After he dies, the congregation asks that he receive the salvation of "thy great eternal love."

The lyrics of "The Three Bells" imply that rather than having a personal relationship with God based on the forgiveness of sins and the acceptance of the Incarnate God as his savior, Jimmy Brown could have lived whatever life he wanted, yet the petitions of the congregation and God's all-encompassing forgiveness would allow him entrance into the eternal kingdom. Though the congregation prayed not to be tempted, one was not necessarily personally responsible for one's own sin. Therefore, the deduction from this point of view was that personal transgression was not a factor in separating one from eternal life in heaven. As in earlier times in popular music history, the vague and civil theology of a heaven open to all is presented.

Pat Boone's eschatological "A Wonderful Time Up There" (no. 4, 1958) is an exception to the theology of civility in songs that invoke an image of a non-exclusionary heaven. The lyrics express a clear theology of the end times. They speak of the second coming of Christ. Boone sings, "The Lord is a-comin' from His throne on high." The lyrics remind the listener of what Jesus Christ said (though of course the name of Christ is not mentioned): "He said He's comin' back again to raise the dead." The song is a sermon. The lyrics are a warning to the listener to be prepared for Christ's return. He cautions, "Brothers, there's a reckonin' a-comin' in the mornin'" so "You better get ready." He insists that there will be a judgment. In the last verse, the narrator as preacher asks, "Are you gonna be among the chosen few? Will you make it through?"

Unlike other popular songs that deal with heaven in their lyrics, in this case, heaven is exclusionary. When the narrator sings, "Everybody's gonna have a wonderful time up there," he does not mean that everybody on earth, or everyone who hears the song, is going to enter the kingdom. Rather, he is saying that everyone who makes it through the judgment, those that are "rewarded for the things we've done," will be in glory. Certainly, on the surface, this can be perceived as an offensive message particularly in the context of the song's contemporaries.

However, due to Boone's image, that is, the idea of being a "safe alternative," the song is perceived more as a novelty song. Though it fit in with the audience's understanding of his lifestyle, it did not mesh with Boone's overall body of work. The lyrics have specific detailed content about Biblical theology, but since they are framed in the context of a novelty song, the meaning is reduced and the result is that the lyrics are perceived by the listener as inoffensive. Further, the message of the song is softened by the title. "A Wonderful Time Up There" is a vague reference to the kingdom of heaven. Although there are specific references to "glory" and "His throne" within the body of the song's lyrics, they are foregrounded by the vague wording of the song's title.

For this recording, unlike some of his other work, Boone did not co-opt an existing rhythm and blues song. And, unlike Don Cornell's "The Bible Tells Me So," Boone's recording does not come off as a Sunday School offshoot. It has elements that actually suggest it could be indigenously authentic and a contemporary rock singer, e.g., Dorsey Burnette, could have made it that way, but Boone's image hinders such a reading. Though not a gospel song, apparently "A Wonderful Time Up There" is derived from the Homeland Harmony Quartet's "Gospel Boogie" (1948) (Curtis 29). Boone's recording does have some rock and roll elements in the instrumental rhythm and the vocal, particularly when he introduces the last two repetitions of the refrain with the phrase, "Well, well, well." On those occasions, his voice is reminiscent of one of Sam Phillips's Sun Studios artists, e.g., Carl Perkins. (The "Well, well, well" phrase may also be a nod to the African-American spiritual "Well, Well, Well.") But the overall effect of the Boone production is one of novelty which reduces the impact of the content-filled message of judgment and an exclusionary heaven.

The analysis of popular records that invoke the theme of heaven illustrates how a theological concept can be made as inoffensive as the civil words that are used to express the acceptance of the Biblical tradition. For the most part, all that is learned of heaven from the lyrics of songs that acknowledge a Biblical sacred order is that it is the final resting place and usually there are few, if any, requirements to pass through the pearly gates. It is assumed that once one has passed beyond this earthly existence, she or he will be found (maybe even with a gold microphone!) in heaven. Heaven is primarily presented as an assurance of the potential for future communication between those separated by life and death and entrance to it is not exclusionary. The reason for this portrayal is to comfort the bereaved Girl or Boy who has lost her or his love or the bereaved fans of a fallen teen idol. Similar to the songs considered in earlier chapters, there is, in the songs of heaven, the modus operandi of cushioning Biblical doctrine within lyrics of civility.

There are exceptions to this idea of heaven in lyrics that became popular in the mainstream marketplace. As indicated in the consideration of the image of heaven in the African-American and country and western musical subcultures, the promise of heaven in the afterlife is not invalidated, but the meaning of this promised land is expanded to incorporate an improved and more satisfactory situation in the present life.

CHAPTER FIVE

Imagine There's No Heaven: Rejection of the Biblical Sacred Order in Popular Music Lyrics

In the previous chapters, the lyrical analysis has primarily considered songs that—at least on the surface—presume the Biblical sacred order. Except for a number of songs that replaced the overwhelmingly other of the Biblical tradition with an earthly other, these songs did not suggest a rejection of the Biblical sacred order. The inoffensiveness of their theology and their lyrics of civility contributed to a subtraction of meaning from the Biblical tradition, but the lyrics did not question the possibility that such a sacred order does not exist.

In this chapter, the investigation turns to those songs that explicitly decline the Biblical sacred order. The analysis begins with songs that did not out-and-out refuse the Biblical faith but pointed to the notion of alternative sacred orders. The denial of the Biblical tradition began with oblique lyric turns rather than clear, offensive statements. The analysis then turns to songs that used clear, meaningful language to underline their posture of renunciation of the Biblical faith. The alternate theologies presented in these compositions are unfolded. The language of the lyrics is noted and contrasted with the language of lyrics that embrace the Biblical sacred order.

The theme of a romantic interest substituting for God in an individual's sacred order was earlier unfolded in the Ink Spots's "My Prayer" (1939). The composition enjoyed a new and even more popular chart run in a remake by the Platters which held down the number one spot for five weeks in 1956. This theme was popular in the 1950s beginning with Nat "King" Cole's "Faith Can Move Mountains" (no. 24, 1952). These two compositions (neither of which was written by the recording artists in question) do not share the same engagement of the African-American recording artists's religious heritage with their earthly concerns. The Biblical sacred order is excluded and is replaced by an earthly sacred order. In the lyrics of Cole's recording, the romantic interest becomes the overwhelmingly other.

The theme of "Faith Can Move Mountains" borrows from a teaching of Jesus to his disciples recorded in the Book of Matthew. He said, "if you have faith as small as a mustard seed, you can say to this mountain, 'Move from here to there' and it will move" (Matt. 17:20, NIV). Correspondingly, the narrator confesses to his love, "I can move mountains if you have faith in me." She is his source of strength: "Kiss me and I'll be strong." And she is his help: "What couldn't I do when I know that you are here to help me along?" The sacred order to which the narrator subscribes revolves around his love interest.

Jimmie Rodgers's "Make Me a Miracle" (no. 16, 1958) continues the theme of a romantic interest substituting for God as the center of the individual's sacred order. "Make Me a Miracle" is a prayer, but it is not a prayer to God. It is a prayer to the narrator's romantic interest. He is open to whatever she would make of him: "You can make a slave or a king of me. . . . You can make a fabulous thing of me or nothing at all." All that the narrator desires is to be in the presence of the one to whom he is devoted. He closes his plea, "I don't care whatever you make of me, just make me your love." There is no place for the Biblical sacred order in the narrator's world view. The idea that she is the center of the narrator's sacred order is underlined by the fact that his romantic interest can transform him into a "miracle." Also, at one point, the narrator sings, "I'm only a cup, make me a chalice." The chalice has a strong religious connotation. Parallel to "My Prayer" and "Faith Can Move Mountains," Rodgers's recording dismisses the Biblical sacred order in a roundabout way.

In Simon and Garfunkel's breakthrough album, *The Sounds of Silence* (no. 21, 1966), a love song titled "Kathy's Song" follows the narrative pattern of abandoning a sacred order with God at the center for an order centering on a romantic love. "Kathy's Song" is addressed to a woman from whom the narrator is separated by an ocean. Like the similar-themed compositions examined above, from the point of view of the narrator, the love of Kathy bestowed upon him is beyond what could be gained from divine love. The narrator tells his love, "I stand alone without beliefs, the only truth I know is you." She is his integration point, that through which all meaning is gained and understood. The lyric of "Kathy's Song" asserts that human love can be as high as or exceed divine love.

At first blush, the phrase about being "without beliefs" may refer to doubts over the narrator's chosen occupation of songwriting. In the prior verse he describes his concerns over writing songs he can not believe. He has "come to doubt all that I once held as true." However, the line that suggests that his unbelief is related to religious matters, and that Kathy is his substitute for religion, is the closing line of the song. The narrator tells Kathy "there but for the grace of you go I." This is his spin on the well-worn phrase regarding the grace of God. In the narrator's life, faith in the Biblical sacred order has been replaced by faith in another human.

Again, in this song, though the ideas may be offensive to those who adhere to the Biblical tradition, the language of the lyrics is not offensive. The lyrics are oblique, like parables, meant for the listener who has ears to hear to gather the meaning of what the narrator is saying.

Several years later, Simon extended the theme of "Kathy's Song" to its logical conclusion in "Bridge Over Troubled Water" (1970), Simon and Garfunkel's third and final *Billboard* number one hit single. Borrowing a spoken phrase from a gospel performance, that is, He (referring to Jesus) is a bridge over troubled water, Simon secularizes the mediation theme. Unlike "Kathy's Song," this is not a love song in the romantic sense. It is a statement of a human substitute for the agape love of God. God's divine love, freely given for all, is replaced with a secular version. From the perspective of the narrator, there is no other hope for humanity. God's love is an illusion. Substituting himself for the work of Christ on the cross, the narrator will lay down his life.

Other critiques of the Biblical tradition were couched in terms relating to the physical presence of the tradition, that is, the church, the minister and the congregation. In the seemingly innocuous lyrics of Donnie Brooks's "Mission Bell" (no, 7, 1960) there is a challenge to the Biblical sacred order. The narrator boasts to his beau that his "love is higher than a mission bell." Like the lyric of Paul Simon's "Kathy's Song," the Brooks's recording asserts that human love can be as high as or exceed divine love. There was a signal moment in art history when Biblical figures in paintings, such as God, Jesus Christ or the Virgin Mary, were no longer located above all other figures in the composition. A similar dynamic operates in Brooks's hit single. In popular music lyrics, the "bell" or "bells" signify the sacred place, be it the chapel or church, the physical location of the divine presence. This is found in the Browns's "The Three Bells" and in "Church Bells May Ring," as recorded by both the Willows and the Diamonds. The narrator's use of the mission bell allusion suggests a challenge to the place of the divine in his life-order.

"Ebony Eyes," the Everly Brothers's single which was noted above in the analysis of teenage death songs, proposes that God's representatives on earth, e.g., the chaplain in this particular narrative, are not infallible. This was a controversial suggestion in 1961. As mentioned earlier, the chaplain gives permission for the narrator's girlfriend to travel to the site of the narrator's military base assignment so that the two lovers can exchange their wedding vows. The plane is lost, as is the narrator's fiancee, so the chaplain is partially to blame due to his assent to the marriage plans. Further, the beacon (which may represent a guiding light such as God), searching the ebony skies for the late arrival, fails to locate the lost aircraft. The failure of the beacon suggests that God is not all-knowing or all-powerful or able to provide guidance.

In 1966, Lou Christie invoked the image of a "chapel in the pines," an image found in earlier popular songs such as the Browns's "The Three Bells" and the Dixie Cups's "Chapel of Love" (1964). Christie utilizes the peaceful contemplation of the small, white chapel in a pastoral setting for a much different use. In "Lightnin' Strikes," a *Billboard* chart topper in early 1966, the main theme is that there is no need to wait for marriage before the couple consummates its relationship. The narrator tells his woman friend that she should carefully decide before making a life-long commitment, but that decision should not stop the two of them from enjoying the physical aspects of their relationship at this moment. The invocation of a religious image, the church, the site of the divine presence, in this context suggests a challenge to the moral tenets of the Biblical sacred order.

Other songs of this era evidenced a hostility to traditional religion or at least to religious practices. But as in the examples noted above, these songs, like those that accepted the Biblical tradition, used lyrics of civility to propel their messages of dismissal. The ideas may be offensive but the wording was not. Englishman Jonathan King's "Everyone's Gone to the Moon" (no. 17, 1965) refers to a "church full of singing, out of tune." In this song, in which the primary lyrical theme is the alienation of the individual from other members of society, King's lyrics refer to hypocrisy within the church or to the hopelessness of belief. He, as well as other lyricists who challenge the religious status quo, is literate in religious images previously used in popular music lyrics. The illustration of the congregation singing in church is found in the Browns's earlier recording "The Three Bells."

Paul McCartney's allusion to a wedding ceremony at Father McKenzie's church at the outset of "Eleanor Rigby" (no. 11, 1966), half of the two-sided hit single released in support of the Beatles's *Revolver* (U.S. version) album, falls in line with the lyrical tradition picturing of church weddings. But, like fellow Englishman King, McCartney observes the out-of-tune church in his song. The character Eleanor Rigby is like one of Paul Simon's "illusion dwellers" (see Simon and Garfunkel's "Blessed" below) for she, according to McCartney's narrator, "lives in a dream." The church is her life. She has no one or nothing else. She lives in the church and dies in the church. Even her pastor wipes his hands of her memory after her burial. The other character in the song, Father McKenzie, lives a life of no more purpose than Eleanor Rigby. No one hears the words of his lessons from the Bible.

Lyrically, the most significant element falls in the last phrase of the last verse. As Father McKenzie retreats from the burial ground, McCartney's narrator closes with the following note: "no one was saved." This is a key element of Biblical theology. If there is no salvation, no redemption, then, perhaps, the narrator is suggesting there is no currency to a Biblical sacred order.

The reference to salvation in the song reflects a diversion from the tradition of treating Biblical images with inoffensive lyrics. McCartney draws attention to a specific Christian doctrine and, through his narrator, refuses it. This was one of the strongest attacks in popular music against the Christian tradition and, oddly, it did not draw any controversy at the time of its release, the same year that McCartney bandmate John Lennon made his comment about the Beatles being more popular than Jesus.

Following Jonathan King and Paul McCartney, Joan Baez also utilized a church setting to denounce the Biblical sacred order. On the back cover of her 1967 album, simply titled *Joan*, there is a note just below the song order that refers to a Paul Simon composition included on the album. The note reads, "Paul Simon asks Joan to note that the line in 'Dangling Conversation' was originally, 'Is the theatre really dead?'" In this song, whose lyric primarily unfolds the day-to-day interaction of two lovers drifting apart, Baez interjects a spiritual dimension to the conversation. More important to her than the institution of the theater among "things that matter" is the death of the church. It may be argued that this expresses a concern for the loss of the church or faith, but I would counter that in the context of Baez's overall body of work, the notion of the church being dead is more of a fact for her than a question. In her delivery of the line, there is no sense of loss or mourning.

Another early illustration of the dismissal of the Biblical tradition is found in John Phillips's "California Dreamin'" (no. 4, 1966) as recorded by the Mamas and the Papas. The narrator stops into a church, assumes the posture of prayer (he gets down on his knees) and pretends to pray. Though this song is not particularly offensive in language used, the idea of pretending to pray, especially in church, the sacred site, was certainly offensive and a harbinger of things to come in the lyrics of popular music.

Phillips is familiar with the vernacular of lyric images that embrace the Biblical sacred order. He invokes the image of prayer. Again, prayer and heaven represent the two most popular images in lyrics with Biblical images. Phillips's appreciation of this tradition was evidenced a year later. In early 1967, the folk-rock Mamas and the Papas had a *Billboard* number two hit with their remake of the Shirelles's "Dedicated to the One I Love" (1961), a song that revolves around the theme of the narrator requesting prayer from her boyfriend from whom she is presently separated. In the Mamas and the Papas's version, they highlight the prayer request even more than in the Shirelles's original. When the folk-rock foursome repeat the first verse of the song after the middle measures, they replace the second line of the first verse with the second line of the second verse which is the actual prayer request, "whisper a little prayer for me, my baby."

Returning to Simon and Garfunkel's *The Sounds of Silence*, not only is there an abandonment of God by the individual, as was unfolded in the examination of "Kathy's Song," but the lyrics of "Blessed" also intimate a desertion of the individual by God. Simon frames "Blessed" with two well-known, though very different, portions of the gospel story of Jesus: the beatitudes portion of the Sermon on the Mount and the crucifixion scene at Golgotha. The first line of the song is almost a paraphrase of the scripture passage. Simon sings, "Blessed are the meek for they shall inherit." Similarly, in the same verse, he alludes to those who, like the Christ, are persecuted. Simon details the persecuted as those who are "sat upon," "spat upon" and "ratted on." In this context of persecution imagery, Simon also invokes the image of the sacrificial lamb: "Blessed is the lamb whose blood flows." This may be a reference to the Christ, whose beatitudes provide a framework for the first three lines of each of the three verses. Or it may be another illustration of persecution that can be more broadly applied to the downtrodden population.

Simon's beatitudes at the beginning of the second verse initially follow the Biblical course. He begins the second verse by singing, "Blessed is the land and the kingdom, blessed is the man whose soul belongs, too." Certainly, one way to interpret the kingdom is as the kingdom of heaven and the image of one's soul belonging to a heavenly kingdom can be viewed easily in a Biblical context. Then, the beatitudes of "Blessed" seem to drift away from the Biblical tack. Simon's blessings are cast upon "meth-drinkers," "cheap hookers," and "illusion dwellers." He views these groups, too, people caught in the binds of drug use and sexual exploitation and others blind to the truth of everyday reality (as Simon's narrator perceives reality), as contemporary victims of persecution.

The catch in the song, the place where it really drifts from Biblical tradition, is within the closing lines of each verse. Though Simon has listed the contemporary persecuted populations who are blessed, the resulting blessing is empty. Almost directly quoting the Christ at the crucifixion, Simon sings in the three refrains, "Oh, Lord, why have you forsaken me?" For Simon, there is no one to bless the persecuted. His narrator suggests that humans live in a closed universe or system. If they think they are going to be blessed, they are amongst the "illusion dwellers." This is the same artist who proclaimed Christ as Savior in "You Can Tell the World" and "Go Tell It on the Mountain" within his duo's previous album.

In "Blessed," Simon's narrator argues that humanity is alone, without direction and hopeless. He has "tended his own garden much too long." There is no companion in the Garden of Eden, earthly or heavenly. He half-heartedly complains, "I got no place to go." But, "it doesn't matter no more." He has "no intention to heal" his wounds, the wounds of living in a world without purpose. The narrator views himself as a crucifixion victim, a victim of empty promises patted on the backs of the persecuted.

Furthermore, there is no content to any blessing that may be bestowed upon these singled-out populations. In the gospel account, the meek shall inherit the earth. In Simon's first beatitude, the line stops at the word inherit. The listener does not know what the meek shall inherit. There is no inheritance to be bestowed. Unlike the Sermon on the Mount, which contains a corresponding blessing for each population group listed, Simon's beatitudes only bless the populations and leave it at that.

Interestingly, Simon does not go as far as to precisely quote the two accounts (the Gospels of Matthew and Mark) that include the "forsaken" statement. In each of the Gospel accounts, the Christ addresses God as "My God," rather than as "Lord." Though Simon preaches a radical message against the Biblical tradition in this song, a message of empty blessing, he still contains his lyric within the popular music practice of not addressing God as "God." Simon breaks from popular music tradition by not containing his images within the framework of common topics such as heaven or prayer, which contemporary songs repudiating the Biblical tradition did.

Simon and Garfunkel's third album, *Parsley, Sage, Rosemary and Thyme* (no. 4, 1966) continued Simon's lyrical interest in the Biblical tradition. The main theme of "Flowers Never Bend with the Rainfall" is the obliviousness of humanity to its mortality. Actually, the song's narrator recognizes his mortal predicament but he refuses to acknowledge it. He denies his human situation. He does not deny the work or truth of God in the universe, but he declines it. The narrator sings, "I am blinded by the light of God and truth and right and I wander in the night without direction." His blindness is caused by himself. Within his pretense of oblivion, he decides to proceed without a course of direction. He denies the need of some common sense order of reality in his life, of religious origin or otherwise.

The use of the word "God" on this track is one of the first on an album that contained a Top Five single ("Homeward Bound"). Again, though, the message is more radical or offensive than the language used to convey it, as was the case in Simon's "Blessed."

The *Parsley, Sage, Rosemary and Thyme* longplayer closes with a track titled "7 O'Clock News/Silent Night." The track juxtaposes a sweetly-harmonized version of the Christmas hymn with a radio broadcast of news briefs. Beginning with the Christmas traditional, the song initially draws the listener into a tranquil mood. But before the first verse is complete, the listener hears something else going on. At first, the listener has the aural impression of hearing one radio station interfering with another. The news announcer's voice is particularly intrusive because a peaceful picture is being framed through the opening lines of "Silent Night." Images of reality begin to unfold: racial discrimination in housing; an overdosed and dead Lenny Bruce; a fair housing march in Chicago led by Dr. Martin Luther King; the indictment of mass murderer Richard Speck; and protests against the Vietnam conflict. As the song goes on, the initially low volume of the news broadcast crescendos until it overwhelms the words of the carol. Thus, the song title, in which the news is listed before the Christmas hymn, rather than the other way around.

In this song, Simon returns to the lyrical ideas he introduced on *The Sounds of Silence*. God has forsaken the world. He is not to be found in a time of dire need. The ingenious juxtaposition presented in "7 O'Clock News/Silent Night" proclaims that the horrors of everyday life overwhelm any hope that may be found in Christ's birth. Though Simon's language is inoffensive, it is not without meaning. Songs that renounce or question the Biblical sacred order can have meaning though they are couched in inoffensive language unlike songs that acknowledge the Biblical tradition. This is because songs that embrace the Biblical tradition (at this place in time) are not created with the same sort of imagination (that can envision the juxtaposition of a news report with a traditional Christmas carol) to make the notion of a Biblical sacred order relevant to the listener.

Simon's lyrical interest in religion continued in the folk-rock duo's second *Billboard* number one hit, "Mrs. Robinson" (1968). The protagonist of the song is one of the "illusion-dwellers" Simon first cited in "Blessed." Though written for the film *The Graduate* (1967), Mrs. Robinson's illusions in the song go beyond that of upper middle class suburban life and her character in the film. She is so out of touch with reality that she is ready to be hospitalized at a psychiatric facility. Simon alludes to this in the first verse of the song: "We'd like to help you learn to help yourself" and "Stroll around the grounds until you feel at home." R. Serge Denisoff and William D. Romanowski's study of film and rock music supports the notion that Simon's presentation of Mrs. Robinson's character in his lyrics surpasses the viewers's comprehension of the personality of the character as presented in the film. They suggest, "the music (of *The Graduate*) . . . contribute[s] to the audience's understanding of characters and the meaning of events" (166).

Further, Simon's suburban housewife is deceived about the reality of a Biblical sacred order as well. Simon and Garfunkel sing phrases that literally could be part of an evangelistic or fundamentalist church service: "Jesus loves you more than you will know" and "Heaven holds a place for those who pray." But the duo quickly follow up these phrases with snickering punctuation marks. To the phrase about Jesus loving the individual, they add "wo, wo, wo." To the phrase about prayer and heaven, they add "hey, hey, hey." These codas mock the beliefs of the churchgoer whether or not her or his belief is nominal or genuine.

Faith in secular gods is shown to be no less an illusion than belief in a spiritual god. Baseball hero Joe DiMaggio is nowhere to be found to provide a ground of being or meaning to life. Secular heroes have vacated the pantheon. But Simon's narrator does not suggest that the illusion-dwellers need let loose their hold on their fantasies. Within the lyrics of "A Hazy Shade of Winter," a Top Twenty single collected on the same album (*Bookends* [1968]) as "Mrs. Robinson," the narrator sings, "if your hopes should pass away simply pretend that you can build them again." The pretense of dwelling in an illusion is superior to living without hope. Though secular heroes like Yankee baseball stars no longer have the capacity to provide hope, a year and a half later, Simon's lyrics would suggest that there was a secular basis for hope as claimed in "Bridge Over Troubled Water."

Lyrically in "Mrs. Robinson," Simon returns to the tradition that has been pointed out earlier. In the use of Biblical images in popular music lyrics, they are often placed in the context of prayer. Simon follows this in his phrase about prayer being a gateway to heaven.

"Mrs. Robinson" was the first Top 40 single to use the word "Jesus" in its lyrics. Ironically, a bestselling song embracing the Biblical sacred order did not use the name of Jesus in its lyrics prior to a song critical of the Biblical tradition.

In the last half of the 1960s, there is the emergence in popular music lyrics of a different idea toward heaven, a rejection of heaven. On her first album, *More Than a New Discovery*, published in 1966 (and re-released by Columbia Records as *The First Songs* in 1973), singer-songwriter Laura Nyro swore "there ain't no heaven" in her composition "And When I Die," made popular by Blood, Sweat and Tears (no. 2, 1969). Despite swearing against the existence of a heaven, Nyro does, however, immediately rejoin, "and I pray there ain't no hell." The narrator begs to not be let to go by Satan. Though there is the ironic juxtaposition of the fact that there is no heaven with the idea of the possibility of prayer, still, the idea is introduced that there is no heaven.

Though there is nothing more offensive in the lyric than the idea that there is no heaven, in another song on the same recording, Nyro reveals the source of her ambivalent feelings. Within the lyric of her composition "Stoney End," popularized by Barbra Streisand (no. 6, 1970), Nyro announces, "I was raised on the good book Jesus, 'til I read between the lines." She discards the source of the tenets of Biblical doctrine.

Though Nyro's first songs were released by Verve/Forecast, a record label that directed its product to the audience of the folksinger movement rather than the mainstream popular music market, the use of the word "Jesus" in 1966 was still a big step toward the entry of offensive or content-filled language in songs that declined a Biblical sacred order. Record labels that traditionally catered to the folksinger movement, e.g., Elektra, Vanguard and Verve/Forecast (an update of Verve's previous imprint, Verve/Folkways), were, at this time, beginning to direct more and more of their product to the mainstream audience. Introducing the name of Jesus was basically unprecedented and, ironically, it was in a song that criticizes and to a certain extent renounces the Biblical sacred order. As mentioned earlier in the analysis of Martindale's "Deck of Cards," there were few references to Jesus Christ through most of the history of recorded popular music. This dynamic was changing in the late 1960s.

Elektra Records was the first of the former exclusively folk record labels to successfully issue an album by a rock band. In the fall of 1967, the Los Angeles-based Doors's second album *Strange Days* (no. 3) was released. It included two Top 30 singles, "People Are Strange" and "Love Me Two Times." The last song on the album, "When the Music's Over" ran for eleven minutes. Closing an album with an extended track was a trend at the time in the sequencing of rock albums. The Doors closed their previous album with a track of similar duration, a track titled "The End."

"When the Music's Over" is an apocalyptic vision of sorts. The lyrics suggest an impending catastrophe. There is the idea of something coming to an end. The narrator wants to hear "the scream of a butterfly" before he "sink[s] into the big sleep." He says, "music is your only friend until the end." The lights are to be turned out when the music ends.

In the third verse of the closing track, the narrator makes a request, one that is possibly a prayer request. He asks, "Cancel my subscription to the Resurrection." He may not be simply rebuffing the concept of a heaven. Similar to the teenage death songs, in which the narrators assumed that their deceased beaus went to heaven, the narrator of "When the Music's Over" implies that he has the opportunity to decline the invitation to enter a non-exclusionary heaven. But the language that is used is more content-filled than the lyrics of civility in songs that welcome the invitation of heaven. Unlike the narrators of the earlier songs, he does not refer to a nebulous "somewhere up above" but specifically refers to the Christian doctrine of the resurrection. Further, and unlike Laura Nyro's narrator who does not want to go by Satan, the narrator of the Doors's track goes on to say that he would rather go to hell. After refusing the resurrection, he asks that his "credentials" be forwarded to the "House of Detention," a place, he notes, where he has friends. He declines the work of Christ on the cross.

Later though, near the end of the song, the narrator screams out a plea for help from Jesus to ward off the night, the "Persian night." He is not dissimilar from the narrator of Nyro's "And When I Die" who, after refusing the idea of heaven, immediately hopes "there ain't no hell." Lead singer Jim Morrison yells, "Save us! Jesus! Save us!" This is the same narrator who has declined the resurrection several verses earlier. He is not as secure in what he thought he wanted as the end approaches.

Again, the use of the word "Jesus" here is one of the earliest in the lyrics of mainstream popular music. Though this song would not have been played on AM radio stations with playlists that consisted of Top 40 singles of two-and-a-half to three minutes duration, "When the Music's Over" did receive airplay on emerging album-oriented FM radio stations, as well as on AM stations that opened a time slot for the era's alternative music in their programming schedules.

Joni Mitchell's "Blue" (1971) suggests that the narrator will examine her options before she rejects hell as an alternative destination in the afterlife. She notes, "Everybody's saying that hell's the hippest way to go." The narrator is not sure if that is the case but she will explore the opportunity.

On the title cut (and opening number) of the Doors's fourth album, *The Soft Parade* (no. 6, 1969), lead singer Jim Morrison starts with a spoken narration. The orator reflects on his days as a seminary student. He recalls hearing a "proposition," a proposition that "you can petition the Lord with prayer." He repeats the proposition, "Petition the Lord with prayer," deliberately thinking over each word as it is uttered. Increasing his volume, he repeats the proposition again. Finally, in a booming resonant voice, he shouts, "You can not petition the Lord with prayer." Here, again, is a clear, offensive declaration from a position that renounces the Biblical sacred order. There is nothing vague in the narrator's statement.

The narrator of "The Soft Parade" does not embrace a sacred order that offers a use for prayer. In the universe envisioned in Morrison's lyrics, there is no God, no hand that can change the course of history. Just as the blessings listed by Paul Simon in "Blessed" are empty, so is the place to which petitions go in the world view of the narrator of the Doors's track. Like Simon's narrator, Morrison's narrator has erected a closed universe or system. It is not an easy place for the narrator of "The Soft Parade" to live. As he begins to sing after his declaration about the deaf ear to prayer, he asks someone (even he may not know who): "Can you give me sanctuary, I must find a place to hide." Unlike Simon's narrator, who does not care that he is alone, without direction and hopeless, the revelation of Morrison's narrator leaves him seeking an escape route from an insecure universe.

The sky pilot of Eric Burdon and the Animals's song of the same name is as different from the heroic sky pilot of Frank Loesser's "Praise the Lord and Pass the Ammunition" as the public perception of the Vietnam conflict was from that of the "good war" (World War II). Whereas the sky pilot at Pearl Harbor took up the wounded gunner's station, Eric Burdon's "Sky Pilot (Part One)" (no. 14, 1968) "feels so tired and he lays on his bed, hopes the men will find courage in the words that he said." For the Vietnam era chaplain described in Burdon's song, faith is only a matter of going through the motions. The chaplain can only hope that his actions have meaning for the soldiers. There is no sense of assurance that he is being empowered by a deity. He attempts to draw his spiritual strength from within, but even his faith in himself is minimal: "He mumbles a prayer and it ends with a smile." The songwriters (Burdon and the four members of the band), through the third person narrator, deny the possibility of a Biblical sacred order. In the refrain, the lyric suggests there is no existence other than the earthly tangible: "sky pilot. . . . You'll never reach the sky." As the soldiers go forth to battle, the chaplain will "meditate, but it won't stop the bleeding and it won't stop the hate."

In the Who's rock opera *Tommy* (no. 4, 1969), the narrator questions how those who do not hear the gospel can be saved if Jesus is the one way, as Christian teachings assert, to eternal life. The narrator of "Christmas" ponders how the deaf, dumb and blind lead character "can be saved from the eternal grave" since he "doesn't know who Jesus was or what praying is." The track does not reject the Biblical sacred order, but it questions the justice of not offering redemption to those who will not hear the message and incorporates the name of Jesus in the lyric. The Who's "Heaven and Hell" (1970) protests the lack of choice available in the afterlife. Why, the narrator asks, is the choice between "fly[ing] . . . round with a harp singing hymns" or "down in the ground" dressed in "horns, tines and tail." He closes both verses asking why humanity has to leave the planet at all. He wants to reject the Biblical teaching of heaven and hell and the relationship between one's moral character and afterlife destination.

Even Elvis Presley, who recorded several albums of gospel music, and charted with "(There'll Be) Peace in the Valley (For Me)" and "Crying in the Chapel," recorded a song that alludes to a crumbling of faith in the Biblical sacred order. In "Where Did They Go, Lord" (no. 33, 1971), the narrator's faith is shaken by the departure of his love, who did not even leave for "another, but Lord, she just walked off alone." A result of this crisis of separation is he can no longer find answers to his questions, the explanations he previously held in his grasp. In the last verse, he pleads, "I cry out my questions, oh, the answers all gone, where did they go, Lord?"

It may be argued that the love who left the narrator was the center of his sacred order. He opens the last verse by singing, "The passion I trusted, the truth that I leaned on, and the hope that would forever keep me strong." Conceivably, the lyric suggests that the narrator's crumbling faith is in his departed love. However, these words are followed by his realization that there are no answers to his questions. He then asks God what happened to these answers. This suggests that the "truth" and "hope" that were his bulwarks are those that are drawn from God rather than an earthly love. He no longer has any spiritual base to stand on. He is alone. Also, the church organ in the arrangement underlines the idea that the erosion of the narrator's faith is in the Biblical sacred order rather than in the woman who walked away.

One year after claiming that the Beatles's "Ballad of John and Yoko" was a prayer, John Lennon declared "I don't believe in Jesus." Nor did he believe in God. On his first solo album after the breakup of the Beatles, *John Lennon/Plastic Ono Band* (no. 6, 1970), in a song simply titled "God," Lennon defined God as a concept, a concept of the human imagination. And, it was not a concept that would lead to inner peace or some sort of transcendence. Rather, to Lennon, God was some kind of rule by which anguish or suffering is measured by humanity. He begins the song by singing, "God is a concept by which we measure our pain." If that is not controversial enough, he sings, "I'll say it again" and repeats his theological observation. This connection of God, or at least Christianity, and suffering was first put into lyrics by Lennon years earlier while the Beatles were still recording as a group. On *Rubber Soul*, released for the Christmas, 1965 season, in his song "Girl," in the first line of the last verse, he asks whether the girl was taught as a child that pain leads to pleasure. In an interview with Jann Wenner of *Rolling Stone* in December, 1970, Lennon stated that he was trying to say something in "Girl" about his view of Christian doctrine, at least of Catholic Christian doctrine, expressing a need to be "tortured" before one can get to heaven (Wenner *Lennon* 130).

Returning to Lennon's 1970 solo album and the song "God," the context of the song within the greater album needs to be considered. During the time the album was recorded, Lennon was strongly influenced by the primal scream therapy teachings of Arthur Janov. *John Lennon/Plastic Ono Band* was his primal scream. God was only one element of distress from which Lennon was attempting to free himself.

The lyrics of "God" clearly present John Lennon's message of his refusal of faith in a Biblical sacred order. He does not replace the names "God" or "Jesus" with vague terms.

Lennon went on in the song to disavow his belief in the Beatles and "Zimmerman," that is, Bob Dylan. In fact, Lennon concludes that he only believes in himself, though he does immediately expand that certainty to encompass his wife Yoko Ono. For him, that is all that is real. Unlike Paul Simon, for Lennon there are no bridges over troubled water that can mediate human pain. After his creed, or non-creed, listing those whom he no longer believes or never believed, the melody shifts and Lennon sings to the listener, who more than likely is a Beatle fan, "The dream is over. . . . Yesterday I was the dreamweaver but now I'm reborn. . . . And so dear friends, you just have to carry on." For him, there is nothing else and his listeners have to accede to the truth that they are alone as well.

The message of John Lennon's solo "Imagine" (no. 3, 1971) is quite similar to that of "God," but the twist that makes the provocative lyrics of this composition so welcome is the sweetness of the instrumental accompaniment. "Imagine"'s lyric is a type of what Berger labels the reductive approach. Berger's "reductive possibility" finds its basis in the "authority of modern thought or consciousness" (57). In the reductive approach, there is a "translation procedure," that is, as Berger elaborates, "References to other worlds are translated into terms referring to this world" (103). In Lennon's "Imagine," there are no other worlds. Everyone and everything operates in a closed system.

The genius of this composition is the marriage of Lennon's controversial lyrics, that is, the imagination of a world without religion or civil states among other things, with instrumental music that could very well have accompanied the sentimental, melodramatic compositions of the pre-rock era. The tension in this song is created by the juxtaposition of a pretty and understated melody with a radical message. The same form of music that supported songs with inoffensive lyrics that embraced the Biblical sacred order in the early rock era is appropriated by Lennon to accompany an offensive lyric. The melody deceives the listener into absorbing the song's message. For example, it has been reported that at least one government assembly has stood up in session and sung this song in tribute to Lennon. Because of the melody and the officials's probable familiarity with the accompanying inoffensive musical elements contained in the recording, they were probably unaware that they, the lawmakers of their state, were singing "imagine there's no countries." Similarly, a witness has reported of being in attendance while an organist played "Imagine" in church prior to a worship service.

Lennon sings, "Imagine . . . nothing to kill or die for, and no religion, too." This is not unlike those who criticize the powers who claim victory in the name of God. Like Bob Dylan's "With God on Our Side" (1964), Lennon is against religious zealots who declare war in the name of God. But Lennon goes beyond the condemnation of wars and conflicts justified by a religious cause. He actually opens the song with the line, "Imagine there's no heaven . . . no hell below us, above us only sky." Lennon's dream is of a world with no heaven. This is the ultimate reductive message. Everything takes place within a closed system. Like others who write lyrics that criticize or dismiss the Biblical tradition, Lennon is fluent with the Biblical images in popular music that predate his composition. This is evidenced in his rejection of heaven (a prevalent theme in songs that contain Biblical images) as opposed to some other aspect of Biblical theology.

CHAPTER SIX

Spirit in the Sky: Spiritual Seekers in the 1970s

In 1965, while filming their second movie *Help!*, the Beatles were introduced to the culture, music and mysticism of the East. In addition to inserting the sound of the sitar, an Indian stringed instrument, in their musical arrangements, the group also became followers of the Maharishi Mahesh Yogi and transcendental meditation. The influence of Eastern thought manifested itself in several Beatles compositions, including John Lennon's "Tomorrow Never Knows" from *Revolver* (1966) and George Harrison's "Within You Without You" from *Sgt. Pepper's Lonely Hearts Club Band* (1967).

As the decade of the 1960s drew to a close, young Americans began to look outside traditional religious orders for life meaning. Tipton notes, "In the atmosphere of disappointment and depression that followed the conflicts and failures of the sixties, many youths sought out alternative religious movements" (30). Some of these seekers became weary with the empty promises and moral bankruptcy of the anti-war protest movement. For many, the anti-war movement was the first real cause that had seized and captured them heart and soul. As they realized that the protest leaders in whom they believed had selfish interests, they became disillusioned. Others were turned off by the movement's relativistic and sexist morals. The student of the 1960s is familiar with the popular slogan, "Girls say yes to guys who say no" (to the military draft). Tipton speaks of the "moral fragility" of the counterculture (29).

Just as the Beatles's musical innovations influenced and raised the bar for their musical peers, the Beatles's interest in Eastern mysticism and transcendental meditation piqued the curiosity of the popular music fellowship. Soon after their pilgrimage to the meditation academy or Ashram at Rishikesh, India, other musicians followed including the Beach Boys and British folksinger Donovan (Leitch). On the back cover of Donovan's two-disc box set, *A Gift From a Flower to a Garden* (no. 19, 1968), the artist is pictured holding hands with the Maharishi. The caption identifies the guru as "His Holiness." The opening song from the set, "Wear Your Love Like Heaven" (no. 23, 1967), contains a prayer to Allah in the chorus. He asks his "Lord" to "kiss" him and "fill" him with song.

The Beach Boys's 1968 album *Friends* contains several tracks steeped in the precepts of transcendental meditation including "Anna Lee, The Healer" and "Transcendental Meditation." The latter track asserts that transcendental meditation will "emancipate" the practitioner. The track's musical arrangement goes against type. One might expect a song with the title "Transcendental Meditation" to have a quiet, contemplative arrangement. However, the Beach Boys track has a rhythm and blues feel complete with horn charts. The same year as the *Friends* release, the Beach Boys added the Maharishi to their tour bill. The lineup consisted of Strawberry Alarm Clock, Buffalo Springfield, Maharishi Mahesh Yogi and the Beach Boys. Several members of the Beach Boys, Carl Wilson, Mike Love and Al Jardine, also collaborated with jazz flautist Charles Lloyd on a meditative piece titled "TM" for his album *Waves* (1971). Over a slow-tempoed arrangement, the Beach Boy members provide wordless vocals.

"He Came Down," a track from *Carl and the Passions-So Tough* (no. 50, 1972), expands the group's religious vision to include not only the Maharishi, but Jesus, Krishna and Guru Dev as well. In the lyric, they are all "saints" singing the "same song of revelation." The embracing of Jesus (the "He" in the title) may be related to the surge of interest in born-again Christianity in the United States in the early 1970s. The expansiveness of the religious embrace illustrated in the song parallels the notion of the individual choosing what she or he finds meaningful from each of various religions. In the lyric, eastern and western thought are merged in the line, "Maharishi gives a lift to every man's Bible." "All This is That," another track from the same release, focuses more on the Eastern religion influence, with mentions of Krishna and "Jai Guru Dev." In the chorus, the songwriters mingle eastern thought with King James English. They sing, "I am that, thou art that, all this is that." The best known translation of the Bible is the King James Version.

The Beach Boys continued to record songs about the Maharishi and Transcendental Meditation into the late 1970s. *15 Big Ones* (no. 8, 1976) included Brian Wilson's "TM Song," a proselytizing for the meditation process. The narrator speaks of how the mantra given to him by his guru "set [him] free" from his cares. The *M.I.U. Album* (no. 151, 1978) is named after Maharishi International University in Fairfield, Iowa, where basic tracks for the release were recorded. The last track, "Winds of Change," which was to be the title of the album before an eleventh-hour change, speaks of the desire of the narrator to be a "shining lighthouse" in the "dark night."

The inside sleeve of Pamela Polland's self-titled debut album (1972) on the Columbia label includes a thumbnail portrait of "His Holiness Maharishi Mahesh Yogi" in the section where she gives her thanks and credits to various collaborators and friends. Polland also joins in the harmonies on the Charles Lloyd track with the Beach Boys vocal contribution. Three of Polland's songs are directly related to the Maharishi's teachings: "Sing-A-Song Man," "The Rescuer" and "Lighthouse." The latter track speaks of how "ships in darkness" will be "saved in the light . . . if you believe." "Sing-A-Song Man" is a direct reference to the Maharishi. Similar to many of the references to the God of the Bible in popular music, it is a somewhat vague image of the Maharishi. Though, by 1972, there had been quite a few references to "Jesus" in popular music lyrics, there had not been direct images to the Maharishi in lyrics. Polland, who wrote all of the songs on the album, may have chosen to make the song more of a parable. The song opens with an exhortation to "listen" to the "sing-a-song man." The central character of the song will "touch you with his voice." He is also described as a "soul, soulful man."

As with artists who were part of the revival rock movement and who were personally committed to the lyrics of their songs, Polland's album encompasses a number of themes. The subjects of the songs include unrequited love ("In My Imagination," "When I Got Home"), a state ("Texas") and listening to the radio ("Please Mr. D.J."). As in African-American music culture, there was not a dichotomy between the spiritual and the secular, or grace and nature. An artist did not have to keep her or his spiritual music separated from earthly concerns. This atmosphere of combining the sacred and the profane was prominent in the late 1960s and early 1970s.

One way that Polland's and Donovan's albums were different from those of artists committed to the Biblical sacred order is that they were able to include photos of their spiritual leader on their record jackets. The mainstream market would not have been as open to an artist including a picture of Jesus Christ on an album targeted to the mainstream audience. That would have been considered too offensive. Though gurus, e.g., the Maharishi, did not represent the overwhelmingly other of the sacred order subscribed to by these artists—the gurus showed the path to God and did not pretend to be God—the embrace of the gurus signified the embrace of sacred orders alternative to the Biblical tradition.

In addition to the Maharishi, other spiritual gurus were adopted by popular musicians as they looked to the East in their quest for meaning. Peter Townshend, leader of the rock band the Who, embraced the teachings of Meher Baba. Townshend's first solo album, *Who Came First* (no. 69, 1972), is a tribute to his spiritual leader. On the front cover, Townshend is pictured standing in his trademark jumpsuit wearing a button that shows the face of Baba. The back cover has a snapshot of Baba riding his donkey. The gatefold cover opens to simply reveal two more pictures of Baba. Townshend recorded a cover version of Jim Reeves's country hit "There's a Heartache Following Me," a favorite of Baba, for the album. Most of the tracks were inspired by the instruction of Baba. The opening track "Pure and Easy" speaks of a musical note that is "eternal." The note is compared to a "breath rippling by." In "Nothing Is Everything (Let's See Action)" Townshend sings, "Nothing is everything, everything is nothing." The narrator states that he is "happy singing in the arms of God" ("Content"). The closing track, "Parvardigar," is an adaptation of Baba's "Universal Prayer." It is a hymn of praise to "the Creator, the Lord of Lords."

The Santana band made their mark on the American popular music landscape with their Saturday afternoon performance at the Woodstock Music and Arts Fair in August, 1969. The same month saw the release of their debut album. Though the band had shown some interest in the things of the spirit on their early albums, e.g., the instrumental "Soul Sacrifice" on the debut, a quote from a Hermann Hesse book on the back jacket of their second album *Abraxas* (1970) and a reproduction of the painting "Man with outstretched hand" as the cover of *Santana III* (1971), it was not until the release of the fourth studio album *Caravanserai* (no. 8, 1972), that Carlos Santana, band leader and lead guitarist, displayed clear evidence of his spiritual quest in both the songs and the liner notes of the album jacket. The album opens with "Eternal Caravan of Reincarnation." Side One closes with "All the Love of the Universe." The inside of the gatefold cover contains a quote from Paramahansa Yogananda about how the body merges into the universe which merges into sound which merges into light which becomes "infinite joy."

The next year saw the release of Carlos Santana's first project without the band. *Love Devotion Surrender* (no. 14, 1973) was a collaboration with Mahavishnu John McLaughlin. The two musicians had become followers of the guru Sri Chinmoy. Music critic Robert Christgau, who has little patience for spiritual things, commented briefly on the album for his "Consumer Guide" column in the *Village Voice*. His remarks were solely based on a photo of Chinmoy, Santana and McLaughlin on the back cover. Christgau describes Santana as wearing an Alfred E. Neuman grin and McLaughlin looking like a man on his way to prison. He then describes the man in the middle: "a man in an orange ski jacket and red pants with one white sock. . . . He looks like the yoga coach at a fashionable lunatic asylum. Guess which one is Sri Chinmoy" (343). Like most music critics, Christgau displayed a cynical attitude to musicians who asserted that they had found what they were looking for.

The next Santana album with the whole band, *Welcome* (no. 25, 1973), continues the themes of the McLaughlin collaboration. There is a track titled "Love, Devotion and Surrender" and another track is co-composed by McLaughlin. As McLaughlin had added "Mahavishnu" to his name, Santana's drummer Mike Shrieve is credited on *Welcome* as Maitreya Michael Shrieve. Prior to the release of *Welcome*, the Santana band recorded a live album in Japan titled *Lotus*. Available in 1975 as an import, the recording was not released in the U.S. until 1991. The recording opens with several minutes of silence which comprise the track "Meditation." (This may be a reason Santana's record label was hesitant to release the album earlier.) The massive five-panel gatefold cover opens to reveal a picture of Buddha in the center with golden rays radiating to portraits of Krishna and Jesus. The outer panels open vertically to reveal images from both Eastern and Western religions. Included are several classic paintings of the Madonna and child, the Annunciation and Christ on the cross. The images contained in the artwork speak of meaningful theology. There is nothing vague in the visual counterparts to Santana's statement of belief.

Beginning with the Santana band's seventh studio project *Amigos* (no. 10, 1976), band leader Santana appended "Devadip" to the front of his name. The name means "light of the lamp of the Supreme" (Evans 620). Through this change in identity, Santana manifested a commitment to his faith. "Devadip Carlos Santana" would identify the leader of the band through Santana's *Shango* (no. 22, 1982) release. Santana's 1980 solo release *The Swing of Delight* (no. 65) is "offered to my spiritual father-guru, Sri Chinmoy, who inspires me to aspire toward the goal supreme." The comments of Robert Christgau reveal that the mainstream market will reject meaningful and civil language from an esoteric sacred order as readily as from the Biblical sacred order if it is perceived that the author of the language is serious about her or his faith.

Joni Mitchell observed the migration to alternative sacred orders in "Roses Blue" (1969). She notes that the main character (Rose) dabbles in "mysterious devotions" including "the zodiac and zen (sic) . . . and tarot cards and potions." To the narrator of the song, the concern is not as much with Rose's internal change, but rather that "she's laying her religion on her friends." It is one thing for the individual to experiment with sacred orders, but another to proselytize.

Jamaica's Wailers, co-led by Bob Marley, Peter Tosh and Bunny Livingston, began recording in 1963. By the time of the band's international record distribution deal in the early 1970s, through Island Records, only Marley was left of the three leaders. Marley's lyrics are imbued with the Rastafarian faith. From the Bible, he draws images of "Babylon," the oppressor, and "Mount Zion," the promised land. Mount Zion represents Zion, the home of the creator ("Jamming"), but the narrator also notifies the listener that Zion is attainable in the earthly life. Marley encourages people to embrace the promise now: "if you know what life is worth, you would look for it here on earth" ("Get Up Stand Up"). Marley's narrator's hope is in "Jah" (a form of Yahweh or Jehovah) who "endureth forever" ("Small Axe"). He states, "They try to keep me down but Jah put I around" ("Duppy Conqueror"). In the same track, he tells those who would block him from the promised land, "Don't try to cold me up on this bridge . . . I've got to reach Mount Zion."

In "Rastaman Chant," from *Burnin'* (published 1973, no. 151, 1975), the same album that contains the aforementioned tracks, Marley borrows imagery from the Book of Revelation including the "angel with the seven seals." He also notes of Babylon that "your throne gone down." Babylon, for Marley, represents the tyranny that suppresses people from attaining their due in this life. Marley returns to this theme through his body of work. He asserts Babylon can be torn down through the power of reggae music ("Chant Down Babylon"). "Jump Nyabinghi," also collected on *Confrontation* (1983), compares the crumbling of Babylon to the falling of the walls of Jericho. Marley sings, "We keep on trodding until Babylon falls." The title track of *Exodus* (no. 20, 1977) speaks of the people of Jah escaping from Babylon. The narrator petitions Jah to "send us another Brother Moses."

Similar to the dichotomy between Babylon and the oppressed is the opposition of the righteous with "stiff-necked fools." Marley states, "The lips of the righteous teach many but fools die for lack of wisdom. The rich man's wealth is in his city [but the treasure of the righteous] is in his Holy Place" ("Stiff-Necked Fools").

The psychedelic drug culture sought transcendence sans an otherworldly deity. The sacred order centered on hallucinogens. Jimi Hendrix preached the gospel of psychedelia in his first album, *Are You Experienced?* (no. 5, 1967). On the title track, the listener is invited to "watch the sun rise" from a vantage point beneath the sea. "Spanish Castle Magic" (1967) bids the recipient to join the narrator in his transcendent experience and "float your little mind around." These tracks express a quest for something outside everyday life. The transcendence proselytized by Hendrix may refer not only to psychedelic drugs but to erotic love as well. The lyrics of the above tracks may be interpreted as words of seduction. Similarly, the opening track of *Electric Ladyland* (no. 1, 1969), "Have You Ever Been," summons the listener to take a "magic carpet" ride over a "love-filled sea" to a site where "electric love penetrates the sky." Like the prophet Isaiah's vision of a land where the lion lays down with the lamb (Isa. 11:6), Hendrix's revelation is of a setting where "good and evil lay side by side." "Voodoo Chile," from the same collection, is a mixture of eros, psychedelia and the occult. In an electric blues arrangement, Hendrix's narrator's vision incorporates "sulphur mines" on Jupiter, "liquid gardens" in Arizona, boasting of sexual prowess and a supernatural birth.

Just as the Beatles led the pilgrimage to Eastern gurus, members of the band from Liverpool were the first to retreat from the gurus's spiritual fellowships. In 1968, John Lennon composed a veiled critique of the Maharishi Mahesh Yogi that appeared on *The Beatles* (White

Album) (no. 1, 1968). The song, "Sexy Sadie," speaks of how the main character made a "fool" of people and did not practice what he preached. In reference to offerings that were required of followers to sit in the guru's presence, Lennon sings, "We gave her everything we owned just to sit at her table." Lennon's biographer Ray Coleman notes, "Lennon admitted that he 'copped out' by not naming the Maharishi in the song" (450).

As young people dabbled with alternative religious ideas, others began to explore the spiritual aspects of their Christian roots. After Laura Nyro read between the lines of the Bible, but before Lennon imagined a world void of heaven and religion, songs emerged with lyrics that clearly embraced Jesus and God as the overwhelmingly other of the lyricists's sacred orders. In the late 1960s, there was an emerging interest among baby boomers in their Christian heritage. This was not a focus on civil religion, or the idea of the United States as a Christian nation but, rather, a fix on personal spiritual exploration.

In an era of revolutionary rhetoric, Jesus Christ was regarded as an early prototypical revolutionary, a radical against the Pharisaic establishment. In the late 1960s, visual representations of Jesus portrayed him not too differently from those who were bent on seizing the Pentagon. Thus, Jesus Christ became an attractive alternative to those who found counterfeit elements in the protest movement. Phy notes that "hippy culture and the youth movement broadly have stressed Jesus as an itinerant teacher, plucking grain for his meals . . . making wine without a license, and socializing with a motley crew" (16). The popular music audience of the late 1960s and early 1970s could identify with such an image as easily as with that of a favorite rock group.

The songs of the revival rock era of the late 1960s embraced the Biblical sacred order. These songs particularly took hold of the Christian sacred order and clearly adopted Jesus and God as the overwhelmingly others of the lyricists's sacred orders. The songs answered the content-filled songs of the late 1960s that rebuffed the precepts of the Bible. There were three important elements to the revival rock era, at least in relation to the history of Biblical imagery in popular music. Unlike earlier popular songs that embraced the Biblical tradition, the lyrics of revival rock songs were not couched in vague, meaningless phrases. Jesus was identified as "Jesus." Secondly, the theology of the songs was more specific. Guilt and the need for forgiveness were themes that surfaced during the period. Thirdly, the instrumental backing that supported lyrics of Biblical faith was not of the inoffensive, easy listening variety that had become identified with songs that accepted the Biblical sacred order. These songs attacked the prevailing aesthetic of civility associated with songs that adhered to the Biblical tradition. Composers combined contemporary rock sounds with lyrics that embraced the God of the Bible and Jesus Christ.

The name of Jesus was the epitome of offensiveness in the history of popular music with Biblical images, particularly in songs that assumed the Biblical sacred order. Though there had been some oblique references to the Christ as the "lamb" and the "light" and to the cross as the "croce di oro," it was not until 1969 and Lawrence Reynolds's "Jesus Is a Soul Man" (no. 28) that a mainstream song that held to the Biblical faith mentioned the offensive name of "Jesus."

This usage of "Jesus" achieved greater popularity in James Taylor's "Fire and Rain" (no. 3, 1970) with the narrator's desperate plea for help: "Won't you look down upon me, Jesus, You got to help me make a stand." Two other tracks from Taylor's breakthrough album *Sweet Baby James* (no. 3, 1970) make reference to the Christ, again using the name "Jesus." The gospel message of salvation is the centerpiece of Taylor's "Country Road." In "Lo and Behold," Taylor's narrator speaks clearly against the idea of a divinely-ordained war: "You just can't kill for Jesus." In Norman Greenbaum's "Spirit in the Sky" (no. 3, 1970), the narrator notes that he has "got a friend in Jesus." And, the lyric has meaningful, theological content. The narrator warns the listener to get ready: "Prepare yourself, you know it's a must." Following the teaching of the gospels, Greenbaum's narrator recognizes Christ as the mediator between humanity and God. If one is prepared, she or he is "Gonna have a friend in Jesus, so you know that when you die, He's going to recommend you to the Spirit in the sky."

"Gabriel's Mother's Hiway Ballad #16 Blues," written and recorded by Arlo Guthrie for the album *Washington County* (no. 33, 1970), is an invitation to employ the power of love (the strength of God) in bringing peace to the generation coming of age at the time. In the chorus, echoing the contemporary interest in Christ, the son of Woody Guthrie sings, "Jesus gonna make you well." Guthrie's composition is a precursor of his spiritual pursuit revealed at the end of the 1970s in *Outlasting the Blues*.

The offensiveness of the theological viewpoints of the lyricists of revival rock songs mirrored their grasp of offensive language. The Canadian band Ocean's "Put Your Hand in the Hand" (no. 2, 1971) made reference to guilt and shame in the relationship between humanity and God, two offensive concepts not popular in earlier lyrics of civility. West Coast rock band Pacific Gas and Electric's "Are You Ready?" (no. 14, 1970) was a warning to be prepared for the coming of the "Son." In the chorus, the lead vocalist asks, "Are you ready to sit by the throne?"

On each of her first three solo albums, Linda Ronstadt included a song with Biblical images and clearly used the name "Jesus" in the lyrics. Her solo debut *Hand Sown . . . Home Grown* (1969) contained a country-music inspired track titled "We Need a Whole Lot More of Jesus (and a Lot Less Rock and Roll)." The followup *Silk Purse* (1970) included "He Dark the Sun" composed by Bernie Leadon of the Eagles and Gene Clark of the Byrds. Both tracks were slotted near the end of the program order, specifically the next to the last track on side two in each case. Her next recording, *Linda Ronstadt* (1971) opened with Jackson Browne's "Rock Me on the Water" (no. 85, 1972). The lyrics speak of people seeking meaning in their lives: "The road is filled with homeless souls . . . who have no idea where they will go." Browne's words allude to the Christian sacred order but do not explicitly suggest it is the path to truth. A "seabird" flying above is compared to "Jesus in the sky." There is a sense of a moral order: "we all must do the best we can" and of the Biblical Godhead: "when my life is over gonna stand for the Father." However, before that, the "sisters of the sun" will comfort the narrator by "sooth[ing] [her] fevered brow" and "rock[ing] [her] on the water." There is a place for God but the Biblical sacred order does not supply all of life's meaning.

Tommy James and the Shondells's "Sweet Cherry Wine" (no. 7, 1969) and "Crystal Blue Persuasion" (no. 2, 1969) reminded the listener of the need to look to a higher place for assistance in bringing peace among the peoples of the earth. "Sweet Cherry Wine" speaks of the futility of war and a refusal to be part of it. The narrator reminds the listener, invoking the specific name "God": "Only God has the right to decide who's to live and die." "Crystal Blue Persuasion" warns of the return of Christ. The narrator voices an alarm: "Better get ready, gonna see the light." The theology of these compositions is indicative of the change in popular music. Lyrics of the revival rock era unfolded an offensive, content-filled view of the Christian tradition.

Psychedelic rock group the Electric Prunes recorded a rock-inspired version of the Roman Catholic mass, *Mass in F Minor* (no. 135, 1968). Though they sing the Latin liturgy, thus masking any offensive terminology, the album cover boldly displays a gold crucifix. Bob Dylan explored his religious heritage. He recorded a modern-day psalm, "Father of Night," a track on *New Morning* (no. 7, 1970). Though he had recorded a number of songs incorporating Biblical images in his career, this was his first track that studied the Bible from a personal vantage point.

The Byrds's recorded "Jesus Is Just Alright" (no. 97, 1970), a track from *Ballad of Easy Rider* (no. 36, 1970). The song was released in a more successful single version by the Doobie Brothers (no. 35, 1972). The use of the name Jesus in the title of a track that was released as a single indicated the acceptability of offensive language in the popular music landscape. "Glory Glory Hallelujah" from *Byrdmaniax* (no. 46, 1971) continued the expression of meaningful Christian lyrics in Byrds's songs. Bud Scoppa, who wrote one of the first credible biographies of rock stars with his work *The Byrds* (1971), addresses the collision of Biblical images with the expectations of the mainstream audience. Writing about "Jesus Is Just Alright," Scoppa notes lead singer Roger McGuinn "was being both satirical (in that he understood the manner in which the listener could most easily accept the song) and sincere (in that he has convictions, and lives by them, in his own way)" (131). Scoppa's observation suggests that he understands the mainstream filter of civility because the audience will embrace the lyric as satire. On the other hand, Scoppa notes that the lyrics do in fact partially express McGuinn's spiritual convictions.

In his discussion of the Byrds in performance, he notes a smile on McGuinn's face hinting to the audience that the band leader may not be completely committed to the words he sings as the band closes a Central Park, New York concert in 1970 with an a capella version of the hymn "Amazing Grace." The crowd was "initially bewildered" by the song choice, but as the band worked through the verses, according to Scoppa, the audience realized the Byrds "weren't joking—but McGuinn's smile gave them an out" (167). The fans were allowed to interpret the performance of the hymn as a novelty.

The title track of Van Morrison's first proper solo album after the breakup of Them, *Astral Weeks* (1968), expresses sentiments that appear to be addressed to either an earthly lover or a deity. At the end of each of the first two verses, the narrator voices his desire "to be born again." He may yearn to be born again both in romantic love and in the spirit. As the song draws to its conclusion, he tells his "darlin'" that he is a "stranger in this world." He has a "home on high . . . way up in the heaven." Morrison is more specific about his faith in "If I Ever Needed Someone" from *His Band and Street Choir* (no. 32, 1970). The "Lord" is the "someone" he longs for. The composition is a psalm to God. He desires to communicate with his God, to be able to call on Him in time of need and to secure protection from his human frailties.

For their eighth studio album, *Late Again* (no. 14, 1968), the folk trio Peter, Paul and Mary, the group who secularized "Tell It on the Mountain," recorded a Paul Stookey-penned track simply titled "Hymn." Unlike the group's earlier versions of songs with religious images, "Hymn" was a contemporary affirmation of personal faith in the God of the Bible. The metaphorical lyrics—the "pretty window picture" is a stained glass window, a "house" is a church, "assistants" are priests and pastors—creatively reveal the object of the narrator's belief. The style is an update of the language of the parables of the gospels.

"Hymn" is a conversation between the narrator and God. Though God is addressed as "you," the context suggests that the lyricist is not veiling his words in civil language. The song opens, "Sunday morning, very bright, I read your book by colored light that came in through the pretty window picture." The line evokes images of the Sabbath and the Scriptures.

The most powerful verse is the last. On a religious holiday (Christmas or Thanksgiving) the narrator visits a church where the preacher espouses a God-is-dead theology. Even without God, the man in the pulpit announces, "the house would go on living." Rather than relying on the scriptures, the preacher recites poetry. Having enough of this, the narrator gets up to leave the church sanctuary. The preacher responds to this act by shaking his head and telling the narrator he will never find God. The action of the narrator in response to the message of the faithless preacher countered the actions of the congregants under the hollow spiritual care of Paul McCartney's Father McKenzie or Eric Burdon's sky pilot.

Paul Stookey employed a similar lyrical tack in "Wedding Song (There Is Love)" (no. 24, 1971) from his first solo effort, *Paul And* (no. 42, 1971), after the breakup of Peter, Paul and Mary. On his concert album *One Night Stand* (1973), he describes where "Wedding Song" came from in his introduction: "[it] comes from just sitting in one place long enough that you get used somehow, you become the instrument of what it is that wants to be said." Stookey explained himself not as the author of the composition, but as a vessel through which the piece flowed into a tangible reality. Content-filled theology flowed not only from the voice of the narrator, but from the composer as well.

In the song, Stookey invokes Jesus's promise to be "where two or three come together in my name" (Matt. 18:20, NIV). Stookey sings, "For whenever two or more of you are gathered in His name, there is love." Stookey also draws from the Genesis account of Creation in the line: "a man shall leave his mother, and a woman leave her home." This reflects the verse, "For this reason a man will leave his father and mother and be united to his wife" (Gen. 2:24).

Supergroup Blind Faith's album, *Blind Faith* (no. 1, 1969), includes a track titled "Presence of the Lord." Again, a content-filled theology is presented. In the opening verse, the narrator reflects, "I know that I don't have much to give but I can open any door." The lyrics show evidence of the composer's understanding of the relationship of God and human as taught in the Christian faith. The narrator does have nothing to give, it is given by God, and once received, there are possibilities open to him that he never dreamed of. Eric Clapton, composer of the track, described himself years later as a "casual Christian" (Schumacher 125). Sweathog's "Hallelujah" (no. 33, 1971) witnessed to the power of God to make a change in the life of the individual. The narrator testifies, "You took me in your hands and like a piece of clay, You made me a man. Now I'm proud to say, 'Hallelujah.'"

The Blind Faith and Sweathog recordings merged the hard rock arrangements of the era with a gospel message. This countered the previous style of supporting lyrics that contained Biblical images with easy listening arrangements. A number of other records merged rock music arrangements with lyrics that adopted the Christian sacred order including the Five Man Electrical Band's "Signs" (no. 3, 1971), Teegarden and Van Winkle's "God, Love and Rock and Roll (We Believe)" (no. 22, 1970) and the aforementioned Norman Greenbaum recording. These songs attested to a new combination permissible to the mainstream: lyrics that affirm the God of the Bible and rock and roll music.

The revival rock era consciousness carried over into the lyrics of two established, high-profile recording artists who did not emerge during the period, but who were influenced by the religious awareness of the surrounding culture. Both George Harrison and Marvin Gaye asserted the need for a change of heart in humanity to restore fellowship with God.

Former Beatle George Harrison staked his claim to move out from the shadow of John Lennon and Paul McCartney with his solo debut, *All Things Must Pass* (no. 1, 1970). Though Harrison's definition of Lord encompasses the overwhelmingly other of each traditional sacred order (following the Eastern influence on his beliefs) in the number one single from the album, "My Sweet Lord" (1970), the theology of repentance that he incorporates in the track "Hear Me, Lord" constitutes a meaningful, offensive posture. He acknowledges a need to change to enjoy a relationship with the Godhead. Harrison does not take lightly the relationship between human and the deity, whoever Lord is. He acknowledges that he has "ignored" his Lord. And, he knows that in his human frailty, he can not alone restore fellowship with God. In the second verse, the narrator pleads with the Lord to help him "rise above this dealing" and "to love you with more feeling." He also is aware of the temptation of sin and the need for the help of his Lord in that area. He closes the song with the supplication, "Help me, Lord, please, to burn out this desire." The lyrical grasp of offensive theology was something birthed in this era of popular music. It ran against the grain of the inspirational "I Believe" and "He."

Marvin Gaye also sings the phrase "my sweet Lord" on *What's Going On* (no. 6, 1971). Gaye's work is a plea for change. He sees hope for transformation in two places, community and God. "Right On" urges a "love for your brother" and a "love for God." "Wholy Holy" recognizes the strength of the community of the church. By being "wholy holy," the community can "conquer hate forever" and "rock the world's foundations." Gaye's narrator reminds the listener that there is a cost (the necessity to be righteous) if there is to be a powerful unity. Using the name "Jesus," Gaye sings of the Christ's promise to return to the earth and he reminds the listener that, in the interim, there is the Bible to guide the listener in doing what is right: "He left us a book to believe in, in it we've got a lot to learn." Just as the lyrics are not vague in their invocation of "Jesus," they are not vague in addressing the cost of discipleship.

The strongest text of Gaye's position is not found within the lyrics of the songs, but in a note on the album's inner sleeve. Like Noel Paul Stookey, Marvin Gaye steps out from behind his lyrical narrator. Gaye writes:

Find God; we've got to find the Lord. Allow him to influence us. I mean what other weapons have we to fight the forces of hatred and

evil. And check out the Ten Commandments too. You can't go too far
wrong if you live them, dig it. Just a sincere and personal contact
with God will keep you more together. Love the Lord, be thankful,
feel peace.

Gaye closes the note, "Thank you, Jesus." Gaye's personal comments
unfold the "love" of which he speaks in the album track "God Is Love,"
the song that is central to his hope for change in the community and
change in the world. Reflecting the moment in popular music history,
Gaye invokes meaningful images in his musical embrace of the
Christian sacred order. *What's Going On* was an African-American
response to the mainstream interest in the Biblical sacred order.

Like other composers in the revival rock era, Marvin Gaye
acknowledged that there was a cost to discipleship. Loving God was
more than an expression or a shallow sentiment. He urged people to
understand the precepts of the Biblical faith. This posture countered (in
the same year) the idea that a world without heaven or religion was a
pleasant dream. At the end of the 1960s and in the early 1970s, there
were signs of the growing impact of Christian tenets on the lyrical
consciousness of popular music.

With the interest in rock music with a Biblical foundation, record
labels sought out musicians with Christian repertoires. Singer-
songwriter Judee Sill recorded two albums for David Geffen's Asylum
Records. "The Lamb Ran Away with the Crown" from her 1971 self-
titled debut album is a parable about the transforming power of Christ
in the individual. She sings, "I drew my sword and got ready" pointing
to the incident at the Garden of Gethsemane when Peter was ready with
his weapon to attack those who had come to take away Jesus. Just as he
was rebuked by the Christ for his determination to answer violence
with the same, Sill's narrator lets go of her resolve to do things her way
and allows "the lamb" (the Christ) to run "away with the crown." On
both her debut and the followup *Heart Food* (1973), the symbol of the
cross is depicted on the album cover. On the first, Sill wears a pin with
a gold cross that is clearly visible in the corner of the photograph. On
the second album, a simple cross necklace is worn. Also, on *Heart
Food* Sill gives "Special Thanks to God."

For the Elektra label, Jeanie Greene recorded the album *Mary
Called Jeanie Greene* (1971). Greene, who contributed backup vocals
to George Harrison's Bangladesh concert in New York City the same
year as her record release and was part of the circle of the Muscle

Shoals Sound Studio musicians in Alabama, wrote and sang "Peter, Put Away Your Sword," a song with a theme that parallels Sill's "The Lamb Ran Away with the Crown." In parentheses, Greene notes that her song is "for Jesus Christ." On the back cover of the album, Greene is pictured with her hands outstretched to the heavens reflecting the stance of a charismatic believer praising the Lord. The diecut front cover, which contains a framed photo of Greene at the center, reveals a classic painting of Jesus Christ and the woman at the well, when the inside sleeve is removed from the album jacket. Husband Marlin Greene, who engineered Jeanie Greene's debut, recorded his own album for Elektra, *Tiptoe Past the Dragon* (1972). The title cut warns of the power of the devil to turn people toward darkness.

From the outset of his career, Ottawa, Ontario singer-songwriter Bruce Cockburn's albums have included Biblical images. On his self-titled 1970 debut, he prays to Jesus: "don't let Toronto take my song away" ("Thoughts on a Rainy Afternoon"). Skyscrapers are compared to "jewels on the Serpent's crown" ("Man of a Thousand Faces"). Cockburn's sophomore effort *Sunwheel Dance* (1972) continued his exploration of Christianity. "Up on a Hillside" addresses a world oblivious to its dark circumstances, a place where "Buicks get bigger." The narrator has an idea of the right path to follow but he doubts: "the cliffs are so high and I might fall." A voice beckons him: "over the mountain I can hear myself called." He alludes to the gospel-recorded miracle of water being turned to wine at the Cana wedding. He describes a sunset that "makes the lake look like wine." The song opens and closes with the same line and hints at the way to lead the world out of its "convulsions." He observes from his vantage point that "the cross does shine." "He Came from the Mountain," from the same collection, is an impressionistic examination of the incarnate God. Cockburn sings of a savior who arrived to "walk among the wounded" but "they couldn't see him."

The songwriter makes use of allegory to sew a fabric of faith that does not pommel the listener but still reveals the artist's beliefs. "All the Diamonds in the World," from *Salt, Sun and Time* (1974) speaks of how seductively temptation takes away one's reason for being. The narrator "ran aground" and "lost the taste for being free." Borrowing the image of Noah's Ark, he notes that "some gull-chased ship," a provision from "God," rescued him. The narrator asserts that miracles continue to happen. Referring to the Holy Land, he sings, "Two thousand years and half a world away dying trees still grow greener when you pray." Cockburn sings a spare-worded direct tale of Christ in "A Life Story" (1975). Tossing out images of strong winds and bent reeds and wild skies, he punctuates each paragraph with a phrase about the life of Jesus culminating with "Christ is risen to lead us free." In the ensuing and final track of *Joy Will Find a Way* (1975), Cockburn again uses a spare lyric to illuminate the self-portrait of the narrator's faith. "Arrows of Light" (the title of the track) "pierce [his] soul," mirroring the sword piercing the side of the crucified Christ. He petitions the Spirit (the "breath . . . of the wind") to unify the peoples of the world. Cockburn was part of a group of artists willing and able to marry their beliefs with songs whose scenes took place in the reality of life and the surrounding world.

The early 1970s period was a critical juncture in mainstream popular music for songwriters who adhered to the Biblical sacred order in their lyrics. Artists had the opportunity to make statements of faith within compositions dealing with other aspects of life and receive airplay on Top 40 radio stations. The melding of the sacred and the secular, a fundamental component of African-American popular music, was evident in the songs of the revival rock era. The idea that nature and grace, the secular and the spiritual, could be integrated into a whole in the life of the individual received a hearing in the mainstream marketplace from artists not affiliated with a particular music subculture. These messages subverted secular expectations that did not allow for adherents to a traditional sacred order, in this case, believing Christians, to be part of the world. In other words, the believing artists could focus on subjects that other pop artists did, but they also sang about the Lord and they were not gospel singers. Their presence did not mesh with the pop music audience's conventional social construction of reality. The lyrics confronted the myths of the non-believers who did not consider that Christians could be interested in earthly day-to-day living.

A continuance and further elaboration of this message of the integration of nature and grace seemed a natural and logical extension from the songs of the revival rock era. The lyrics melded life concerns with tenets of the Biblical sacred order and, furthermore, the sound undergirding the lyrics was contemporary. There also was no sense of the statements of faith being the justification for the art. That is, the impetus for the message was not to evangelize the listener but to naturally present the alternative lifestyle of the songwriter. These messages of the integration of one's adherence to the Biblical sacred

order with earthly concerns continue to exist to the present, but after the
first years of the 1970s, they no longer enjoyed the mainstream
popularity of the recordings that defined the revival rock era.

The year 1972 saw fewer songs that extended the themes of the
revival rock genre. The popularity of "I'll Take You There" by the
Staple Singers, a Billboard number one bestseller, was related to the
popularity of Bible-based lyrics. *Chi Coltrane* (no. 148, 1972), the
debut Columbia label album released in support of Coltrane's
bestseller, "Thunder and Lightning" (no. 17, 1972), includes a number
of songs that hold to the Christian sacred order, including "The Tree"
and "Go Like Elijah." The hit single and the track "Turn Me Around"
can be interpreted as being directed either to a deity or to a romantic
love. In "Thunder and Lightning," she sings, "I wouldn't try to run
from it, no, it reaches everywhere." "Turn Me Around" is a petition for
forgiveness. Coltrane starts, "I know I hurt you." She tells the one to
whom she is singing, "you know that you can mold me to you." "Go
Like Elijah" may be a tribute to America's gospel tradition. The
narrator petitions God to let her be assumed into heaven as the prophet
Elijah was. She wants to "ride right up into the sky . . . and for my sins
I apologize." The arrangement of "The Tree" is a quiet, almost
whispered vocal with a simple piano accompaniment. The first three
verses may be interpreted as a tale of the narrator communing with
nature. She takes her "troubles to the tree," tells her "story to the
breeze" and "lays down in the sun." In the last verse, when the narrator
takes her "troubles to the tree," she sings, "and God's own Son looked
down at me." She goes on to sing that she was "blind and now I see"
echoing the words of the traditional hymn "Amazing Grace."

Coltrane continued with Biblical themes on two tracks from her
second and final studio album for Columbia, *Let It Ride* (1973). The
opening track, the title cut, is a plea to a desperate friend to seek the
Lord for help. She exhorts the downtrodden to "just reach up to His
light." The final track on the album is a cover version of Sweathog's
"Hallelujah." Coltrane chooses to end the album (and her Columbia
career) with a praise to the Lord.

Rick Springfield's "Speak to the Sky" (no. 14, 1972) spoke of
prayer but returned to the tradition of using inoffensive terminology to
address God. Ljubica Popovich states, in her essay on Biblical imagery
in the visual arts, that artists are obliged to employ "iconographic
traditions already known and widely accepted by [the] audience" (215).
Thus, the songwriter who uses language that is offensive distances

herself or himself from the mainstream. Popovich notes "highly imaginative or individualistic . . . interpretations of biblical scenes are . . . likely to be rejected" (215). Thus, the lyricist who speaks in vague terms will be rewarded with the most success.

Country and western recording artist Tom T. Hall barely cracked *Billboard*'s "Hot 100" with "Me and Jesus" (no. 98, 1972). Jesus was no longer hot in the mainstream. Some artists continued to present messages that integrated faith and the earthly walk. Stookey, Coltrane and Judee Sill followed Christ's model of using parables to express their faith in their lyrics.

More prominent were songs that replaced God with an individual as one's overwhelmingly other. This was evident in Bill Withers's "Lean on Me" (no. 1, 1972), Bread's "Everything I Own" (no. 5, 1972) and the Carpenters's "I Won't Last a Day Without You" (no. 11, 1974). The most blatant example of this progression toward depending on another individual to provide meaning in one's life that began over 35 years earlier with the Ink Spots's "My Prayer" was found in Michel Polnareff's "If You Only Believe (Jesus for Tonite)" (no. 48, 1975). Polnareff's narrator asserts he will be the Savior and Messiah of his paramour. He is not the Son of God—he "can't walk on water" or "raise the dead"—but he can turn his romantic interest's "tears to smiles like water into wine," making reference to Jesus's first recorded miracle. He offers to carry the burdens of his lover's "sadness" away, as the Christ took away the sins of the world. Polnareff's recording stated in no uncertain terms that an individual could be another's god.

The popularity of revival rock coincided with the emergence of the evangelical and charismatic Jesus Movement in the late 1960s. The Jesus Movement first grew to prominence in southern California and, as the movement gained momentum, recording artists and songwriters from the area saw the opportunity to express the convictions of the new believers. As the movement spread to other areas of the country, the potential for garnering a nationwide hit with a lyric that embraced the Christian sacred order increased. The hit records of the revival rock era reflect the early spread of the gospel message to baby boomers in the late 1960s and early 1970s. As the Jesus Movement made the transition from a popular fad to a more-insulated religious subculture, the chance of attaining a hit record with Jesus lyrics lessened.

Several singer-songwriters commented from outside the Jesus movement circle on the cultural phenomenon. Joni Mitchell, in "Banquet," the opening track of her fifth album, *For the Roses* (no. 11,

1972), sang "some turn to Jesus and some turn to heroin," reflecting both the emergence of the born-again phenomenon and the Marxist viewpoint of religion as the opiate of the people. In "Lesson in Survival," from the same album, she expands her posture toward Christianity to include other sacred orders, "Guru books, the Bible, only a reminder that you're just not good enough." Several years later, the narrator of one of Mitchell's compositions softened her contrary stance toward religion. "The Same Situation" (1974) is the story of a woman who wonders if she should trust the one who desires to romance her. She will accept help from anyone (even a deity) who can assist in her quandary. At several points in the song, the narrator prays hopefully "wondering who was there to hear." In a search for love (agape or erotic), "millions of his lost and lonely ones" never cease to "search." Like these myriad followers of Christ ("the Lord on death row"), Mitchell's narrator begs to be "released" from a world without love.

Noting the same gravitation to born-again Christianity in the early 1970s, Bernie Taupin, the lyricist for Elton John's compositions, wrote, "Jesus freaks . . . handing tickets out for God" in the hit recording "Tiny Dancer" (no. 41, 1972). The "tickets" are a reference to the small tracts, e.g., *The Four Spiritual Laws* published by Campus Crusade for Christ, that born-again young people would hand out in public places. Even Stevie Wonder, who was more of a participant observer in things of the spirit than Joni Mitchell or Elton John, warned evangelizers and proselytizers to not live a "lie" in "Jesus Children of America" from *Innervisions* (no. 4, 1973). Wonder does not limit his warning to Jesus freaks, but also aims at "holy rollers" and those who preach Transcendental Meditation. He closes the song by stating, "Jesus died on, cross for you." With these words, Wonder's narrator affirms his spiritual position and provides a reminder to those who would use the name "Jesus" to understand the sacredness of it. Five years earlier, there were limited references to Jesus Christ in popular music. By 1973, however, there were no barriers to invoking the name of Jesus in recordings that rejected or accepted the Biblical sacred order.

Heavy metal music expanded the exploration of spiritual pondering to embrace spiritual warfare, Satan and death including suicide and execution. In addition to lust and sex, individual bands also explored their personal themes. Judas Priest focused on biker culture. Iron Maiden expressed a fascination with native Americans, science fiction and World War II history. *Black Sabbath* (no. 23, 1970) introduced the grim vision of the seminal British heavy metal band. The title track is the blueprint for their tracks that address the shadowy portion of the spirit. The narrator is assailed by a "figure in black" (Satan) and calls to God to rescue him. "N.I.B.," from the same collection, parallels the Rolling Stones's "Sympathy for the Devil" (1968) in that the narrator is Lucifer himself. He entices the listener, promising "those things you thought unreal." As Christ beckoned fishermen along the Sea of Galilee to come with him (Matt. 4:19), Lucifer lures the listener with similar language: "Follow me now and you will not regret leaving the life you led before we met." Later, Judas Priest also cast the devil as the narrator in the band's "Burn in Hell" (1997).

Black Sabbath's lyrics contain numerous images of Satan, but they do not glorify the devil. For the most part, despite the band's name, the tracks that deal with the devil are warnings against the enticement of evil. "Who Are You" (1973) asks who "in the name of hell" is the one who will "cast our souls into the dust." "Lord of This World" (1971) acknowledges a creator God and explicates the choice given to walk away from God toward evil. For the character who has chosen the way of the wicked, the "lord of this world" is "possessor" and "confessor." The narrator wonders if those who were lured to Satan by their lust for power and wealth will "turn" to the devil when their earthly walk comes to an end.

"After Forever" (1971) is Black Sabbath's evangelistic altar call, not to the altar of Satan, but to the Christian altar. The lyrics assert that love can only be found in God. God is the "only one who can save you . . . from . . . sin and hate." The narrator has "seen the light and . . . changed his ways." The track does not fit with the image of the band, though it does go along with the groups's interest in spirituality. The narrator challenges the listener to ward off pressure from peers who mock those who believe in God. Similarly, Led Zeppelin, a band whose lyrics drew more from Norse mythology ("Immigrant Song") and ancient sacred orders of the British Isles ("The Battle of Evermore"), recorded a prayer to Jesus. "In My Time of Dying" (1975) is a blues-based plea for salvation. Written by all four members of the band, Robert Plant sings, "Jesus gonna make up . . . my dyin' bed." The twist in the song is that in addition to the narrator's petition to the Lord, he is simultaneously involved in an erotic embrace with "Georgina" and is approaching two out-of-this-world climaxes at once. The track is heavy-handed in underlying the mingling of the sacred and the secular in the American blues form.

Australian band AC/DC re-mold the Led Zeppelin idea to suggest that in lovemaking if the woman "play[s] a demon" and "brings out the devil" in the man, then "Hell Ain't a Bad Place to Be" (1977). Lust is the central theme of the band's lyrics. Several tracks in AC/DC's work focus on Satan and hell, including "Hell's Bells" (1980) and "Highway to Hell" (no. 47, 1979). In the latter track, the narrator boasts of being on the road to damnation with his friends, paralleling Jim Morrison's narrator's desire to enter the "House of Detention" where his comrades reside in the Doors's "When the Music's Over." Playing on the myth of rock and roll as the devil's music, AC/DC's narrator sings, "Hey Satan, paid my dues playing in a rocking band." To the narrator, hell is the "promised land," appropriating the Biblical image of heaven and applying it to the underworld. Gilmore notes that in the mid-1980s hysteria over heavy metal lyrics promulgated by Tipper Gore's Parents Music Resource Center, rumors spread that the band's name stood for "Anti-Christ/Devil's Child" or "After Christ, the Devil Comes" (259).

Reflecting society's interest in end times theology in the early 1980s, Iron Maiden recorded "Number of the Beast" (1982). The theme finds its basis in the Book of Revelation in the Apostle John's vision of the "beast" whose "number is Six hundred and sixty six" (Rev. 13:18). The narrator observes a scene of blazing torches, chants of praise and sacrifice to the Beast. He finds himself helplessly drawn to the "evil chanting hordes." In the final verse, the singer has been possessed by the Beast who has become the narrator. Menacingly, the Beast vows in the final line to "return . . . to make my evil take its course."

For Black Sabbath, AC/DC, Iron Maiden and Led Zeppelin (who conjure up the image of "Satan's daughter" in the track "Houses of the Holy" [1975]), the use of the names Satan or Lucifer and the idea of being attracted to eternal damnation are meant to shock the mainstream listener. Unlike "Lord," Satan and Lucifer are explicit terms without vague connotations. The notion of describing the abyss as a "promised land" is meant to stun and disturb the receptor of the lyric. These words are meaningful. Otherwise, they would not have shock value. In the late 1990s, the band Marilyn Manson attempts to draw similar reactions from the mainstream both in performance and on record. During their Spring, 1999 tour, the leader of the group tore pages from the Bible while standing behind a "makeshift pulpit" (DeSantis 46). The title of the band's breakthrough album, *Antichrist Superstar*, not only was a take-off on the name of the early rock musical *Jesus Christ Superstar* but also used a shock term for effect.

Thrash-metal group Metallica debuted with *Kill 'Em All* (published 1983, no. 155, 1986). Following earlier heavy metal bands, they used the device of the devil as narrator in several songs. In "Jump in the Fire" (1983), the narrator beckons the listener to come join him in the "pit." Similarly, in "Devil's Dance" (1997), the narrator summons, "come down to me . . . take the chance . . . let's dance." Satan is also the narrator of "Master of Puppets" (1986). The opening line of the song, "End of passion play, crumbling away" suggests the victory of evil over the persecuted Christ on the cross at Golgotha. "The God That Failed" (1991) suggests that there is no hope in Christianity. Pointing to the incarnation of Jesus, the narrator chides, "trust you gave a child to save left you cold and him in grave." With Christ in the grave, the lyric denies the possibility of resurrection.

Several Metallica tracks find their root in the scriptures. "Creeping Death" (1984) makes use of the Passover episode (Exod. 12) to examine the death theme. The lyrics closely follow the story line of the Bible passage. Creeping death takes the first born of the Egyptians, but "lamb's blood painted door, I shall pass." The lyrics of "To Live Is to Die" (1988) also emulate the Biblical sacred order. The singer petitions the "kingdom of salvation" to rescue him from the world. The basis of "Thorn Within" (1996) is uncovered in the Apostle Paul's description of the "thorn in the flesh, the messenger of Satan" (2 Cor. 12:7). In the Metallica track, the thorn is the sin nature of humanity. The narrator sings, "true guilt is from within." The song opens with the first words of the Roman Catholic Act of Contrition: "Forgive me Father for I have sinned." Following earlier heavy metal bands, Metallica does not outright deny the possibility of the Biblical sacred order. The lyrics show the end results of evil and muse over the possibility of redemption from evil.

At about the same time that music of the revival rock genre was vanishing from the charts, the contemporary Christian music (CCM) industry was emerging. Seeing the popularity, albeit short-lived, of Christian messages in the mainstream market, record labels that catered to the Christian subculture, e.g., the Word label in Waco, Texas, saw the opportunity to expand their market into a younger demographic segment. Ironically, rather than continuing to experiment with the merger of a rock music foundation with lyrics drawn from Biblical truths, the productions of the early 1970s returned to inoffensive instrumental arrangements that were more comfortable to the producers of music targeted to the religious market. One nod to the times was for the arrangements to use acoustic guitar instrumentation instead of orchestra arrangements to evidence contemporaneity. Barry McGuire (who sang the bestseller "Eve of Destruction" [1965]), Mike Johnson and Larry Norman were early CCM artists who toured the nation equipped with a guitar for accompaniment and a box of albums for sale after their concerts.

Larry Norman had been with the Capitol Records band People, who had a minor hit with "I Love You" (no. 14, 1968). He wanted to name the accompanying album "We Need a Whole Lot More Jesus (and a Lot Less Rock and Roll)," after one of the tracks on the longplayer. Capitol did not want to have the name "Jesus" in the title, so Norman left the band. Norman recorded an early CCM album as a solo artist that was initially released on Capitol. The album became more successful in the CCM market when it was picked up by a label that had superior distribution in the religious marketplace, which for CCM artists was primarily Christian bookstores. With long blond hair, Norman presented the early 1970s "Jesus Freak" image. He played straight ahead rock music to accompany his evangelical lyrics. On *In Another Land* (1976), one track describes Jesus as the "rock that doesn't roll." By the mid-1970s, CCM musician ensembles began to resemble traditional rock groups at least in appearance. The bands Love Song and the Way emerged on the West Coast.

Andrae Crouch and the Disciples represented a more traditional approach in the CCM market. Rooted in the band's African-American heritage, the ensemble presented a contemporary gospel approach in tracks such as "Jesus Is the Answer," with a melody closely resembling Billy Preston's "That's the Way God Planned It." Recording for Light Records, based, like the Word conglomerate, in Waco, Texas, the group released a successful concert album, *Live at Carnegie Hall* (1973).

Word's subsidiary label Myrrh released the first album by the 2nd Chapter of Acts, *With Footnotes*, in 1974. The vocal trio of two sisters and their brother were named after the Bible episode in which the Holy Spirit manifests itself to the early believers on the day of Pentecost and adherents begin to speak in tongues. Each of the songs on the album refers to a portion of the chapter. Therefore, as with most CCM songs, all the tracks refer to the God of the Bible and Christian teachings. The arrangements were soft rock in nature. The following year the band recorded *In the Volume of the Book* (1975). The subjects of the songs again remained close to scripture teachings. One song, "Hey Whatcha' Say," used a harder rock arrangement than the band had been backed with before. The guitar solo on the track was played by Phil Keaggy, who began his recording career with the mainstream band Glass Harp.

Living in a Christian fellowship called Free Love in the Southern Tier region of New York, Keaggy recorded his first CCM album, *What a Day*, in 1973. The record was the first release for New Song, a private label that would eventually release recordings for other musicians from the same community of believers, including Nedra Ross, one of the original Ronettes. The album cover depicts the bearded Keaggy in flannel shirt with acoustic guitar, the typical early 1970s CCM troubadour. Keaggy's next album, *Love Broke Thru* (1976) began to reveal the artist's electric guitar prowess that had labeled him as a "musician's musician" in his secular career. Buck Herring, husband of the leader of the 2nd Chapter of Acts, produced the album.

The next release for the 2nd Chapter of Acts and Phil Keaggy was a joint live recording, *How the West Was One* (1977). A three-disc set, the recording opens with one side of the vocal trio, continues with three sides of Keaggy and closes with two sides of the 2nd Chapter of Acts. The recording presents the hardest rock arrangements heard in CCM to date. Though the vocal trio still sings its harmonies over soft rock arrangements and Keaggy uses his acoustic guitar on a number of tracks, the album signals a turning point in CCM arrangements. Still, the lyrics focus on the three persons of the trinity and the relationship of the believer with God. Keaggy's "My Life" is his personal testimony. Anne Herring's "Dance with You" presents the story of King David dancing before the Ark of the Covenant. "Now That I Belong to You" deals with commitment to Christ.

The lyrics of CCM artists did not stray from these topics through most of the 1970s. Keaggy expands into social issues with "Little Ones" (1980), a pro-life song. Not until his fifth solo album, *Town to Town* (1981), does the artist sing about romantic love, specifically marital love, in the track "What a Wonder You Are." This is an early instance of a CCM artist singing about a love that is not agape. The same album includes a song about Keaggy's reunion in the Cleveland area with his former bandmates from Glass Harp. This was no small step in the CCM environment to incorporate a song that does not have to do with Christianity.

After two solo albums, Noel Paul Stookey left Warner Brothers and began to release albums on a private label. He expanded the CCM repertoire to incorporate subjects that would not be out of place in contemporary folksingers's repertoires, e.g., "Garden Song." Stookey

composed a track titled "Building Block." He sings, "the building block
that was rejected became the cornerstone for a whole new world"
closely following the words of the Psalmist: "The stone which the
builders refused is become the head stone of the corner" (Ps. 118:22).
In the late 1970s, I witnessed Stookey perform the track several times,
once solo at the Lamb's Club, a Christian venue in midtown Manhattan
and later on a reunion tour with Peter, Paul and Mary at the Garden
State Arts Center, a "summer shed" in central New Jersey. Before the
secular crowd at the Peter, Paul and Mary concert, he told a story of
how he converted a henhouse on the coast of Maine to a home. There
was no discussion of the Christian implications of the song. Rather, he
explained that he saw the promise of an old building that no one wanted
as a new abode for his family. In front of the Christian audience,
Stookey, in addition to unfolding the tale of his conversion project,
explained that the song followed the scripture teaching of the Christ as
the cornerstone.

Stevie Wonder explains in his liner notes that *Songs in the Key of
Life* (1976) is "only a conglomerate of thoughts in my subconscious
that my Maker decided to give me the strength, the love + love - hate =
love energy making it possible for me to bring to my conscious an
idea." During the 1970s, in a number of tracks, Wonder made clear who
his "Maker" is. In "I Believe (When I Fall in Love It Will Be Forever)"
(1972), the narrator finds romantic love. Commingling the secular with
the spiritual, toward the end of the song, he witnesses to the hand of
God in aiding him in his quest for romance. Wonder testifies that God
answered his prayer for love. Then, he turns to the listener and declares,
"God always will answer your prayers, believe in one who will answer
my prayer." In the African-American religious tradition, grace is not
separated from nature. God's hand works in romantic relationships and
Wonder is willing to incorporate that into his love song.

On *Innervisions* (no. 4, 1973), in the track directly before he chides
the "Jesus Children of America," Wonder sings of striving for the
"higher ground" in a lyric that echoes the words of the Apostle Paul: "I
press toward the mark for the prize of the high calling of God in Christ
Jesus" (Phil. 3:14). "Higher Ground" (no. 4, 1973) is a warning to be
ready for the coming of righteousness "cause it won't be too long." He
ends all four verses with the phrase underlining its importance to the
theme of the song. The phrase echoes the promise of the Christ to
return. The narrator is thankful that he has gone from the darkness to
the light. He is glad he has another chance: "I'm so darn glad he let me

try it again." For the African-American community, the "higher ground" is akin to the "promised land." It may be heaven in the Biblical sense or it may be freedom from oppression. Wonder focuses on the former in this hit single. He says his "last time on earth I lived a whole world of sin." Voicing the precept of a sin nature is a clearly communicated assent of a sacred order. At the close of the track, if the message is still vague to the listener, Wonder specifically mentions that "God is gonna show you higher ground." Wonder makes it clear that for him the "higher ground" is a new life with his Maker.

"Heaven Is 10 Zillion Light Years Away" from *Fulfillingness' First Finale* (no. 1, 1974) claims that people are not yet prepared to see the handiwork of God. As long as there is no healing of racial strife, as long as people "don't believe," then they will go on thinking they can not rise above their "evil souls," and heaven will continue to be an inconceivable distance away from humanity. Baffling to Wonder's narrator is that people can picture heaven at an insurmountable distance from them (a place "just" for the "pure at heart"), yet they can not envision "hate" being as remote. For Wonder's narrator, heaven is not so far away: "In my heart I can feel . . . His spirit." He entreats the listener to strive for the spiritual life he has experienced. For Wonder, the healing of the problems of humanity begins when people "let God's love shine within."

Stevie Wonder's *Songs in the Key of Life* (no. 1, 1976) has a number of tracks with Biblical images. "Have a Talk with God" simply reveals the opportunity for access through prayer to the "One" who can help in time of need. Wonder clearly communicates what God means to him. God is a "free psychiatrist" who is "always around" to bring "peace of mind." The acceptance of Wonder's espousal of the Biblical sacred order, as evidenced by the fact that the four albums whose tracks are discussed here were huge bestsellers, may relate to the mainstream audience's recognition of Wonder's African-American heritage. At this juncture, there were few artists who could use the name "God" in the title of a popular song and sing as enthusiastically and meaningfully about the power of prayer.

The lyric of "As" (no. 36, 1977), a single culled from *Songs in the Key of Life*, is primarily about the narrator pledging his love eternally to his romantic interest. In the middle of the seven-minute mid-tempo track, Wonder transforms his vocal style from smooth-voiced love man to a gravelly-voiced preacher style. Echoing his chiding of those who would preach the gospel in "Jesus Children of America" three years earlier, he chastens those who attempt to proclaim the word of God yet "make this earth a place sometimes called Hell." His words are specifically directed to those who announce that they are "in it but not of it." These words mimic a common phrase used in the evangelical church about being in the world but not of the world. The Apostle Paul wrote "Do not conform any longer to the pattern of this world" (Rom. 12:2, NIV). The Apostle John admonished early believers, "Do not love the world or anything in the world" (1 John 2:15). Yet, at the same time, Christ commanded his followers in the Great Commission to "Go and make disciples of all nations" (Matt. 28:19). So, there is the tension for the believer to keep a distance from the world but be active in the things of the world.

Before Wonder lectures those who aspire to share their truth, he declares that "God knew exactly where he wanted you to be placed." The narrator of "As" is convinced that the purpose of the believer is not to bring harm and hate to the world. Rather, the called are to "change [their] words into truths and then change that truth into love." For Wonder's narrator, the gospel is worthless if the end result is not love. Again, as in "I Believe (When I Fall in Love It Will Be Forever)," Wonder combines eros love with agape love. He asserts that the two can not be separated. He places his sacred messages within the context of everyday life. There is no dichotomy between the spiritual and the secular.

In the mainstream market, aside from the recordings of Stevie Wonder, there was little in the way of songs that identified an approval of the Biblical sacred order from the end of the revival rock era until the late 1970s. Debby Boone sang her number one "You Light Up My Life" (1977) to the God of the Bible, but the vagueness of the reference to God glossed over its message. The phrase "you light up my life" has a different connotation for the lonely teenager suffering from an unrequited love, than it does for the listener familiar with Debby Boone's religious commitments. The message of Boone's bestseller was further veiled by the fact that her reading was a cover version of a title song of a film romance. Only those familiar with the biography of the daughter of Pat Boone knew who Debby Boone meant by the address "You."

CHAPTER SEVEN

Slow Train Coming: Following the Path of Dylan through the 1980s

Bob Dylan's immersion in Christianity should not have been so surprising as he had explored spiritual and, in particular, Biblical images since the early years of his recording career. In the mid-1970s, he used metaphors based in Biblical texts in his lyrics. "Shelter from the Storm," from *Blood on the Tracks* (no. 1, 1975), incorporates a narrator who is a Christ figure. The twist in the story is that the Christ figure is not the "shelter" but a woman who provides sanctuary for him. The woman frees him from his "crown of thorns." Villagers "gambled for [his] clothes," mirroring the acts of the soldiers at Calvary. Like the Christ, the narrator "offered up my innocence and got repaid with scorn." Dylan's lyrics attest to his fluency in the texts of the Bible.

From the same collection, "Idiot Wind" is a vengeful complaint against a former lover and/or a former audience. The narrator rails against his target whose every word breathes "idiot wind." Again, the lyrics focus on Jesus Christ. Dylan sings of a "lone soldier on the cross" who "in the final end . . . won the wars after losin' every battle." As in "Shelter from the Storm," the narrator relates to Christ. He is telling his enemy it may appear she or they may be winning now, but he will be victorious.

The next release *Desire* (no. 1, 1976) again reflected Dylan's spiritual dabbles. In a non-fiction narrative, "Joey," about the assassination of the mob boss Joey Gallo, Dylan sings that if there is a God, the assassins will be brought to justice. The first person narrator of "Oh, Sister" sings to his lover who is his "sister" in a common faith. God is referred to as "Our Father." The two have had a common salvation: "we died and were reborn and then mysteriously saved." The two have a common calling. The narrator asks, "is our purpose not the same on this earth, to love and follow His direction?" The words of "Oh, Sister" clearly imply a spiritual transformation and are congruent with the doctrine of the Christian faith. Though Dylan was yet to publicly express his conversion, certainly his lyrics revealed his interest in a relationship with God.

The subsequent album *Street-Legal* (no. 11, 1978), the third release of the trilogy that began with *Blood on the Tracks*, evidenced an interest in end times theology. Dylan's narrator asks if he is on the way to Armageddon ("Senor"). "No Time to Think" is an apocalyptic revelation of a moon the color of blood, of betrayal where the lion should be living in peaceful harmony with the lamb and of leaders who will "offer their heads for a prayer" (but will not experience redemption). The narrator does note a glimmer of hope: "starlight in the East and you're finally released," referring to the coming of the Christ. On another track Dylan warns against the practice of the occult arts ("New Pony"). Dylan's foreboding lyrical vision precurses the theology of an angry God that he would espouse with his next release.

With the unexpected lyrical content of *Slow Train Coming* (no. 3, 1979), a proclamation of Dylan's spiritual renewal in Christ, the mainstream music market found itself in a state of instability. In the early rumors of Dylan's conversion, it was even remarked that the 1960s icon had been baptized in Pat Boone's swimming pool! In an album review of rare length for *Rolling Stone* magazine (two full pages), Editor and Publisher Jann S. Wenner dissected Dylan's album. Though recognizing the religious, and specifically Christian, content of the work, Wenner, near the end of his essay, is convinced and satisfied that Dylan did not convert to Christianity. He states, "neither the album itself . . . nor any firsthand reports . . . say that Dylan has been 'born again'" (Wenner "Bob" 94). Wenner opened the essay stressing the theme of faith that pervades the longplayer: "Faith is the message. Faith is the point. Faith is finally all we have" (95). However, he can not or will not define the object of Dylan's faith. Despite the allusions in the lyrics suggesting the embrace of Christianity and the visual metaphors of crosses on both the back and front of the album jacket, Wenner is close to suggesting Dylan's new music is inspirational in nature—"I Believe" or "You'll Never Walk Alone" with a folk-rock sensibility. Wenner asserts the "religious symbolism is a logical progression of Dylan's Manichaean vision of life and his pain-filled struggle with good and evil" (95). The born-again Dylan did not fit in with the rock and roll myth. Dylan's work was an extension of his religious pondering and unfolded the answer he found. Ruminating on Dylan's Biblical thoughts, Wenner ponders the embrace of a sacred order to provide meaning. He writes, "Maybe there is a personal and communal text that offers explanations, laws and practical notions that make sense where there has not been sense" (95) He is not ready to change his life, but accepts that after "long years of disrepair . . . maybe the time for religion has come again" (95).

Just as Dylan had explored spiritual images through his career, he also used the image of the "slow train" in the past. In his liner notes for the back album cover of *Highway 61 Revisited* (1965), he opens his prose with the line, "On the slow train time does not interfere." He uses the image several more times in the notes. One character in the tale notices the slow train and "prays for rain and time to interfere." Later, Dylan writes that the "subject matter" of the lyrics on the longplayer includes the "*holy* slow train" (emphasis added). He did not clarify the meaning of the slow train anymore than it being holy and that time had no meaning on the train. Even in 1965, the slow train was a type of spiritual image to Dylan.

Slow Train Coming encompasses a wide range of Biblical themes. "When He Returns" addresses the second coming of the Christ. Dylan draws out images from the Bible related to the Christ's teachings and His promise to return. He sings of the "thief in the night" who will "replace wrong with right." The lyrics re-mold images from the gospel texts. Notifying the listener that there is a holy other that has the power to "reduce" him "to tears," Dylan's narrator addresses "all those who have eyes and all those who have ears," alluding to Christ's teachings about the interpretation of his parables. The second verse begins with the line, "truth is an arrow and the gate is narrow that it passes through," echoing Jesus's teaching that it is easier for a camel to pass through the eye of the needle than for a rich person to enter the kingdom of heaven (Mark 10:25). Though Dylan sings of a "mighty God," Christ is only referred to as He in the track. Dylan reflects back on his pursuit of justice as a protest singer in the early years of his career and recognizes that "there'll be no peace, that the war won't cease until He returns."

Dylan more specifically addresses the return of Christ in "Gonna Change My Way of Thinking." He quotes the Christ: "Jesus said, 'Be ready, for you know not the hour in which I come.'" He also quotes

Christ saying, "'He who is not for Me is against Me.'" The lyrics also include a verse about the passion of Christ. Dylan sings of the "stripes" suffered by the persecuted Christ and of the "swords piercing [his] side" at Calvary.

"Precious Angel" combines a story of faith with romantic love. The first-person narrator is grateful to his lover for showing him the path to Christ. Dylan uses specific Christian dogma in the lyrics. Of he and his love, he says "we are covered in blood," referring to the substitutionary death of Christ and to the Passover experience of the Israelites. Dylan's vision is apocalyptic. He warns of "darkness that will fall from on high when men will beg God to kill them and they won't be able to die." His is not a vision of peace. He notes that there is "spiritual warfare" going on.

In "When You Gonna Wake Up," Dylan attacks "spiritual advisors and gurus [that] guide your every move." He chides, "counterfeit philosophies have polluted all of your thoughts." The narrator is sermonizing. He views the world as in need of redemption. He chastens those who think God is "just an errand boy to satisfy . . . wandering desires." He closes the song by clearly stating that the way of Christ is the way of change from the litany of sins that encumber society. He sings, "there's a Man up on a cross and He's been crucified."

Every track on the *Slow Train Coming* longplayer contains Biblical images. "Do Right to Me Baby" uses Jesus's teaching of doing unto others as you would have done to you as the basis for its chorus. "Slow Train," from which the album title comes, warns of impending judgment. The symbol of the train echoes the train of freedom of the Impressions's "People Get Ready" and the "sweet chariot" of the gospel hymn. "Gotta Serve Somebody," the opening track on the album, simply states that people serve either the darkness or the light. For Dylan, it is black and white: "it may be the devil or it may be the Lord." For John Lennon, Dylan's conversion was so upsetting that he composed an answer song to Dylan's track titled "Serve Yourself." Strumming angrily on an acoustic guitar, Lennon, in a solo home recording from 1980, replies to Dylan, "Ain't nobody gonna do for you." The individual may trust "devils" or "laws" or "Christ" or "Marx," but in Lennon's purview, "you're gonna have to serve yourself."

The album cover is a drawing of early railroaders laying track for a steam-powered locomotive waiting to continue its journey across the country. In the foreground a worker stands with his pick raised high above his head. The pick is a symbol of the cross. It echoes Jesus's words that the Christ must be raised up as the serpent was raised up by Moses in the wilderness. The back cover of the album is a photograph of a sunset over a body of water. On the right side of the photograph in the shadow is a sailboat with a sail-less mast silhouetted against the sky. Again, the mast represents the cross.

Those who had hoped the message of *Slow Train Coming* was allegorical in nature and did not truly evidence a commitment to Christ on the part of Dylan were sorely disappointed with the release of the followup *Saved* (no. 24, 1980). Dylan clarified his life change, clearly proclaiming the gospel of Jesus Christ. Dave Marsh called the album a "caricature of fundamentalist cant-it prevents anyone else ever doing an effective satire of the Christian Dylan, because he's satirized himself" (Marsh "Bob" 157). "Are You Ready" continues the theme of being prepared for the hour of judgment and the coming of the Christ. Though the track has the same theme and the same title as Pacific Gas and Electric's hit single of 1970, Dylan's composition is a completely different song. The narrator asks pointedly, "Are you ready to meet Jesus?" He again draws from the well of the New Testament in the lyrics. Dylan asks, "Will He know you when He sees you or will He say, 'Depart from me'?" following Jesus's vision of the judgment (Matt. 25:41). He chides individuals for privatizing their religion: "Have I surrendered to the will of God or am I still acting like the boss?" As in his previous album, Dylan's lyrics focus on the end times. In "Are You Ready," he asks if listeners are prepared for "judgment" and "Armageddon." He warns "there's no time" for goodbyes for "destruction cometh swiftly." His is a harsh vision.

"Saving Grace" speaks of the agape or undeserved love of God. The narrator marvels at the favor he has received from on high. He points to the Christ as the path to find the grace he has experienced: "there's only one road and it leads to Calvary." "Covenant Woman" is addressed to the same woman of "Precious Angel," a woman who showed the narrator the path to light. In the chorus, he expresses his gratitude to her for praying for his salvation. He is a new creation in Christ. His old life is nothing but dross. He explains that he has been "shattered like an empty cup." He awaits the Lord to "rebuild and fill [him] up."

"In the Garden" has the same title as the traditional hymn but does not have a like theme of God leading the believer and showing the way. Rather, Dylan asks whether people believed in New Testament times when they witnessed the signs of Christ. Using a more literal adaptation of the same scripture that formed the basis for Stevie Wonder's "Higher Ground," the narrator of "Pressing On" moves toward the same "high calling" as the Apostle Paul (Phil. 3:14). The "Solid Rock" of the track of the same name is Jesus Christ. Christ said that those who do as He said were comparable to one building their home on a solid foundation (Luke 6:48). The primary motif of the lyric is that the narrator "can't let go" and he "won't let go." The title track "Saved" is Dylan's testimony of redemption in Christ. Subscribing to the Biblical doctrine of original sin, the narrator opens the lyric by singing, "born already ruined, stone-cold dead as I stepped out of the womb." By God's grace, he has been "healed" and "delivered" from the judgment. In the chorus, he sings, "I've been saved by the blood of the lamb," reflecting a phrase repeated in hundreds and hundreds of fundamental church services weekly. Dylan did not mince words in his songs of new-found faith.

A little more than a year later, Dylan released *Shot of Love* (no. 33, 1981). In addition to the musician credits handprinted on the inner sleeve, Jesus's prayer to His Father thanking him for revealing truth to "babes" rather than the "wise and prudent" is quoted in its entirety (Matt. 11:25). Unlike the previous two Christian albums, Dylan began to write about topics other than the Biblical sacred order. Earlier in his career, Dylan had written songs about men who had died unjustly, including the prisoner George Jackson ("George Jackson") and the civil rights activist Medgar Evers ("Only a Pawn in Their Game"). He had also turned his lyric hand to the plight of Reuben "Hurricane" Carter, a New Jersey boxer unjustly sentenced to prison. On *Shot of Love*, one song focuses on the martyrdom of Lenny Bruce.

"Watered-Down Love" begins with phrases from 1 Corinthians 13, the "love" chapter that is often quoted at wedding ceremonies. Dylan sings, "Love that's pure hopes all things, believes all things," drawing from verse seven of the chapter. But the lyricist's intent is not to focus on the pure love, but rather on what those who have no need for God (the "wise and prudent" of Matt. 11:25) desire. They want love on their own terms-a "watered-down love." In the verses he describes the "love that's pure," and then follows in the chorus, scolding the listener for wanting something less.

In "Property of Jesus," Dylan comments on the reaction of non-believers, friends and fans alike, to his born-again faith. Using a third-person narrator, he sings, "laugh at him behind his back just like the others do, remind him of what he used to be when he comes walkin' through." He claims his freedom from the past. He does not need to be compared to his earlier artistry. The narrator declares that the one who is the "property of Jesus" no longer has the values of those who criticize. He "doesn't pay no tribute to the king that [they] serve."

The album closes with "Every Grain of Sand," a track which evidences the maturation of his faith. In contrast to some of the evangelical cliches used on the prior album, e.g., "I'm pressing on to the higher calling of my Lord" or "I've been saved by the blood of the lamb," Dylan uses a more poetic approach to share his faith. Reflecting on his past life, he sings, "the flowers of indulgence and the weeds of yesteryear, like criminals, they have choked the breath of conscience and good cheer." Borrowing from Jesus's parable about the sower whose seeds were choked by thorns (Luke 8:7), he uses the same image to describe how past "indulgences" affected him morally. The narrator is indebted to his Master for saving him from his past. Unlike Dylan's visions of judgment and apocalypse, his focus is on the agape love of God. Dylan draws from the teachings of Jesus as he stands in awe of a watchful guardian: "every hair is numbered like every grain of sand" and "I am hanging in the balance of the reality of man like every sparrow falling." The words parallel Jesus's teaching about the care of God for believers in the Gospel of Luke:

> Are not five sparrows sold for two farthings, and not one of them is forgotten before God? But even the very hairs of your head are all numbered. Fear not therefore, ye are of more value than sparrows. (Luke 12:6–7)

Dylan continued to record songs about his faith in later years, though not with the fervor witnessed in the three albums released directly after his conversion to Christianity. From *Infidels* (no. 20, 1983), "Man of Peace" warns of the deceptive character of Satan. "I and I" speaks to the relationship between God and the believer. Basing the chorus on the Book of Exodus, Dylan sings, "I and I in creation." When Moses asked God his name, He responded, "I AM THAT I AM" (Exod. 3:14). So, the "I and I" refer to God and the narrator. The chorus also quotes God's words to Moses at Mount Sinai, "no man sees my face and lives." Bob Marley also made use of the "I and I" imagery in a number of tracks ("Give Thanks and Praises," "Positive Vibration," "Jamming"). The imagery in the context of the exodus of the Israelites from Egypt parallels the Rastafarian image of the escape of Jah's people from Babylon. Marley's "Zion Train" (1980), released the year after *Slow Train Coming*, borrows similarly from the lyrical ideas of Curtis Mayfield's "People Get Ready" and the hymn "Swing Low, Sweet Chariot."

Dylan's *Down in the Groove* (no. 61, 1988) includes the track "Death Is Not the End." The lyrics are addressed to those who are searching for meaning in life and who are not comforted by the thought that there is nothing beyond the earthly walk. In the middle measures, he points to the hope for the sad, the lonely, the comfortless and the dreamless. Dylan sings, "the tree of life is growing where the spirit never dies and the bright light of salvation shines in dark and empty skies." Almost a decade after his conversion, Dylan was still pointing to the God of the Bible as his hope.

Under the Red Sky (no. 38, 1990) includes a track about the position of God in the universe simply titled "God Knows." Almost every line of the song starts with the title phrase and notes the omniscience of God whether it be in the way the world will come to an end or the uniqueness of the individual. Dylan tells the listener that "God knows the secrets of your heart" but "there's a purpose" and "a heaven" open to those who "weep" and open their hearts. In *Time Out of Mind* (1997), Dylan's first studio album of new compositions in seven years, several songs include references to the Biblical sacred order including "Standing in the Doorway" and "Trying to Get to Heaven." In a song of unrequited love titled "'Til I Fell in Love with You," the only thing that keeps the narrator from becoming unglued is his God. He sings, "I feel like I'm comin' to the end of my way, but I know God is my shield and he won't lead me astray."

Dylan's conversion, albeit indirectly, opened the doors for evangelical Christians to again record whole-life messages on mainstream record labels. In the late 1970s, Van Morrison, Teena Marie and Arlo Guthrie among others ushered in a new era of specific religious images in popular music lyrics. The doors that a number of singer-songwriters had tried to open in the early 1970s were opened by Dylan, the same artist who had introduced electric instruments to the world of folk music 15 years earlier. In the 1980s and 1990s, artists as diverse as U2 and Amy Grant, as well as Bruce Cockburn and Lauryn Hill, were able to present gospel messages to the mainstream market within songs that were more than just praise or worship songs.

Carlos Santana dropped the name "Devadip" for the cover of his 1983 solo release *Havana Moon*. In the liner notes he writes, "First and foremost, I would like to offer my deepest gratitude to our Lord Jesus Christ." Santana had experienced another spiritual transformation, three years after Dylan went public with his conversion. Nowhere on the jacket is there a mention of Sri Chinmoy.

In the same year that Dylan's *Slow Train Coming* was released, Arlo Guthrie's *Outlasting the Blues* (1979) debuted. The first three tracks, all written by Guthrie, contain a number of Christian images. The opener, "Prologue," takes a look at the legacy of the protest movement of the 1960s. People who dreamed of "rearranging" society are now "drunk in a world of material wealth." Near the end of the song, he asks, "Who'll be awake when the master returns." The following track, "Which Side," makes clear who the narrator means by the "master." The lyrics contain images of Moses leading the Israelites in the desert and of Jesus on the cross at Calvary. Echoing the gospel story of the Crucifixion, one of the thieves asks the Christ "what lay beyond." The next line identifies Christ as the "master" responding to his fellow crucified. Guthrie ends the song singing, "Me myself I'm satisfied to sing for God's own son." A later track on the album, "Drowning Man," studies the dilemma of doubt. The narrator wonders "How far down the road to glory must we go without a sign." He insists that it is "too late for new beginnings." But in the last line of the song, he requests that he not be "abandoned in this dark night of the soul." The narrator is affirming that there is something outside himself that he needs. On the title track of Guthrie's followup album *Power of Love* (no. 184, 1981), composed by T Bone Burnett, the "power of love" is a metaphor for Jesus. The song opens, "the power of love can make a blind man see." In the chorus, dueting with Phil Everly of the Everly Brothers, Guthrie sings that the "power of love is the Name of Names," echoing the scripture verse about the Christ having a name above all names (Phil. 2:9).

Bruce Springsteen's scenes from the souls of common folk rarely address the relationship between God and the individual. But his examinations have studied the spirit of humanity on its path through the alleyways and highways of existence. He has employed Biblical images to flesh out his tales of human relationships. "Adam Raised a Cain" confronts the tension between father and son. From the same album, *Darkness on the Edge of Town* (no. 5, 1978), the narrator voices the common faith that there is something better out there and it is reachable in "Promised Land." Introducing "Pink Cadillac" (1984) in concert,

Springsteen offered a tongue-in-cheek interpretation of the creation story.

The broodings of *Nebraska* (no. 3, 1982) contain a number of Biblical images. "Open All Night" sets a counterpoint between the redemption offered by Christian radio stations and the deliverance offered by the rock music disc jockey. In an opposing parallel to the promised land, "Mansion on the Hill" reflects the idea of striving for the unattainable—transcendence on earth or in heaven. The image of the mansion echoes the teachings of Christ. Jesus promises, "In my father's house are many mansions" (John 14:3). The same Bible verse resounds in the track "My Father's House." But the bleakness of Springsteen's vision counters the promise of the Christ. Like the narrator on watch in "Mansion on the Hill," he realizes that there is no admittance, no deliverance. The protagonist only dreams that he has access to the refuge of his father's home, a safe house that can represent the hearth or the promised land of heaven. The last verse identifies the house as something more than the residence of a son's earthly father. Redemption is across a great divide, "a dark highway." The narrator discerns that his transgressions will not be forgiven: "our sins lie unatoned." Faith has vanished. When there is no redeemer to turn to, there is no hope.

Paralleling Bob Dylan's experience, Van Morrison began to write with clarity about his faith in 1979. "Full Force Gale" speaks of the narrator's encounter with God. The narrator compares being "lifted up again by the Lord" to being carried along by a powerful wind. He was protected from a "fall" and finds his "sanctuary" in God. From the same album, *Into the Music* (no. 43, 1979), Morrison creates a pastoral scene ("Rolling Hills") where the narrator communicates with his God. He promises to "read his Bible" and "live my life in Him among the rolling hills." Morrison's Christianity is mystical in nature. The magic of the old ways and the legend of the holy grail at Avalon mingle with the stories of the Bible in the artist's vision. "Ancient of Days," from *A Sense of Wonder* (no. 61, 1985), takes its name from the title given to God the Father by Daniel in his vision of the Son of Man (Dan. 7:9). The track is a hymn of praise written in the fashion of David's psalms. Wherever the narrator goes, his God is to be found. "A New Kind of Man" is an exhortation to the listener to communicate with God. Morrison opens the track with the words, "There's a voice crying out in the wilderness," drawing forth the image of John the Baptist (Matt. 3:3). He encourages the listener to look toward the "mountaintop" and follow the "light that keeps shining up ahead of you." Such is the way to become a new creation or "a new kind of man."

Morrison composes another idyllic scene of communication with God in the track "In the Garden" from *No Guru, No Method, No Teacher* (no. 70, 1986). The album title is drawn from the song. The narrator and his love together commune with God in this quiet place: "just you and me and the Father and the Son and the Holy Ghost." The tranquil space is akin to a Garden of Eden. The couple "felt the presence of the youth of eternal summers" or Christ who Morrison identifies as the "Youth of 1,000 Summers" in a later composition. "Give Me My Rapture" is a prayer to be let loose from the shadows of night. The narrator prays, "Let me purify my thoughts and words and deeds that I may be a vehicle for thee."

The lead track from *Avalon Sunset* (no. 91, 1989) is a testimony and an exhortation. When he is deep in the "dark night of the soul," the place from which he desired to be unbound in "Give Me My Rapture," the narrator is assured that God will be available during his "confusion" and "despair" in "Whenever God Shines His Light on Me." This is his witness of God's work in his life. In the following verse, the singer preaches to the audience to do the same to get "back on higher ground." *Hymns to the Silence* (no. 99, 1991) combines church anthems with personal reminiscences. Morrison performs the old Irish hymn "Be Thou My Vision." The theme of nostalgia pervades several track including "On Hyndford Street" and "Take Me Back." The song "See Me Through Part II (Just a Closer Walk with Thee)" combines a church hymn with visions from the narrator's past in one production. The hymn bookends the song. The narrator reminisces of listening to music on the wireless "before rock 'n' roll, before television." He compares the simplicity of youth with the innocence of his faith in God. The Christ taught his disciples that one must accept God with the innocence of a child. In the gospel, Jesus says, "Except ye be converted, and become as little children, ye shall not enter into the kingdom of heaven" (Matt. 18:3). Morrison is concerned with the lack of faith in the world. In "No Religion," from *Days Like This* (no. 33, 1995), he examines his surroundings and declares "the whole world has gone astray." People "doubt" the offering of God's "unconditional" love.

As he had done since his career began, Bruce Cockburn continued to record his observations of faith in the God of the Bible. "Lord of the Starfields" (1977) is a psalm of praise to the "Ancient of Days, Universe Maker." He prays that he will continue to follow the light of

God. He asks, "O Love that fires the sun, keep me burning." Half a year after Dylan expressed his faith in Christ with *Slow Train Coming*, Cockburn enjoyed his only Top 40 hit in the U.S. market, "Wondering Where the Lions Are" (no. 21, 1980). In the early 1980s, Cockburn's lyrical purview expanded to incorporate the plight of oppressed peoples. "Justice" (1981) is a reshaped version of Dylan's "With God on Our Side," expanded to encompass all world powers that employ their Godhead or ideals as an excuse to carry out their interpretations of "justice." He opens the track with pointed questions about the horrors accomplished in the name of Jesus, Buddha, Islam and liberation. On the same album, *Inner City Front* (1981), he paints the world as a "Broken Wheel." Cockburn's prayer reflects the healing of the blind man by the Christ on the sabbath at Siloam (John 9: 1–7). To repair the "bleeding wound" on the wheel, he prays to the Lord, "spit on our eyes so we can see."

"Dweller by a Dark Stream" (1981) is the narrator's testimony of salvation in Christ. He realizes that he is no less guilty than those who attended the crucifixion at Golgotha. The lyric speaks clearly of the work of God in the narrator's "convict soul." At the end of the decade, "Shipwrecked at the Stable Door" (1989) again underlines Cockburn's narrator's conviction that the Christ is the passage from darkness to light. Cockburn contributes his account of the Christmas story in "Cry of a Tiny Babe" (1991). Through this child, "redemption rips through the surface of time." The lyrics update the story and hint at its parallels with the dark conditions of the modern world. To kill all the young male children in Bethlehem (Matt. 3:16), King Herod sends "death squads."

Donna Summer emerged at the cusp of the disco era with the orgasmic dance track "Love to Love You Baby" (no. 2, 1975). She was the most popular vocalist of the disco era. Between May, 1978 and January, 1980, she placed eight singles in the *Billboard* Top Five, including "Last Dance," "Heaven Knows," "Hot Stuff" and "Bad Girls." Beginning with *Bad Girls* (no. 1, 1979), the two-record set that spawned "Hot Stuff," "Bad Girls" and "Dim All the Lights," her album liner notes began to reveal a commitment to the God of the Bible. Ironically, the photos on the inside and outside cover depict Summer as a street-corner prostitute under a streetlight with a "trick," being watched by a cop, or carousing with other hookers and street characters. The front cover photo shows the artist dressed in a revealing black negligee. In her thanks to the people who helped with the album, just after she thanks her husband and daughter, she offers her final thanks to "GOD for all the wonderful things above, behind, beneath and in front of me."

Her next album, *The Wanderer* (no. 13, 1980), produced for her new label, Geffen Records, was Summer's declaration of independence from disco music. The final track is "I Believe in Jesus," a statement of faith that borrows from the hymn "Onward, Christian Soldiers" and the nursery rhyme "Mary Had a Little Lamb." The placement of the track at the end of the album is indicative of the mainstream record companies's desire to not be overt with religious messages. The image of the disco diva did not mix with a commitment to Christ. Penned by Summer, the song opens by focusing on a Los Angeles street corner preacher named Mother Mary. The narrator swiftly turns the focus to herself in the chorus and affirms she is "going to heaven by and by 'cause I already been through hell." In the second verse, she identifies Jesus as the lamb and notes that "this lamb" (herself) will follow Jesus. In the liner notes, at the close, she offers a "special thanks to the Supreme Being, the Creator; without Whom there would be no beginning and no end." On her next album, *Donna Summer* (no. 20, 1982), produced by Quincy Jones, she again concludes her thank-you notes with a nod to God. She thanks "GOD, the Father" for bringing together the various singers and musicians who helped to create the album and finishes, "I PRAISE THE LORD and surrender all unto HIM."

Completing her contractual commitment to her former label (Casablanca), Summer recorded *She Works Hard for the Money* (no. 9, 1983), which was released on Polygram's Mercury subsidiary, the label that had purchased Summer's old record company. The album was produced by Michael Omartian, a contemporary Christian artist, who was responsible for a number of successful mainstream productions, including Exile's number one hit "Kiss You All Over" (1978). A Geffen Records executive feared that the combination of Omartian and Summer's growing faith would produce a Christian collaboration that would completely sabotage her mainstream image (Bolettieri 32). However, this was not the case. The lyrics are populated with a cast of urban characters and their relationships. The main character of the title track, a number three single in 1983, was a waitress. The lyrical idea of the reggae number "Unconditional Love" (no. 43, 1983), the followup single and the track that leads off side two of the album, is rooted in the agape or undeserved love of the Biblical God. Musical Youth, a group of young Britons of Jamaican heritage, provide backing vocals. Summer and the British vocal group sing, "my torn heart to discern, this agape love to learn." In the liner notes, Summer adds scripture quotations for the first time on an album. She quotes an excerpt of John 3:16 and a larger portion of the book of the prophet Isaiah. She thanks the "body of believers" that has prayed for her during the making of the album and offers the album to the "Lord, Supreme Being." She expresses that she is giving "back the talents which You have given us as a witness." The third single from the album, "Love Has a Mind of its Own" (no. 70, 1984), is a romantic ballad that paired Summer with Matthew Ward, a member of the 2nd Chapter of Acts contemporary Christian vocal group. The recording may have been the only time Ward sang a love song or a lyric without specific Christian images.

Donna Summer wrote or co-wrote all but two tracks on her next album release, *Cats Without Claws* (no. 40, 1984). One of the songs not penned by her, "Forgive Me," was composed by Reba Rambo and Dony McGuire, artists in the contemporary Christian music market. Summer describes the song as "divinely anointed" in the notes. She opens her notes with a prayer. She asks that "God will bless [those] who buy or possess this record with the truth and the Holy Spirit."

Teena Marie, like Donna Summer, reveals her religious faith more explicitly in her albums's liner notes than in her compositions. Signed to Motown Records in the late 1970s, she debuted with *Wild and Peaceful* (no. 94, 1979). Her final thanks on the album jacket is to "the Master of heaven and earth." She prays, "Perish me not Lord until my sermon is preached, for as yet, I am not worthy to permeate the gates of heaven." She humbly states that she does not believe she is yet at the point she needs to be in her spiritual walk. She recognizes the need for spiritual preparedness.

On the followup *Lady T* (no. 45, 1980), Marie includes a poem in the liner notes that borrows from the Genesis story of Abraham negotiating with God over the preservation of Sodom if a few righteous inhabitants can be found. She speaks to the "sweet children of Yaweh (sic)." She preaches equality: "You and I are no more or less than each other-small fragments of the master's imagination." Echoing the concerns of the patriarch Abraham, she prays, "Grant that I may save at least one soul, even if not mine." She is not self-righteous. Paralleling the liner notes of her debut, she does not consider herself worthy of the agape love of God. "Irons in the Fire" (1980), the title track of her third album, continues the idea of the individual as a "fragment of God." In the same song, she addresses her Heavenly Father and prays He will help her overcome the trials of life: "with you as my desire the spirit is gonna lift me higher."

On her last album for Motown, *It Must Be Magic* (no. 23, 1981), Marie offers her thanks "most of all" to "the Master Jesus Christ . . . the only light." In "Opus III (Does Anybody Care)" she admonishes those whose faith does not lead to action: "It's not enough to say you care." She illustrates with her Master's life. She sings that Jesus "gave more than just his hands." Teena Marie includes these words amidst lyrics that deal with romantic love and social issues. She did not present a dichotomy between the secular and the spiritual. On "Portuguese Love," she presents a ballad reminiscence of making love on a beach on the Iberian coast.

Teena Marie's first album for her new label, Epic, was *Robbery* (no. 119, 1983). She had left Motown in a dispute over royalty payments. In her notes, her first thanks are to "Jesus Christ for continuing to bless me through all my faults and shortcomings." Again, she presents a humble character who continues on a spiritual quest. *Starchild* (no. 31, 1984) contained Marie's only Top Ten hit single, "Lovergirl" (no. 4, 1985). The poem "Starchild" on the inner sleeve speaks of the "Creator," the only one who is "new and innovative." The poem lists those who show the path to the light of God:

> We walk upon the same hallowed ground that Jesus walked upon/ can you imagine the intensity of a light so bright/ can you fathom the place where the Gandhis/ and the Yoganandas/ the Chinmoys/ and the Buddhas/ the Shivas/ and the Blessed Virgin Mary dwell/ Have you heard Steveland's "Higher Ground."

Though she personally has embraced the Biblical sacred order, she asserts that there are other paths to truth, to find meaning in life.

"Help Youngblood Get to the Freaky Party" presents a tale of temptation. The guy (Youngblood) is flirting with the narrator and confesses that he wants to "make" her. She defends herself by reading "Romans 8:14" and later "Galatians Chapter 4" to the enamored fellow. The scripture passages she chooses to defend herself with speak of the believer as a child of God. She is explaining to her accoster that she is an heir of her Creator. Somewhat tongue-in-cheek, Marie presents the struggle between the spirit and the flesh in facing the temptation of lust on a daily basis.

The final track, "Light," is a lullaby of thanksgiving to God the Father and God the Son. Marie sings of a vision from "Jesus" of "a heavenly light [shining] through [her] window" revealing "all of the joys that love could bring." She praises Jesus for giving his life for her and thanks the "Father for all the songs you've given me." Like Noel Paul Stookey, she views herself as a vessel through which the Creator sends the beauty of music in song. In the liner notes, Marie "thanks Jesus Christ who makes it possible for me to thank the rest."

"My Dear Mr. Gaye" (also from *Starchild*), written shortly after Marvin Gaye was shot and killed, suggests that Gaye is in heaven. Marie sings, "Trouble Man now you're home." ("Trouble Man" is a reference to a film soundtrack composed by Gaye.) A poem in the liner notes of *Naked to the World* (no. 65, 1988) also references Marvin Gaye as well as two other rhythm and blues singers, Minnie Riperton and Donny Hathaway. She writes of the "sensual sexuality of Marvin" and the "purity of Minnie." And, she testifies that she "drown[s] in still waters when Donny sings." Because these three rhythm and blues singers who died tragically young have passed on to the other side, "heaven rocks."

"Opus III-The Second Movement" parallels the format of the teenage death songs of the late 1950s and early 1960s. Again she mentions the three deceased recording artists voiced in her poem. In the midst of the track, she sings from the liturgy of the Roman Catholic mass: "Kyrie Elieson Christe Elieson." These Greek phrases translate to "Lord, have mercy" and "Christ, have mercy" respectively. Per Catholic theology she lifts the souls of the departed to the Lord. She prays that the three departed musicians are in heaven. The track closes with a promise to God from the narrator to secure her place in heaven when she is called: "whilst trouble arise I'll hasten to your throne." (Marie connects the track through its title to "Opus III (Does Anybody Care)" from *It Must Be Magic*. The first line of that track is "Memories past but not forgotten.") Again, in her liner notes, Marie affirms that the music she creates is from God. Her music "is not as much mine as it is his and yours."

Prince (or The Artist) focuses on the apocalypse in "1999" (no. 12, 1983) from the album of the same name (no. 9, 1983). Like the Biblical prophets, his vision comes in the form of a dream. He underlines the sacredness of his vision by noting it seemed like "judgment day." For Prince, the end-of-the-world catastrophe is more man-made than the destruction described in the Biblical revelation of John. Because of the weapons that can bring about a world-wide holocaust, Prince's narrator suggests humanity enjoy the sensual pleasures of life while there is still time. From the soundtrack of his semiautobiographical film *Purple Rain* (1984), "I Would Die 4 U" (no. 8, 1985) outlines the messianic character of the rock musician. The narrator of the track is neither "woman" or "man" nor "lover" or "friend" or "human." He has the ability to pardon "evil." All he asks is that the adherent to his character have faith in him. He closes the track with the words, "All I really need is to know that you believe that I would die for you." Belief is the turnkey to receive strength and forgiveness from this worldly overwhelmingly other.

On the back cover of Steve Arrington's Hall of Fame's second release *Positive Power* (no. 141, 1984), Arrington writes in the liner notes: "Brothers and Sisters, In the middle of this album a change came over me. I found God. So this album shows where I've been and where I'm going." The following year Arrington went solo and released *Dancin' in the Key of Life* (no. 185, 1985). The opening track and the title track express Arrington's new found faith. In "Feel So Real" the narrator explains that he owes everything to God. In the final verse, Arrington sings, "I'm right here on my knees to thank you for the air that I breathe." The single "Dancin' in the Key of Life" (no. 68, 1985) is a testimony of the hand of God in the life of the narrator. God is his power over temptation. He sings, "when the demon tries to make a play, you know you always pull me through." He tells the listener it is impossible to disregard the "vibe" of the gospel. The "good news" makes the adherent hungry for more of the word of God.

Steve Winwood's "Higher Love" (no. 1, 1986) asserts that there must be an overwhelmingly other to provide order for life. The narrator searches to find the meaning of his existence. He states, "Without [higher love], life is wasted time." He knows there is something out there but, at least for him, it is yet to be discovered.

The Hooters, a pop-rock band from Philadelphia, had a number of Top 40 singles in 1985 and 1986 including "And We Danced," "Day by Day" and "Where Do the Children Go" culled from their debut *Nervous Night* (no. 12, 1986). The first single release from the longplayer, "All You Zombies" (no. 58, 1985), centered on Old Testament images of Moses and Noah. The song unfolds the resistance to the prophets. Pharaoh was unyielding to Moses as were the people of God when the leader of the exodus met God on Mount Sinai. The lyric notes that

Moses "went to get the Ten Commandments, he's just gonna break them in half." Similarly, as Noah prepared for the great flood, the narrator sings, "they all laughed at him."

The narrator is a contemporary prophet. The song is a warning to the "zombies" who "hide their faces" and leaders "in high places" who ignore God. He chastises leaders informing them the "rain's gonna fall on you." The song closes with a prayer to the "Holy Father" asking where the believers have gone. He encourages the children of God to come out: "you don't have to hide anymore." The song recognizes a sacred framework for life as noted in other popular songs of the mid-1980s.

The Los Angeles band Mr. Mister defined mid-1980s pop with their back-to-back number one hits "Broken Wings" and "Kyrie" from the number one album *Welcome to the Real World* (1985). Each line of the chorus of "Kyrie" begins with the Greek phrase "Kyrie elieson" which translates to "Lord, have mercy." The narrator asks God to be with him as he walks the paths of life. The first verse hints at the work of the Holy Spirit in the life of the narrator. He sings, "The wind blows hard . . . into my soul." In the Bible, the rushing wind represents the spirit of God (Acts 2:2). Though the lyrics reflect the fellowship of God with humanity, the use of the Greek masks the relationship of the narrator with the Biblical overwhelmingly other. The listener unfamiliar with the Greek "Kyrie" phrase may comprehend the song as a search for meaning without a ground for being in the narrator. At the time the track was popular, I heard a WPLJ-FM, New York City disc jockey explain that "Kyrie elieson" was the Greek translation for "Mr. Mister."

Los Angeles cowpunk/country rock band Lone Justice, led by Maria McKee, released its self-titled debut in 1985. The album closed with McKee singing the ballad "You Are the Light," composed by band member Marvin Etzioni. The track is an homage of thanksgiving to the one who "shine[s] when everything seems hopeless." The identity of the recipient of the hymn is vague. It could be God or an earthly love. On the title track of the band's second album *Shelter* (no. 65, 1986), the narrator offers to be the recipient's overwhelmingly other. McKee's narrator will provide a refuge "from the endless night." The opening cut of the same recording is a testimony titled "I Found Love." The narrator sings of how "somethin' jumped up and it grabbed my heart." The second verse opens, "The beginning and end of every wish is balanced in the center of a vision like this." These words mirror the statement of Christ in John's revelation, "I am Alpha and Omega, the beginning and the end, the first and the last" (Rev. 22:13). In the same verse, the narrator is ready to "surrender to the notion of a glorious kind." These phrases suggest the narrator speaks of a theistic love, but, as in "You Are the Light," the understanding of the type of love can be either agape or erotic. In the bridge, though, McKee sings, "The Power's got me and it won't let me be." The capitalization of "Power" in the lyric sheet suggests she is singing of a higher love, a deity.

On her first solo album, McKee's "Breathe" (1989) sounds like the words of someone who has been filled by the Holy Ghost. Her body, her life has been taken over by a strong force. The narrator sings, "My heart beats your blood, your breath fills my lungs." The words illustrate John the Baptist's reflection about the Christ: "He must increase, but I must decrease" (John 3:30). McKee's song may not be about God but a more earthly lover with whom she has become one. McKee has revealed more of her personal spiritual stance in her extracurricular recording activity. She sang a duet with Tim White titled "Cover Me" for a compilation of praise songs on the Maranatha! Music label.

In the opening song from U2's debut album, *Boy* (published 1980, no. 63, 1981), "I Will Follow," the singer promises to dedicate himself to the one he addresses. The target of his vow may be God. At the end of the first verse, he admits, "I was blind but now I see," mirroring the words of the blind man healed by Jesus (John 9:25). At the end of the third verse, he allows, "I was lost, I am found." Together the two couplets match the second half of the first verse of John Newton's hymn "Amazing Grace." U2 biographer Eamon Dunphy suggests the lyric may be about the singer's mother, who passed away when Bono was 14 years of age (155).

The band's sophomore effort, *October* (no. 104, 1981) opens with "Gloria." This is not a cover version of Van Morrison's paean to the woman he lusts for, but an expression of the majesty of God in relation to humanity. In the face of the glory of God, the narrator is speechless. He can not find the words to speak to the overwhelmingly other. He admits to God, "only in you I'm complete." The narrator will give his God anything He requests.

"Tomorrow" is a psalm of desire for the hand of God in the life of the narrator. He asks rhetorically, "Who heals the bounds? Who heals the stars?" He knows the answer. As the song closes, his plea is for Jesus to "come back." The title track, "October," speaks of the never-changing character of God. Though the seasons change, as everything else on the earthly plane, God is the one constant. Dominions emerge and collapse but God goes "on and on."

"With a Shout" indicts those who stand still in the face of injustice and ignore the plight of the oppressed. Bono's lyrics use the scene at Calvary to illustrate the message: "Blood was spilt . . . we were doing nothing." Bono sings, "Jerusalem, Jerusalem" mirroring the words of Christ, "O Jerusalem, Jerusalem, thou that killest the prophets" (Matt. 23:37). He sings of the love of God that was offered to humanity through the Christ. The narrator states he is "filled" with agape love. The next to the last track of the album is "Scarlet." The lyric consists of one word, "rejoice," repeated over and over. The scarlet of the song title refers to the completed work of the Christ whose blood was shed to save the world according to Biblical teaching. The singer's recognition of the sacrifice of the Paschal lamb for his redemption leaves him awestruck. He can only respond by reveling in the undeserved love of God.

In June, 1983, the Irish band played at the Red Rocks amphitheater outside Denver (Dunphy 224). As they closed the performance, lead singer Bono asked the audience of 8,000 to join in singing the anthem "40." Over a somber, rhythm-heavy beat, Bono opened with the words, "Waited patiently for my Lord, He inclined and heard my cry." These words and the remaining lyrics of the song are closely drawn from the first three verses of Psalm 40. The Psalmist writes, "I waited patiently for the Lord, and He inclined to me, and heard my cry" (Ps. 40:1). In the chorus, the band and the audience (captured on the concert documentary *Under a Blood Red Sky* [1983]) sing together, "How long to sing this song?" As the song closes and the audience is left alone singing the words a capella, it is a poignant moment—a sense of cautious and exhausted optimism pervades the atmosphere.

Though the band has recorded a number of tracks in its career that draw from the scriptures, in the U2 repertoire "40" most closely follows a Bible text. Interestingly, the band chose not to call the track "Psalm 40." This falls in line with a type of song titles used by U2 in their early years (the aforementioned "Scarlet" and "Gloria," for example, and "MLK," a song about Martin Luther King) and also the way the band uses Biblical images in their music. The manner in which they blend these images into their songs reflects an understanding of the scriptures, but it also points to the fact that U2 carefully walk a path that does not clearly reveal their spiritual posture.

Early in their recording career the band struggled with the integration of their Christian commitment with rock music. From before the release of *Boy*, three members of the band, Bono, Edge and Larry Mullen, attended a charismatic Christian bible study and worship circle in Dublin called Shalom. At one point, between the release of *October* (1981) and *War* (1983), guitarist Edge announced to his fellow band members that he was quitting the band to devote himself to the radical Christian lifestyle taught in the Shalom gathering. Singer Bono and drummer Mullen also grappled with how to blend their devotion to Christ with the music and lifestyle of rock. Early on Bono knew his vision was for U2 not to be labeled as the band that sang about God (Dunphy 170). The end result of Edge's anguish was the composition of "Sunday Bloody Sunday" (Dunphy 204). Dunphy suggests that the song was the substance of Edge's revelation that the mind and the spirit can not be compartmentalized (Dunphy 205). In the last verse of the track, released on *War* (no. 12), Bono sings, "The real battle just begun to claim the victory Jesus won." The song was a signal for the future of U2's recordings. It recognized a sacred order, but rather than being evangelical, it showed that one could subscribe to the Christian faith and live in the secular world, following the African-American music tradition.

In their breakthrough album *The Joshua Tree* (no. 1, 1987), U2 make mystical and vague references to the Biblical tradition. In the opening track, "Where the Streets Have No Name," the lead vocalist sings, "I want to touch the flame where the streets have no name." In the hit single "I Still Haven't Found What I'm Looking For," from the same album, lead singer Bono intones, "I believe in the kingdom come, then all the colors will bleed into one." In the last verse the narrator gets more specific. Bono sings, "You . . . carried the cross of my shame," acknowledging that the "you" he is singing about throughout the song (the "you" he has "climbed [the] highest mountain" for and "scaled . . . city walls for") is the Christ. Still, the song ends ambiguously. After he mentions the cross, he goes back to singing the title line. Though he "believed" Christ died for him, he is still seeking.

The Christian members of the band are careful to keep their spiritual lives at a low profile when they are in the spotlight. Labeled on the cover of the March 14, 1985 issue of *Rolling Stone* as the magazine's choice for "Band of the 1980s" as the group stood on the threshold of stardom, they did not want to be labeled a Christian band.

It is a taboo in rock music culture for artists to admit that they have found what they have been looking for.

"Bullet the Blue Sky," also from *The Joshua Tree*, details the horrors of war and the plight of its innocent victims. The narrator draws a parallel to the scene on Calvary. Bullets and artillery shells are a "stinging rain" that "drive[s] nails into the souls on the tree of pain." In the live version from *Rattle and Hum* (no. 1, 1988), Bono goes into a monologue as the song draws to a close. He uses his observation of the cult of American televangelists who rob the "sick and the old" as a springboard to describe his God, one who "isn't short of cash."

On the same album Bono re-molds the words of Psalm 23 to create a perplexing statement of faith. He sings, "Yea, though I walk in the valley of the shadow, yea, I will fear no evil." These phrases are drawn directly from the scriptures. He immediately follows, "I have cursed thy rod and staff, they no longer comfort me." The words of solace to the Psalmist are rejected by U2's narrator. Once he has rejected the rod and staff, the singer promptly entreats, "love rescue me" (the title of the song). The words reflect the tension between faith and doubt. Further, it is not made clear if the love that has the power to deliver him (or the narrator has the power to reject) is of a deity or a fellow human.

Blues artist B.B. King collaborates with the Irish band on the studio track "When Love Comes to Town" (1988). The lyric is a statement of release and of new life. Love has caused the narrator to turn from a wicked past. In the previous track in the album order, the narrator's plea was for love to rescue him. In this song, in the first verse, the singer affirms that "love rescued me." The love that transformed him could be the love of the Biblical God. The narrator was "lost at sea" and "under the waves" when love renewed him. These images are congruent with the testimony of a repentant sinner. He broke promises and left his woman stranded. He recognizes wrongdoing or sin. The chorus opens with the line, "When love comes to town I'm going to jump that train." Again, there is the traditional image of the train of salvation on its way to take the believer home.

In the last verse, the lead vocal duties shift to B.B. King. The blues singer evokes the scene at Calvary and confesses to being an accessory to the crucifixion of Christ: "I held the scabbard when the soldier drew his sword, I threw the dice when they pierced his side." Intriguingly, Bono does not sing these words but rather offers them to an African-American blues singer. Though the words sung by King do not necessarily define the love that has come to town as the love of Christ, it is interesting that Bono chose not to sing the words. The narrator has numbered his sins but the identification of his deliverer is cloudy.

"God Part II" is a creed with a twist. The narrator lists the things he does not believe and then admits he is still drawn to these objects of rejection. He does not believe in "excess" or "riches" but concedes "you should see where I live." He dismisses "forced entry" and "rape" but acknowledges "every time she passes by wild thoughts escape." His words resound with the teaching of Jesus Christ in the Garden of Gethsemane: "the spirit is willing, but the flesh is weak" (Matt. 26:41). In opposition to the lyrical structure of dismissals combined with confessions, each verse ends with an affirmation of what the narrator does believe. He sings, "I . . . I believe in love." And he repeats the same profession at the end of each verse. But Bono does not clarify what this love is, though "God" is the significant element in the song title.

"God Part II" is an answer song to John Lennon's non-creed "God" (1970). Lennon stated that he did not believe in Jesus, Kennedy, Buddha, the Bible, Elvis or the Beatles among other sacred icons. The former Beatle declared he only believed in his wife and himself. The U2 track differs in its focus. The sense is that the love the narrator believes in is not one that emanates from within himself. It may not be a divine love, but what he believes in is external. Bono alludes to Lennon in the song. The narrator rejects "Goldman," the author Albert Goldman, who wrote an unflattering biography of Lennon. The U2 singer continues, "instant karma's going to get him [Goldman]," referring to Lennon's hit single "Instant Karma."

From *Achtung Baby* (no. 1, 1991), the ballad "One" (no. 10, 1992) is an examination of the sacrament of matrimony that finds its basis in the scripture verse about the "two becoming one." Bono sings, "we're one, but we're not the same." The lyric is a sobering scrutiny of wedlock. In marriage, one partner can transfer his or her shortcomings on the other. The narrator asks, "Will it make it easier on you now? You got someone to blame." On a positive note, he sings, "we get to carry each other." One can rely on the other for support. The singer observes the complication of two becoming one when one's companion has his or her own demons to deal with that keep the person from being one alone. Using the New Testament image of the healing Christ, the narrator asks his mate, "Have you come here to play Jesus to the lepers in your head?" The key to the couple's union is "love." The narrator declares that love is a "temple" and a "higher law." This suggests that a divine canopy covers their marriage. Again, though, the employ of the term "love" is vague.

In the late 1990s, the band continued to utilize Biblical images in their lyrics. From *Pop* (1997), the track "Mofo" incorporates the image of the individual attempting to "fill that GOD shaped hole." Several tracks on the same album suggest that such an endeavor may be in vain. Bono sings, "God has got his phone off the hook babe, would he even pick it up if he could?" ("If God Will Send His Angels"). In another lyric he sings, "God is good but will HE listen" ("Staring at the Sun"). "Last Night on Earth" relates the story of a woman who is not interested in or has given up the quest for God: "she's not waiting on a saviour to come." These thoughts signify a turn in the outlook of U2 toward the Biblical sacred order. Despair has overcome hope. Past songs recognized an underlying foundation of assurance in something, maybe love, that would at the minimum offer a lifeline to drag people out of the morass of existence. These tracks signal that there may be no exit.

The songs of *Pop* present a God who is not very different from the God of Dog's Eye View's "Everything Falls Apart" or Tori Amos's "God." The collection portrays an unresponsive God. U2 uses this theme as the basis for the closing song of *Pop*, "Wake Up Dead Man." The song is a plea for help to Christ, the "dead man" of the title. The narrator directs his entreaties to "Jesus." Bono sings, "I know you're looking out for us but maybe your hands aren't free." The narrator suggests that Christ go back to the Bible for a rescue plan: "listen to your words they'll tell you what to do." In this song, not even God knows where to turn. *Pop* paints a picture of a desperate people pursuing the unattainable.

Unlike the nascent days of contemporary Christian music (CCM), when songs had a simple acoustic accompaniment, by the mid-1980s, CCM borrowed from a number of musical forms. CCM instrumental tracks differed little from their secular counterparts. The magazine *Contemporary Christian Music* classified their record reviews of CCM releases as: Rock/Pop, Metal, New Country, Inspirational. There was also CCM rap and CCM "New Age" instrumental music. When aerobics records were popular, there was a CCM alternative with the title *Firm Believer*. An article in *Rolling Stone* magazine about Sam Phillips, a woman who left CCM for the mainstream, referred to CCM as a "parallel universe" (Woodard 24).

Like earlier CCM, the lyrics still dealt with the God in three persons: the Father, the Son, or the Holy Spirit. Though CCM emerged in the late 1960s, it was almost a decade before a CCM artist dared record a song about something other than the triune God. Earlier it was noted that Phil Keaggy, who started recording CCM in 1973, did not sing a song about romantic love until his fifth album in 1981. When CCM artists addressed romantic love, it was clear that the love represented was that between a husband and wife rather than a couple dating.

In the late 1970s, Word Records signed a young woman from Tennessee named Amy Grant to Myrhh, one of the firm's subsidiary labels. Grant was the youngest artist ever signed to the label. She became popular with her second album and, in particular, with a song called "My Father's Eyes." Her career and music illustrate the tenuous relationship between nature and grace outside of African-American music culture. Precursing her future in CCM, her second album was controversial because of the back cover photo of her with the top three buttons on her blouse unbuttoned.

Since the release of *My Father's Eyes* (1979), Grant has recorded eight studio albums. In this time, her music has evolved from simple acoustic guitar accompaniments to synthesizer dance pop to adult contemporary to modern rock. After *My Father's Eyes*, Grant released *Never Alone* (1980) and two volumes of a concert longplayer (1980 and 1981). Musically, the albums were similar to *My Father's Eyes* in both instrumental and vocal arrangements.

In 1982, Grant released *Age to Age*. It became the most successful CCM album at the time. It was the third gold record and the first platinum record in the CCM realm. The instrumentation, still conservative, revealed a new maturity in the music. The music was labeled Contemporary Praise. The album contained "El-Shaddai" (God Almighty) which became Grant's signature song. The lyrics speak of the unchanging nature of God: "age to age you stay the same, El-Shaddai."

Grant's next album, *Straight Ahead* (published 1984, no. 133, 1985), added more of a beat to the instrumentation. This was particularly evident in the opening cut, "Where Do You Hide Your Heart." The song's position at the beginning of the album announced a new direction for Grant. Though still firmly rooted in CCM, her music and the subjects of her lyrics were veering from the "Contemporary Praise" mold.

Unlike the religious motifs presented in the graphics of the prior *Age to Age* release, the back cover revealed Grant in blue jeans in poses uncharacteristic for female CCM artists at the time. The same year Grant, barefoot, sang the song "Angels" (from *Straight Ahead*) on the nationally-televised Grammy Awards show. The next morning, a New York area disc jockey, Jim Kerr, of the morning shift on WPLJ-FM, commented that he felt guilty for being physically attracted to a gospel singer while watching the awards show.

In 1985, Grant made her first inroad to the mainstream with *Unguarded* (no. 35). Unlike her previous albums, the instrumentation was for the most part uptempo and the percussion was upfront in the recording mix. Much use was made of synthesizers in the arrangements. Grant was aiming for the Contemporary Hit Radio (CHR) format. The phrase "Love of Another Kind" from the opening song on *Unguarded* can be interpreted as referring to divine love or romantic love.

Unlike her previous albums, there were no songs in the "contemporary praise" category. References to the deity were occasionally made through the use of the capitalized pronoun. For example, in "Love of Another Kind," Grant sings, "I've found in *You* a love of another kind" (emphasis added). In "Find a Way" (no. 29, 1985), she says there is no "circumstance that *He* can't see you through" (emphasis added). However, there were also specific references to the Incarnate God in "Love of Another Kind" ("Jesus' love is like no other"), "Fight," and "Find a Way" ("God His Son").

Grant did not hide her religious persuasion. On the lyric sheet, four of the album's ten cuts have scripture references attached to them. Another song Grant calls her "own version of Psalm 139." Aside from one love song dedicated specifically to her husband, all of the songs relate in some way to a facet of the Christian life. "Everywhere I Go" and "Stepping in Your Shoes" can be interpreted as praises to God. Despite this, the CCM audience was in an uproar over the release of the album. It was viewed as a "selling out" of sorts. One characteristic that caused the response was the aforementioned instrumentation and the arrangements of the songs. One could dance to these tracks.

Another characteristic that added to the negative reaction was the album graphics. The cover is done in black and white except for Grant's name in large, bold, fluorescent pink letters. Secondly, Grant is dancing in the cover photo. Thirdly, the artist is wearing a leopard-skin jacket over her blouse. In rock music history, leopard-skin has strong sexual connotations. In Bob Dylan's "Leopard-Skin Pill-Box Hat," the former lover sees the woman who wears the leopard-skin pillbox hat "making love" with her "new boyfriend" in the garage.

Three buttons on the blouse unbuttoned was one thing. Posing bent over in jeans was another. But dancing in a leopard-skin jacket was too much for the CCM audience. Despite the visible references to God and His Son, some of the CCM audience reacted in a strong negative manner to Grant's attempt to court the mainstream audience.

Because of the vast gap between the CCM and mainstream markets, it was necessary for *Unguarded* to be distributed by two different labels. Myrhh Records, her original label, was able to market the album in its traditional manner, primarily through Christian book stores. However, the label could not break into the mainstream market. So, A&M Records was chosen to introduce Amy Grant to the secular city. Don Cusic wrote about this odd process in an article titled "Moving Music Through a Double Pipeline" (G-16). Double meaning songs (about romantic or divine love or both) were marketed through a "double pipeline." In the opening cut, "Love of Another Kind," Grant sings,"they say love won't last, I say love is never ending, 'cause in You I have a love of another kind." Except for the capitalized pronoun, the song could be about the guy next door.

"Everywhere I Go" is Grant's "version of Psalm 139." Here again, the interpretation can relate to the sphere of divine love or human love. In the bridge, Grant sings, "I have seen you in the evening, in the morning light you hold me, closer than the air around me, you surround me always." Though this closely parallels the Psalmist saying, "if I make my bed in the depths, you are there" (Ps. 139:8) and "When I awake, I am still with you" (Ps. 139:18), the lyrics are not far from dealing with embracing one's lover through the night.

The opening song on the 1991 *Heart in Motion* tour was "Fight." This song led off the second side of the *Unguarded* album. It was in a prominent location on the album, indicating that the artist wanted the audience to know she had an important message to share. And the fact that a six-year old song was even more prominent in concert evidenced the song's continuing importance to the artist. "Fight" is a story of oscillation: "You know some days I like me, some days I don't, some days I try with passion, sometimes I won't." She delivers the vocal in an aggressive, forthright manner. Grant affirms the importance of "everyday life."

Grant sings of wanting to "hold [her] guard up," that is, to defend against God or Jesus coming into her life: "I used to sit and ponder if I'd be fine if Jesus lived his own life and I lived mine." On the other hand, there is a desire to be "unguarded" and to "let in the light." She understands that it is "a holy struggle." The artist is expressing a need to fight to enjoy life, to not be pigeonholed into a narrow definition of the Christian life. But she oscillates. Sometimes, she wants to "hold [her] guard up" and other times she wants to "stay open." At the close of the song, she says "Don't want to be hiding when the love comes around." The song ends with the sense that though the artist wants to experience her humanity, at the same time, she is willing to do this under the will of a divine power. She asserts that it is alright to be human within a divine framework and to oscillate and not stay static behind the fortress walls of "churchianity."

Casually listening to this song, the listener may think the lyrical focus is on fighting to be righteous. Really, though, the "fight" is against those who would bar one from escaping the born-again subculture to experience the surrounding world. The artist says this can be done in the framework of love. In "Stepping in Your Shoes" from the same album, Grant again refers to this "fight." She sings, "Evil and light caught in a fight, they're trying to capture me." The implication is that she does not desire to live solely in one realm or another. She does not want to be captured by evil *or* light. Somewhere between the sacred and the secular is where she desires to be found. In summary, *Unguarded* reveals the artist's desire to swing from the realm of grace to that of nature. The tension in "Fight," as well as the lyrical elements of "Love of Another Kind" and "Everywhere I Go," reveal the movement of the artist in an environment outside the "mighty fortress" walls.

After *Unguarded*, in an article in *Rolling Stone*, Grant mentioned that she sunbathed nude on a West African beach (Goldberg 9). And the context was such that it was not mentioned in a confessional manner. This reinforced the beliefs of those in the CCM audience who interpreted *Unguarded* as a revelation of the "backsliding" or falling away of a sister.

The opening notes of Grant's next release provide a clue as to the album's intent to placate the CCM audience. Several songs, including "1974" and "Saved by Love," reveal a shift back to more traditional instrumentation. The graphics included with the album package are much more subdued, as is Grant's wardrobe.

"1974," the opening number of *Lead Me On* (no. 71, 1988), is Amy Grant's personal testimony. Sharing one's personal testimony, that is, how the believer came to the knowledge of Christ and the salvation experience, is a long-standing tradition in churches. "How did you come to know the Lord?" is a greeting often extended to the recent adherent to a body of believers. It is no accident that this song starts the record after the controversy over *Unguarded*. Grant reestablished herself with the CCM audience by returning to the basics. Apparently autobiographical, "1974" relates the tale of her conversion experience in the mid-1970s.

Unlike the percussive power pop which opened the *Unguarded* album three years earlier, "1974" opens with 12–string guitar and zither in a mid-tempo flowing beat. Young enough to not know "quite what to say," the artist remembers that they "had crossed a big line." Grant uses the first person plural in relating her experience rather than the singular. Though it is her story, she seeks rather to focus on the experience of a community of believers. Ironically, she chooses to do her own background vocals on the recording.

In the title song "Lead Me On" (no. 96, 1988), Grant focuses on two of the great sins of humanity: the slavery of Africans ("Shoulder to the wheel for someone else's gain") and the holocaust ("Echoes of a slamming door in chambers made for sleeping forever"). In the bridge, she asks, "Somebody tell me why." She questions why humanity inflicts pain and suffering on itself. Unlike the song "Ask Me" from *Heart in Motion*, the artist does not ask where God was in the midst of the suffering. God is not blamed in the story of this song. God is the redeemer of the victims of these sins. At the end of the day, for the slave, "freedom was a song" directed "to the holy one." Locked in the gas chamber, the "voices" of the victims "cry to the Lord."

"Saved by Love" presents another testimony. Unlike the personal character of "1974," Grant starts by singing of a woman who has been "saved by love." The woman, Laura, has a husband and child and, sometimes, the "world rests on her shoulders." But because of the love that has saved her, Laura "can't imagine ever leaving now." As Donna Summer did in her song "I Believe in Jesus" with her street corner preacher character Mother Mary "down on Vine Street in L.A.," Grant begins the song by projecting the salvation message onto a created character for the song. Like "1974," "Saved by Love" is backed with traditional instrumentation, including acoustic guitar and mandolin.

As "Saved by Love" continues, Grant applies the message of the song to herself. She admits even though there are lonely times (her admissions question the notion of the eternally-smiling believer), it makes her "love Jesus more." The song builds to a crescendo, with an instrumental arrangement akin to a Tom Petty and the Heartbreakers tune. (Keyboardist Benmont Tench, from Petty's band, plays the B-3 keyboard on the recording.) Finally, Grant leaves no doubt that she is singing, not about Laura, but herself, when she intones, "Amy, she's been saved by love." At this point, the tempo slows, and Grant, soberingly, testifies in an improvisatory manner that the work has been completed: "Nothing I can do, nothing I can say." The evangelical Christian believes that the Incarnate God has completed the work of salvation. No good works on the part of the believer are significant to "crossing the line" to Christ.

Though *Lead Me On* signals the return to the fold, it reveals more about oscillating to the secular than *Unguarded* did. The song "What About the Love" asks the second major question on the album. In "Lead Me On," Grant asks why man hurts man. Here she sings, "Is this all there is, just the letter of the law? Something's wrong."

In "What About the Love," the top CCM artist questions the denial of the body, the idea of learning to submit, the act of praying to be made worthy and the act of tithing. Even though Grant echoes the centuries-old words of the Apostle Paul, the voice of the questioner asks things that are not expected. Paul wrote to the Romans: "we are delivered from the law . . . that we should serve in newness of spirit . . . ." (Rom. 7:6). Further, he wrote: "the letter killeth, but the spirit giveth life" (2 Cor. 3:6).

Grant, as the song unfolds, comes to the realization that the point is not to condemn her sister or brother. She looks in the mirror and sees her "pointing finger pointing back at [her]," paralleling Christ's admonition to remove the log from your own eye before you remove a speck from your brother's eye (Matt. 7:3–5). The singer expresses her understanding that not everyone can do what she desires to do. She may not be accepted for what she wants to do, but she is willing to accept others.

A number of contemporary Christian recording artists have successfully crossed over to the mainstream market, including Amy Grant, Michael W. Smith, dc talk and Kathy Troccoli. In doing so, these artists have continued to maintain their presence in the CCM market. They have not turned their backs on their first audience. Sam

Phillips, who recorded four contemporary Christian albums as "Leslie Phillips," left the CCM field to, as she put it, "explore spirituality, not dispense God propaganda" (White 195). Leslie Phillips recorded her CCM albums for Myrrh, the same subsidiary of Word that signed Amy Grant in the late 1970s. Phillips first album *Beyond Saturday Night* (1983) presents an image of the artist as one whose music has an "unmistakable edge of reality" (Seay). In his liner notes, Davin Seay quotes Phillips's desire to not incorporate "bland candy-coated cliches" in her lyrics (Seay). One of the tracks, "Gina," is, according to Phillips's notes, "a true story about a girlfriend of mine who burned to death in a car accident before I could tell her about Jesus" (Phillips).

Her sophomore effort *Dancing with Danger* (1984) presents a "caught by the flash bulb in the middle of the night" image of the musician. The theme of temptation threads its way through the lyrics. "Light of Love" addresses the challenge of being chaste. "I Won't Let It Come Between Us" notes that "the wine of recklessness can taste so sweet." In a third-person narration, "Hiding in the Shadows" displays a woman who "is not what they (the CCM audience?) assume." The subject of the song "played her role but it wasn't from her heart." The album also includes a hymn of praise by Phillips, "By My Spirit," a duet with Matthew Ward of 2nd Chapter of Acts. Her third album in three years, *Black and White in a Grey World* (1985), continues in a similar lyrical vein. The title track embodies a jazz-inflected arrangement. "Psalm 55" adds music to the words of King David. The effect of the breaking down of a marriage on the children of the home is examined in "Walls of Silence." The album suggests Phillips had gone as far as she could in her initial musical direction.

To steer a change in focus, T Bone Burnett was retained to produce Phillips's final studio album for Myrrh, *The Turning* (1987). Burnett had been part of Bob Dylan's Rolling Thunder Revue tour in 1976. He was a member of the Alpha Band in the late 1970s and recorded a number of solo projects including *Truth Decay* (1980). He was a successful producer, having recently produced Los Lobos's *How Will the Wolf Survive* (1984). The most noticeable shift in the resulting work by Phillips was in the music. Burnett aimed for a leaner sound with less emphasis on the synthesizers that dominated her prior albums. Though there are references to the faith and overwhelmingly other of the artist, e.g., "river of love that runs through all times" ("River of Love"), only one track mentions "God" in its lyrics ("God Is Watching You"). White describes the recording as "a postorthodox folk epiphany" (White 195).

"Down" paints a picture of the awesome glory of God in the face of the self. She sings, "Down I hit the dirt when I see who You really are." Face to face with God, she realizes her "religion" has little to do with God's design for His people. Her "religion" falls like "leaves on winter trees." Personal beliefs that she thought "reflected" God are "shattered" ("Convictions"). The revelation that God came down with His "love on hands and knees" opens her eyes to the entrapment of the baggage that comes with religion and its traditions. Seven years later Phillips would write, "I need god not the political church" ("I Need Love"). Her composition "Expectations" is a veiled critique of the CCM industry and her goodbye to her record company. The narrator pleads, "Loosen the pressure you choked me with, I can't breathe." She offers to "pull down" the "high ideals" of the one she addresses.

With Burnett continuing as producer, Phillips left CCM for the pop mainstream. She signed with the Virgin label and began recording under the name Sam Phillips. Her mainstream debut *The Incredible Wow* (1988) includes "Flame," another exploration of temptation. The narrator wonders why she is so attracted to the flame. She feels "pain if I hold you or let go." Her stance is nebulous. She is not convinced as to which way to turn. From *Martinis and Bikinis* (no. 182, 1994), "Signposts" reflects on her experience in CCM circles. She genuinely desired to explore "beauty and truth . . . [she] could breathe like air" but had to travel to a "strange land" (the mainstream) for the opportunity.

Religion and sex are married in the image of Madonna Louise Veronica Ciccone. Though the number of songs with Biblical images are a small portion of her total recorded output, Madonna has used her given name, her Roman Catholic heritage and her erotic charisma to create an image from which the sacred can not be separated. Her first greatest hits compilation was titled *The Immaculate Collection* (1990). An advertisement for *Like A Prayer* (1989) in *Billboard* proclaimed "Lead Us into Temptation" (Andersen 270).

The first maneuver toward the addition of a religious quality to her image was with her second album titled *Like a Virgin* (no. 1, 1984). In a sepia-toned photograph on the album cover, Madonna rests against a satin pillow partially dressed in a risque wedding gown with a bouquet of flowers nearby. Simply viewing the album title and the artist's name on the cover, the connection is made between the original Madonna (the Virgin Mary) and the dance-pop singer. The lyric of the title track, "Like a Virgin," includes several images that echo Biblical religion. The song opens, "I made it through the wilderness." In the Old

Testament, Moses led the exodus of the Israelites through the wilderness. In the New Testament, Jesus was tempted by the devil in the desert. In the second verse, she announces, "you made me feel shiny and new." This reflects the idea of the believer being a new creation in God, having turned away from the old life. Primarily, though, the song is a love song. The narrator's love interest has redeemed her. She has been "saving" her love for him "like a virgin." Singing the song live at the MTV Music Video Awards in 1985, Madonna eroticized the sacrament of marriage, rolling around the stage in a revealing wedding dress.

"Papa Don't Preach" (no. 1, 1986), the single that led off *True Blue* (no. 1, 1986), did not include any Biblical images, but gave evidence of Madonna's interest in her Roman Catholic upbringing. The protagonist in the song is unwed and expecting a child. She refuses to have an abortion or give up the baby for adoption despite the urging of friends who say she "ought to live it up." Her choice to not terminate the pregnancy is clearly in line with Roman Catholic teaching. The artist described the song as a "celebration of life" (Andersen 211).

The cover photo of Madonna's next studio album *Like A Prayer* (no. 1, 1989) only shows the part of the artist from about six inches above her waist to the bottom of her pants's zipper. Ironically, rather than being solely directed at the body, the recording was her most thoughtful and religious at the time. Again, the images reveal the influence of her faith heritage on this self-described "roller-coaster Catholic" (White 310). Madonna dedicates the album to her mother who she says "taught me how to pray." The opening track, the title cut "Like a Prayer," starts with a hard rock guitar solo that represents the world of confusion. A door shuts, removing the sound of the guitar and there is a sense of being in a sanctuary. As angelic voices harmonize wordlessly in the background, the narrator stands by herself before her God. She notes "everyone must stand alone," reflecting the Biblical teaching that all will be judged. There is the feeling of being called as the narrator hears her name spoken by the overwhelmingly other. In this refuge, in communion with God, she feels she is home. The track is full of religious references. The narrator is on her knees, she hears the sound of an "angel sighing," God and faith are mysteries and a gospel choir enters in the midst of the track to sing the chorus.

The track uses references to past hit recordings to mingle the carnal and the sacred. In the chorus, the narrator sings, "In the midnight hour I can feel your power," referring back to the Wilson Pickett 1965 hit single "In the Midnight Hour." In the following line, she states, "Just like a prayer, I'll take you there." The phrase "I'll Take You There" is the title of the gospel group the Staple Singers number one single from 1972. For the Staple Singers, the place they would take the listener to was a land of salvation, a promised land, a site free from oppression.

For Madonna's narrator, the place of redemption may be closer to home. Release may come through the act of lovemaking. This idea comes to mind particularly in the chorus line, "I'm down on my knees, I wanna take you there." The song became controversial upon its issue, not because of its lyric, but due to the accompanying video. In a Catholic church, the Madonna character helps to bring a statue of a saint of African descent to life. Shortly after, Madonna's character bleeds from stigmata wounds like those Jesus suffered on the cross. The animated statue and the Madonna figure enter into a romantic embrace. Madonna was dropped from a Pepsi television ad campaign that utilized the recording (with a different video storyline) because of the spiritual and sexual imagery combined in the music video. The content of the "Like a Prayer" lyric is meaningful and assertive. The narrator sings of the experience of faith and finds in her spirituality a key to her sexuality and vice versa.

In the next to last track, "Spanish Eyes," the narrator's romantic interest is missing. He may have been taken away in the middle of the night against his will by an oppressive force. Again, echoing Roman Catholic practice, she lights a candle for him. The narrator does not look for consolation from stars or heaven, but specifically looks to "Christ." She asks for prayer from the Christ for her love, "Spanish eyes." Oddly, she does not pray to Christ or God, but asks them to join her in prayer for he who is yearned for. Again in the chorus, she asks God, "if he exists," to "help" her in her petitions for her man.

"Act of Contrition," the final track on the album is a montage of sounds that reprises and samples the opening title track. The hard rock guitar solo from the introduction and a backward tape loop of the choir singing the word "prayer" from "Like a Prayer" are evident in the mix. "Act of Contrition" is liturgical. Madonna first recites the Roman Catholic prayer of confession and petition of repentance and, then, calmly and softly sings it over a cacophony of hard rock guitar, hand claps and tape loops. Produced by, as the liner notes indicate, the "Powers That Be," the track speaks of the goodness of God and the sin nature of humanity. *Like a Prayer* signals the closure of a chapter in Madonna's career. Five years earlier, she was a dance-pop "Boy Toy."

With *Like a Prayer,* Madonna proved she was an artist who could think with more than her body.

After John Lennon's "Imagine" the number of recordings that clearly rejected the Biblical sacred order or religion in general waned. Ian Hunter's "God (Take 1)," the final track from *All-American Alien Boy* (no. 177, 1976), is a conversation between the narrator and God. Hunter, whose musical arrangements and vocal intonation echo the style of the 1960s Dylan, suggests that the people who walk the earth, the crown of creation according to the Book of Genesis, are, in fact, only pawns or toys in a game between God and the devil for "galaxies." God tells the narrator that there are no religions, they are only an invention of man. Hunter's musings are not a rejection of any sacred order as much as an attempt to understand the meaning of humanity and the origins of belief in the sacred.

David Bowie's "Modern Love" (no. 14, 1983) ends with three sets of three lines that progress from "modern love" to "church on time" to "God and man." Each of these phrases is repeated at the beginning of three lines in a row and then the next phrase starts the next three lines and so forth. The progression in the lines is circular. The narrator sings that "modern love" carries him to the church which "terrifies" him. Being in church causes him to place his "trust in God and man." However, being at this juncture, he discovers or demands "no confession" and "no religion." The rejection of confession suggests the dismissal of a sin nature in humanity. With no sin, there is no need to admit fault and, thus, no place for forgiveness. It is interesting that it is in a church where he comes to the conclusion that there is no need for religion. The idea of "God and man" leads him to believe that there is no need for a formal worship structure. Bowie's narrator never rejects the idea of God in the song. However, he does reject the idea that there may be times when fellowship has to be restored, a significant principle in the Biblical sacred order.

At the time of the passing of Sting's father, the former lead singer of the Police wrote a song about the interaction of religion and the impending death of a loved one, in this case, the father of the narrator. In "All This Time" (no. 5, 1991), priests come to administer last rites. The two clergymen are described as "a murder of crows." The narrator chuckles at what his father would think about the Beatitude that speaks of inheriting the earth. He muses that his father would find absurd the idea of inheriting a world not worth possessing. At the end of a chorus, the narrator asks, "Father, if Jesus exists, then how come he never lived here." Not only does the song question the place of religion in the life of a common man, but it also questions the existence of the sacred order that the men of the cloth represent.

Unlike lyricists who write songs that acknowledge the Biblical tradition, Sting questions belief in the God of the Bible in clear, meaningful language. In "If I Ever Lose My Faith in You" (no. 23, 1993), Sting's narrator expresses his trust in his romantic interest, but, at the same time, notes his loss of hope in the "holy church," paralleling the ideas of "All This Time." Another English recording act, Genesis, recorded "Jesus He Knows Me" (no. 23, 1992), a scathing attack on televangelists. Though the focus is on the church or religion, rather than the Godhead, still the name "Jesus" is up front in a song that attacks part of the Christian subculture.

XTC's "Dear God" from *Skylarking* (published 1986, no 70, 1987), labeled an "agnostic diatribe" by one writer (M. Coleman), may be the strongest complaint against the Biblical sacred order. In a letter to God, the narrator makes a case for why God does not exist, or at least why God does not deserve to exist. He tells God he "can't believe" because the "people that you made in your image" starve and suffer with disease and go to war over "opinions" about God. The narrator attacks the Bible, saying that "us crazy humans wrote it" and that people accept "that junk is true."

In the final verse of the song, the narrator lists tenets of the Biblical faith that he rejects including heaven, hell and the "thorny crown." He repudiates the work of Christ on the cross and the promise of salvation. He rejects the triune God: "Father, Son and Holy Ghost is just somebody's unholy hoax." In very clear, meaningful language, XTC proclaims its refusal of Christianity.

CHAPTER EIGHT.

One of Us: Defining Gods in the 1990s

From his self-titled debut album, Marc Cohn's "Walking in Memphis" (No. 13, 1991) documents a tour of the City of Memphis as a spiritual and transcendent experience. In the first line of the song, the first-person narrator puts his blue suede shoes on (a reference to the song popularized by Elvis Presley), suggesting that he is preparing to walk on sacred ground. Arriving at his destination, he offers a petition to the self-proclaimed "Father of the Blues," W.C. Handy, asking him to watch over the blue boy. Walking on the best-known avenue in the city, Beale Street (made famous in Handy's 1916 composition, "Beale Street Blues"), the narrator explains that he is walking ten feet off the pavement.

He makes a pilgrimage to Graceland, the home and final resting place of Memphis's most famous son, Elvis Presley. The narrator watches Elvis's ghost pass unnoticed through the gates of Graceland, much as gospel authors chronicled how the risen Christ moved through doors to appear to his disciples in the forty days after his death. In another allusion to the Christ, Cohn's narrator notes the security at Graceland did not see Elvis's ghost, but only kept watch around his tomb. This echoes the resurrection of Christ from his tomb, and specifically, the image of the Roman guards keeping their vigil to prevent zealots from stealing the body of Christ.

The imagery turns specifically Christian in the bridge of the song. The narrator speaks of the presence of gospel music and of the Reverend Green. The reference to the Reverend Green is to Al Green, the soul singer who had seven Top Ten singles on the *Billboard* popularity charts between 1971 and 1974. In the late 1970s, Green left the popular music scene for a season and solely recorded gospel music. He also became pastor of the Full Gospel Tabernacle in Memphis, a ministry he is involved with to this day.

As the bridge draws to a close, Cohn slows the tempo of the song almost to a stop to emphasize that Reverend Green's church has a place for the hopeless, for those who "haven't got a prayer." But there is hope in Memphis (one can walk "ten feet off of Beale"), and as the tempo picks up and the song moves into the third verse, the scene shifts to a club (the Hollywood) where the musician narrator is asked to perform an impromptu piece. After his number the narrator is asked by the piano player, "are you a Christian, child?" Here is an infrequent use in popular music lyrics of the term used to designate the followers of Christ. The narrator's response is sung enthusiastically, but ambiguously, "Ma'am, I am tonight!" His level of commitment is vague. He does not say whether he is a long-time Christian, or if he is only caught up in the transcendent atmosphere of Memphis and, as a result, is a believer for just one night.

Cohn's recording does not adhere to a specific viewpoint in regard to the Christian faith. It does not embrace or reject the Biblical sacred order. Rather, it is an observation of some of the spiritual forces at work in the "land of the Delta blues." The lyrics describe the atmosphere in the city and mix the transcendence of being caught up in the musical heritage of Memphis with the transcendence of the manifestations of the Christian or gospel faith there. The narrator's personal religiosity is evident in that he can both pray to W.C. Handy or to the God of the Reverend Green's congregation. Personal religion is a common thread in the popular music of the 1990s that addresses sacred orders.

Rapper Kool Moe Dee defends his chosen vocation in the track "I Go to Work." He asserts, "I don't write I build a rhyme I draw plans draft the diagrams an architect in effect." His spiritual blueprint combines images from Christianity and Islam in the title track of *Knowledge Is King* (no. 25, 1989). Moe Dee warns the audience against the pursuit of riches, drugs and lust. In "Knowledge Is King," he states, "chasing butt or trying to get a dollar" is an empty quest. The knowledge he promotes is uncovered in "the Holy Koran or the Bible because it's liable to be revival for the weak." He exhorts listeners to stop listening to leaders without morals and begin listening to the "prophets." He closes the track pointing to the overwhelmingly others of Christianity and Islam. He raps, "whether your faith is Christ or

Allah the knowledge of God will teach one thing . . . knowledge is king." Moe Dee suggests that the meaning of life is not monopolized by one sacred order. Released in the same year as Madonna's "Catholic" album, the success of Moe Dee's spiritual musings hints at an upturn in religious images in popular music.

The 1990s witnessed the widespread acceptance of the rap music genre in the mainstream marketplace. The soundtrack of the summer of 1995 was Coolio's three-million-seller "Gangsta's Paradise" (no. 1). The track opens with the words of verse four of Psalm 23. The neighborhood where the narrator lives is his "valley of the shadow of death." The event that underlined the popularity of rap music was the presentation of five awards to Lauryn Hill at the Grammy Awards program in February, 1999.

Rap group Arrested Development's "Tennessee" (no. 6, 1992) is a prayer to God. The narrator wonders why the Lord has returned him to a land where he can "climb the trees my forefathers hung from." It is certainly not the promised land. His plea follows the age-old question by believers of why God places them in the circumstances they encounter. He asks, "Let me understand your plan." When he begins to comprehend his situation and that he has been sent to the "country" to fathom the history of his people, he states God was "there to quench my thirst." But he wants more: "I am still thirsty." As the track closes, he realizes his quest for "ultimate truth" was a dream. He repeats his desire to understand God's plan for his life.

On his first solo work *Return of the Boom Bap* (no. 37, 1993), KRS-One applies an Afro-centric perspective to American Christianity in the track "Higher Level." He explains that God is not found in the Bible, not if it is the book that legitimized slavery. He speaks of the "scripture that whipped cha'." KRS-One observes the "European version of Christ" and wonders, "Where is . . . the God that looks like me?" Like Bob Dylan, he rejects the notion that the United States is the Biblical city on a hill. He states, "I don't want a God that blesses America."

The veneration of the cross is questioned in "The Truth" from the singer's more successful self-titled sophomore effort (no. 19, 1995). The rapper, whose name stands for Knowledge Reigns Supreme Over Nearly Everybody, observes the cross as a means of execution much as an electric chair or a tree used for lynching or a gun. He challenges the adherent to the Christian faith. After absorbing his message, the believer may wonder why she or he sings the old hymn "When I

Survey the Wondrous Cross." KRS separates Jesus from the cross. To the rapper, Jesus "was all about the revolution," but the cross is an abomination. KRS-One connects the lifting up of the cross to organized religion which he differentiates from a relationship with God. He sings, "God is not down with religion." Though he accepts the existence of God, KRS's narrator does not find a need for the Bible. He tells the listener to find God in his or her own self.

KRS-One's strongest critique of the Biblical sacred order is found in "Fourth Quarter-Free Throws" from *I Got Next*. He interprets the Bible from an astrological perspective. To him, the gospels of Matthew, Mark, Luke and John represent the seasons and Jesus's disciples symbolize the 12 months of the year. KRS's narrator also rejects the notion of the Christ as the son of God. He asserts the idea is drawn from the sun around which the earth revolves. Further, the symbolism of the fish in the scriptures, e.g. the miracle of the multiplication of the fish to feed the 5,000 followers, is related to the past 2,000 years being the age of Pisces. He does not accept scripture as the word of God.

The most creative artists in the world of country music in the 1990s were the women of country. In the issues grappled with in their lyrics and in their interpretations of songs from rising composers, Kathy Mattea, Mary-Chapin Carpenter, Rosanne Cash and others continued the tradition of the folksinger-songwriters of the 1960s and 1970s including Judy Collins, Joan Baez and Joni Mitchell. Mattea's third release, *Walk the Way the Wind Blows* (1986), includes a psalm of praise to the Lord titled "You're the Power." Though the lyric does not refer to the overwhelmingly other any more specifically than the "power," the metaphors suggest the song is directed to the divine. The power is a "beacon" and a "shelter," it "heals [her] soul" and its "spirit" (the Holy Spirit) is "part of [her]." Mattea's Christmas album *Good News* (1993) reflects a faith deeper than the ephemeral character of the holiday season in her song choices for the collection. The second track from Mattea's 1997 release *Love Travels*, "Sending Me Angels," is a testimony to God's protection of His people. When the narrator feels she can not "take any more," "He" directs aid to her. The repentant narrator, "amazed at the number of times we've all sinned," is overwhelmed at the constant love of her God. Beginning in a somber, confessional mood, the arrangement transforms to a gospel-inflected celebration of faith.

In the past decade, Rosanne Cash has contemplated the nature of God and the relationship between God and humanity. In her collection of short fiction, *Bodies of Water*, one of Cash's characters asks herself, "What prayer did one offer up when one had more questions than requests?" (Cash 92). Two major themes weave through Cash's recorded output in the 1987 to 1996 decade: the image of crawling and the domination of woman by man. The strains are not mutually exclusive. In "I Don't Have to Crawl," from *King's Record Shop* (no. 138, 1987), Cash states, "I don't have to be nobody's fool . . . I don't have to crawl, I can just walk away." The song conjures up the image of the oppressed female. The same album opens with a track that addresses domestic violence ("Rosie Strike Back").

Interiors (no. 175, 1990) begins, "We crawled night and day through the tears and debris." "On the Inside," the opening track, puts forth the idea of both partners struggling to make it through. On another track from *Interiors*, an album that documents the breakup of her marriage to country singer Rodney Crowell, Cash sings, "I don't want to hide my light so your's keeps shining" ("Real Woman"). In "Change Partners," from *The Wheel* (no. 160, 1993), Cash sings, "I crawl through an abyss, I struggle and resist, somehow I break free, someone becomes me." The oppressed female frees herself from the male.

Cash's work reveals an uneasy relationship between God and humanity. She observes people oppressed by God. "This World," from *Interiors*, opens with a nightmare scene of a raging father killing his infant. The song moves on to the importance of the narrator and her husband committing to care for their child whether or not the parents stay together. In the last verse, she sings of a "world . . . spinning out of control" and wondering "who's at the wheel." Comparing God to the abusive father of verse one, she sings of the inhabitants of this world awry "feeling beat up by someone who looks like dad."

The Wheel closes with four liturgical questions that ponder the idea of God as female: "If there's a God on my side (the title of the closing song), why don't she show me her face? . . . could she live in this place? . . . is she inside these walls? . . . could she not hear me call?" Cash continues the idea of God as female, but with a twist, on *10 Song Demo* (1996). In "Western Wall," a story of the protagonist paying a visit to the Wailing Wall or Western Wall in Jerusalem, she ends: "I don't know if God was ever a man but if she was I think I understand why he found a place to break his fall near the western wall." Maybe there was an historical Jesus, the narrator ponders and if so, he was sent down by his mother in heaven rather than his father. Though Cash's God may be female, this deity is no less forgiving than the Old

Testament God of Abraham, Isaac and Jacob. Rather than crawling before a man, with a man, or away from a man, the narrator of "Price of Temptation," the opening track, finds herself crawling before God, a God who happens to have a feminine face. Cash sings, "God says here's a lesson and a kiss, you can walk through fire or *crawl* through this" (emphasis added). God does not give his people much of a choice in Cash's purview. In "If I Were a Man," the narrator sings, "If I were God, I guess I'd know, I guess my friends would tell me so." This suggests that God does not even know who she, he, or it is.

On the title track from *When Fallen Angels Fly* (no. 60, 1994), Patty Loveless offers a tale of redemption. The narrator confesses of looking for love in the wrong places. Thus, she describes herself as a "fallen angel." She asserts that the romantic love she now experiences has placed her on the true path of love. The claim of the narrator is that this experience has given her a revelation. Similar to the theology of songs that describe a non-exclusionary heaven, Loveless's narrator declares "all their sins will be forgiven" when the fallen find true romantic love.

"Somebody Stand by Me," the closing track of Faith Hill's 1998 release, is a plea for help from someone, even someone who may be in the form of the divine. Composed by Sheryl Crow, the track is unlike that of other country artists in that it does not express with surety that there is a divine framework. The narrator "know[s] the sound of nothing and no one and yet everything." She describes herself as "twisted and turned and broken down." In desperation, she makes an appeal to the divine, "if God's here tonight," for rescue from her condition. For Hill, the mention of God is a turnabout from the type of songs included in her repertoire. Unlike Cash or Mattea, her songs primarily deal with romantic love. Knowing this, her record label chose to place the song that names God as the last of the twelve tracks.

At the first Presidential inauguration of William Jefferson Clinton on January 20, 1993, evangelist Billy Graham prayed in clear, meaningful terms to the God of the Bible. He addressed the "Mighty God, the Prince of Peace" and closed his prayer "in the name of the Father and the Son and the Holy Ghost" (Fishwick 221). This suggested more than the idea that the United States was a blessed nation. It also revealed an atmosphere open to offensive terminology in the description of the character of the Biblical religion. At the same time, the 1991 International Social Survey Program study of religion showed a wide embrace of theism in the United States. According to the survey,

78 percent of Americans believe in an afterlife, 86 percent believe in a heaven, 71 percent in a hell and 65 percent pray weekly (Greeley 85). The mid-1990s showed a significant increase in the place of religion in the lyrics of popular music artists. Mariah Carey's "Make It Happen" (no. 5, 1992) used a gospel framework to preach her positive thinking message. Joni Mitchell recorded her paraphrase of the Old Testament story of the plight of Job, "The Sire of Sorrow (Job's Sad Song)" on *Turbulent Indigo* (no. 47, 1994).

The hit single "Shine" (no. 11, 1994) by the group Collective Soul was a harbinger for the group of songs with images of God that would become popular in the mid-1990s. Over a modern rock music arrangement, the narrator sings a prayer. Like the lyrics of the 1950s and 1960s, the prayer is not to God but to "Heaven." The narrator seeks a "sign" or a "word." He wants to know where he will find "love." He wants to learn to "speak" and "share." In the chorus, he beseeches the one who can do these things: "Heaven, let your light shine down."

On several other tracks from Collective Soul's *Hints, Allegations and Things Left Unsaid* (no. 15, 1994), the longplayer that contains "Shine," the spiritual is narrowed to the secular as the narrator views his romantic interest as his overwhelmingly other. In "Heaven's Already Here," the narrator expresses his lack of need for a change in his heart to find "heaven." His love is his heaven, as he muses, "Who's gonna bring me heaven when heaven's already here." He does not need to heed any warnings about how he should act. He has found meaning in romance. In the closing track, "All," the narrator takes on the characteristics of the Godhead. He will "walk on water" for his love. He tells his romantic interest that his "kingdom is all yours to receive."

On the cover of Live's *Throwing Copper* (no. 1, 1994), a weary pastor, the Good Book held tightly to his chest, walks determined toward a cliff while four women (the *Sisters of Mercy* of the title of the painting) surround him. Their activity is ambiguous. One "sister" points toward the cliff encouraging the preacher to walk over the edge into the abyss. Another tries to hold him back. The other two, one with a boombox and the other holding an envelope up to the light (as if looking for money), do not appear to care about his fate. The artwork depicts an ambivalent attitude if not toward the God of the Biblical sacred order, then at least toward the organized church. In "Selling the Drama," the narrator presents his own view of salvation. The Bible teaches that Christ paid the ransom for humanity by his death on the cross. The singer states that Christ gets a "cross" while he gets a "chair," and that he "will sit and earn the ransom from up here." He suggests that the individual has the power to be her or his own savior. He will make his peace with God on his terms and does not need a sacred propitiation for his sins.

The opening track of Jann Arden's *Living Under June* (published 1994, no. 76, 1996) is a confusion of spiritual images that reflects the process of the individual creating her own sacred order from a variety of sources. Some lines of "Could I Be Your Girl" sound as though they pertain to God or Jesus, e.g., "He's bringing sweet salvation" or "He's the universe" or "He's the very breath you feel inside." But in the chorus, the narrator states, "I am Jesus" and follows with the request "could I be your girl." The lyric does not appear to have two narrators. She may be asserting that she is her own Messiah. The narrator identifies herself as a "girl" rather than a "woman" possibly to reflect the way the teachings of the Bible have been used to oppress womankind.

There are images of darkness and sin that reflect the turning away from fellowship with God, though, in this text, God is an actor in this turning away. In the first verse, Arden sings "love is a demon." Often, in popular music lyrics, the term "love" represents God or Jesus. Yet, a demon is a sign of that which is the opposite of God. Not only is the "He" of this song the "breath" of life, but he is the "darkness" that takes away the light. Arden's track is interesting in its amalgam of images of good and evil and reflects the tension between body and soul.

Another track from the same recording, "Looking for It (Finding Heaven)," is more straightforward in its unfolding of the pursuit of meaning and of the sacred. The narrator has "lost her way" but is trying to get back on the path to find both "it" and herself. The second verse opens with a reference to a messiah who may be Jesus: "A savior sent to save the world." In the chorus, the narrator says that she finds "heaven" under the "stars" and with "every breath." "Heaven" represents the sacred order that she wishes to embrace and that will lead her to find meaning, or herself. Again, as in the opening track, the individual is the catalyst for finding her or his own sacred order.

Amy Grant's five-time platinum (5,000,000 units sold) *Heart in Motion* (no. 10, 1991) was controversial in contemporary Christian circles because there were few songs with any direct scriptural reference. According to Grant, it was an album about relationships and was written to communicate to a younger audience. Musically, *Heart in*

Motion is more akin to the uptempo pop of *Unguarded* than *Lead Me On*, its predecessor.

In the evangelical weekly, *Christianity Today*, Grant's attempt to successfully crossover to the mainstream caused her to be the focus of an editorial, "Once in Love with Amy." Ken Sidey's column was sympathetic, but was also couched in concern. Sidey reviews the Christian response to Grant's rise to the top: some Christians refuse to play her music because its "too upbeat" or "too controversial." Basically, and Sidey states this, the whole controversy is over the fact that Grant has "gone secular" (17).

Grant, according to Sidey, was not denying she is attracted to the mainstream. She says, "that's the whole point" and she would "rather do a record chock-full of great songs that make it to hit radio and have one song at the end that says 'Have I earned the right to say something really important to you?'" (17). Grant's statement hints that her base motive is still the same as her colleagues in CCM—that is, to have a ministry to others.

Sidey likens the concern of the Christian world to the worried parent watching the "child leaving home, heading out into the world" (17). Sidey mentioned, further, that Grant was being marketed with different images to Christian and mainstream retailers. Apparently, a photo with a more "demure pose" was used at Christian retailers, while a "slightly more provocative look" was used in mainstream outlets (17). From the provocative graphics of *Unguarded* to the more subdued presentation on *Lead Me On*, Grant, with *Heart in Motion*, became the subject of a schizophrenic image media campaign.

Like Madonna, Grant presents the tension of spirituality and sensuality. The difference is that Grant wrestles with the tension from the opposite direction, adding a human quality, i.e., sexuality, to a spiritual base. The mixture is just as volatile except, in her case, she is handicapped by the CCM audience who expects her to emit almost virginal qualities. She is a successor to the female singer-songwriters of the early 1970s who dealt with more than solely presenting their beliefs in their songs.

"Ask Me" is a sobering song about the sexual abuse of a young girl by her father. Grant paints a scene of a child who repeatedly bathes and "sprays her momma's perfume" to remove the "scent" of her father. Grant asks how such an evil can exist if there is a God: "Ask me if I think there's a God up in the heavens, where did he go in the middle of her shame?" And she adds, "I see no mercy." Significantly, CCM's most prominent messenger begins the song by questioning the existence of God. Unlike "Lead Me On," from the prior album, in which the artist asked why peoples hurt each other, in "Ask Me," the question is more serious. If there is a God, where was he in the midst of the girl's nightmare? Later in the song, she says God, indeed, has been the healer of this victim and that, in itself, is a proof of God's existence, just as she sang in "Lead Me On" that God is the redeemer of the victims of slavery and the holocaust.

In "Ask Me," Grant deals with a problem of an acquaintance. Over the years, Grant has lyrically considered concerns which come from encounters with friends or from letters she receives. On *Straight Ahead* (1984), Grant addresses a song to a friend: "I call you on the phone but you're not at home, where do you go when you're hurting . . . ? Where do you hide your heart?" Similarly, on *Unguarded*, there are two songs in which Grant ministers to specific wounded victims. In "Sharayah," she reminds a "childhood friend" that God is still there: "He loves you . . . He cares for you . . . He wants you to come home." "Find a Way" is a response to "hopelessly sounding letters" she receives "from people whose lives were in shambles." Despite continuing this ministry on *Heart in Motion* in "Ask Me," Grant was still opposed in Christian circles because of the musical path she has followed.

"You're Not Alone," also from *Heart in Motion*, is an upbeat rock tune with a message similar to "Everywhere I Go" and "Never Alone" from her 1980 album of the same name. No matter where one walks, in the church or out, in the realm of grace or that of nature, "you're not alone in this world." Like "Everywhere I Go," "You're Not Alone" does not specifically mention the Deity. And, even more so than in "Everywhere I Go," the lyrics can be interpreted as both romantic love and divine love. In the third verse, the singer addresses the person to whom she is giving this message as "baby." She also describes romantic love as healing: "come on let me hold you close because love can soothe what love has burned." On the other hand, the listener is told, "You're like a fallen soldier, but you just can't lay down and die." Here, the singer invokes the image of the Christian soldier (e.g., "Onward, Christian Soldiers").

Listening to the song on record, lyric sheet in hand, the listener can interpret the song in either way: romantic or divine. In a Toledo, Ohio concert during October, 1991, Grant told the Savage Hall crowd within minutes of singing this song that "her prayer" is that the audience will "know the deep love of Christ." Her message is not vague. She does not say this to placate her "old" audience. The old fans already have a relationship with Jesus. She understands something that masturbatory televangelists have not figured out in speaking to their audiences. She understands Jesus's response to the Pharisees and the teachers of the law when they asked why he rubbed shoulders with the tax collectors and "sinners." Christ responded, "It is not the healthy who need a doctor, but the sick. I have not come to call the righteous; but sinners to repentance." (Luke 5:30–31, NIV) Grant speaks to her new audience and tells them it is okay to experience the sacred. Unlike *Lead Me On* or *Unguarded*, there is no sense of stumbling or being on the wrong track present in the lyrics of the songs on *Heart in Motion*. Grant has found that she can face the day-to-day world with power, wholeness and love.

Amy Grant followed *Heart in Motion* with *House of Love* (no. 13, 1994). Unlike the previous bestseller aimed at contemporary hit radio, the 1994 album was directed at an older demographic segment. It was targeted to the adult contemporary music radio format. Most of the tracks are concerned with romantic relationships, including two tracks directly related to her marriage: "Our Love" and "Oh How the Years Go By." Two tracks emphasize the narrator's relationship with God. "Love Has a Hold on Me" speaks of the security of the believer in God's fold and the responding commitment of the singer to the one who offers her protection. Whether the narrator "run[s]" or "hide[s]," "love" will still surround her. Whether she is told "yes" or "no" by this "love," her "heart will follow." She identifies the love that covers her as one that passes from age to age: "long before my life had come to be." Though she does not explicitly mention God or the Christ, Grant sings that the meaning of her life is to "know the one who made me," her Creator, the God of the Bible, the "light" to which she will return after her sojourn on earth.

In 1998, television viewers listened to Grant's performance of "The Power" (also from *House of Love*) as the underlying music for a commercial for Century 21, the nationwide real estate firm. The vagueness of the term "power" allowed the performance to be adapted to promote the strength available to housing market customers from real estate agents. Viewers were unaware of the identity of the "power" referenced in the lyric. In the chorus, the narrator sings of a power that "touches," "helps," and "holds." The four background vocalists mimic a gospel choir as they repeatedly sing the word "power." Through history and through the agony and ecstasy of life this power remains and is more potent than anything known: "stronger than any bomb any man has ever made." In the booklet accompanying the album, Grant illuminates the identity of this force. In a note above the song's lyric, she writes, "The Power . . . spoke the world into existence . . . raised the Son of God from the dead . . . saves us from ourselves" and she adds a scripture reference from the Book of Acts. She clearly acknowledges the Power she sings about. Without the note, though, the listener may think she is singing about the local electric company.

In many of Sarah McLachlan's lyrics, there is a yearning for truth or meaning beyond the visible and concrete, though she confesses to being "not a particularly religious person" (White 190). Her songs contain a number of images drawn from the Bible. She speaks of a "world as pure as Eden's sixth day" (perhaps, prior to the creation of God's companion, Adam) ("Back Door Man" [1991]). She asserts, "I will walk into the fire until its heat doesn't burn me" on "Into the Fire" (1991), echoing the placement of Daniel and his comrades into the fiery furnace by Nebuchadnezzar (Dan. 3:20–27), as well as her comment that she finds human spirituality to be "very sensual" (Woodworth 1).

McLachlan's narrator wonders if this place called heaven, whatever it is, is worth the striving. She asks "am I in heaven here or am I in hell" ("Hold On" [1993]) and in another track discovers that "heaven is a stranger place than what you've left behind" ("Drawn to the Rhythm" [1991]). She questions the pursuit of a sacred heaven. A heaven on earth that the individual can append to her own sacred order may be sufficient.

Though McLachlan has recorded a cover version of XTC's "Dear God," her narrator is yet unsure of what should center her sacred order. In the same track that she asks whether she is in heaven or hell, she prays for a love who is departing from this earthly plane: "Oh, God, if you're out there, won't you hear me." And, she admits, while offering this petition, she has never bothered to converse with God before. She is not ready to abandon the idea of holding on to an order that gravitates around God.

McLachlan introduces alternative sacred orders in "Building a Mystery" (1997). She describes a religion that made use of the symbol of the cross before Jesus arrived on earth. The main character, who is building this mysterious sacred order, keeps "voodoo dolls" in his residence, a church, and has a "secret god." Unlike the singer-songwriters of the late 1960s and early 1970s who witnessed of their embrace of Eastern faiths, McLachlan describes a different form of personal religion.

In "The Christians and the Pagans" (1996) by Dar Williams, the songwriter sets up a creative tension between opposing sacred orders and discovers that there is a "common ground" between the traditional and the alternative. The tale takes place on Christmas Eve. A young woman named Amber who has been celebrating Solstice calls her "Christ-loving uncle" to secure a place for Jane and her to stay. At the dinner table, entreaties are made to "all their gods and goddesses." Jane tells Amber's young cousin Timmy that Amber is not a Christian and explains "you find magic from your God and we find magic everywhere." By evening's end, the impressionable Timmy asks his father if he may become a pagan. Rarely, in the lyrics of twentieth century popular music, is there a statement that someone is not a Christian. Artists will unfold their beliefs in other faiths, but they do not directly say they do not subscribe to the Biblical sacred order. Though Williams's song reveals there is common ground between the faiths, it also points to the possibility of or opportunity for rejection of one sacred order in favor of another.

Todd Snider's *Step Right Up* (1996) opens with a creed titled "I Believe You." Almost every line starts with the phrase "I believe." In the first verse, he states his belief in "Karma," "Soul," "Heaven," and "Rock and Roll," in that order. His canon covers an expansive territory including "wrestling," "gangster rap" and his "girlfriend." Snider's litany is reminiscent of John Lennon's non-credo in his composition "God." As a matter of fact, Snider also mentions that he believes in the Beatles. Perhaps, not coincidentally, he inserts Lennon's former group right after his conviction, "I believe that Jesus Christ died for all my sins." Unlike Lennon, though, Snider's narrator does not reject any dogma. The juxtaposition of the Hindu Karma and Jesus Christ in the song again suggests that one can choose the tenets one wants from opposing sacred orders. The wide sweep of the narrator's canon suggests that an individual's sacred order can include the secular, e.g., rock and roll and wrestling. Snider's creed parallels the thought of Lippy regarding personal religiosity: "acceptance of specific beliefs coming from a particular religious tradition may be only a part of the religion of the people" (xiii).

In 1996, there were a number of popular recordings that focused on the character of God. Not since the Jesus rock of the late 1960s and early 1970s was the presence of God so audible on the contemporary hit radio format. Dishwalla's "Counting Blue Cars," Jewel's "Who Will Save Your Soul," Dog's Eye View's "Everything Falls Apart," Jars of Clay's "Flood" and Joan Osborne's "One of Us" were all best-sellers in 1996.

In the group Dishwalla's first bestseller "Counting Blue Cars" (no. 15), from *Pet Your Friends* (no. 89, 1996), there is an encounter with someone who seeks the feminine face of God. Repeated several times in the chorus is the request: "Tell me all your thoughts on God 'cause I would really like to meet her." Lead singer J.R. Richards denies he is pressing any feminist agenda with the song. He says the lyric is "about questioning things we're spoon-fed. My main point is that you should think for yourself" (Kelly 39). Though we live in an era when churches wrestle with changing the hymnbook to emphasize the genderless character of God, it is still no small step for a she to be God in the Top 40. Richards's lyrics not only contemplate the character of God but also demonstrate humanity's quest for meaning and the desire to make sense of the world. The narrator asks the person who encounters God to "ask her why we're who we are."

In her breakthrough release *Under the Pink* (no. 12, 1994), Tori Amos puts a different slant on the character of God in a track simply titled "God" (no. 72, 1994). The daughter of a minister, Amos's concern is not with the omnipotence of God, but with the impotence of God. She complains directly to God (who is perceived to be male by the narrator): "God, sometimes you just don't come through." She wonders, "Do you need a woman to look after you?" Though Amos is not presenting the idea of a feminine God, she still breaks new ground with the idea that God needs a female to be God.

God is a commuter on an "uptown train" in the group Dog's Eye View's debut hit single, "Everything Falls Apart" from *Happy Nowhere* (no. 77, 1996). God is depicted as a bureaucrat who creates work for himself. The narrator corners God: "don't you have better things to do?" God responds that he has let the world "go to hell" to give himself "something to do." If God was the God of the Biblical tradition and did his "job," the accuser would have nothing to "complain" about, according to the God-commuter.

The group Jars of Clay presents a more traditional, Biblically-based image of God in their debut hit "Flood" (no. 37, 1996). In a rare crossover, "Flood" broke out of the CCM market to become a hit on mainstream contemporary hit radio stations. Jars of Clay (the name is taken from the Biblical image of believers as vessels of clay holding the treasure of God's word [2 Cor. 4:7] and being molded by God [Rom. 9:21]) are unabashedly Christian and do not hide their faith in the God of the Bible, which is reflected in the song "Flood." Using images of being on the water for 40 days, the narrator makes his appeal to God: "lift me up when I'm falling" and "I need you to hold me." Unlike the songs discussed above, God is not mentioned in "Flood," so there is the chance that a listener not attuned to the Biblical imagery in the lyrics can hear this song as a plea to a romantic interest to save the narrator from loneliness, rather than as a call to God for rescue.

In an article covering the Christian rock market, *Rolling Stone* writer Eric Boehlert speaks of how Silvertone Records, a mainstream label, "discreetly promoted" the song after picking up the rights to the group's album (24). Still in the mid-1990s, songs that affirm a Biblical order present their position with lyrics of civility. The recordings by Dishwalla, Dog's Eye View and Tori Amos, all popular at the same time as the Jars of Clay track, all pointedly use the word "God." These recordings all question the tenets of the Biblical sacred order. The one song that embraces the teachings of the Bible carefully and vaguely unfolds its position. "Flood" can be interpreted either as a praise song to God or as a love song to a significant other. With such a lyric, a record company can promote the song without radio or MTV programmers being aware of or concerned with the spiritual significance of the song.

Jewel's "Who Will Save Your Soul" (no. 11, 1996) suggests that it is upon the individual to redeem her or his self. Frustrated by the lies she sees people absorb from the television set and the paralysis that comes from holding onto the vestiges of a once-meaningful sacred order, she chides listeners to be active in unfolding their own fate. She complains, "There are few leaders who teach us to know our hearts and our spirits without dogmatic, fear-based, or segregated thinking" (Woodworth 219). The perception of God by humanity that Jewel's lyrics address is not unlike the character of the God of Rosanne Cash's "This World," a God who will "beat up" on his people. In Jewel's purview, people are immobilized by fear of a "God [who] will take his toll." Her song is a call for people to take control of themselves and act. Jewel says, "in our hearts and in silence all answers may be accessed" (Woodworth 219). A similar theme is revealed in her poem "You Are Not." She writes, "looking for god in answers you seek through others instead of being the answers" (Kilcher 70).

Jewel suggests there may be more than one path to commune with God. She observes in "Who Will Save Your Soul" that "we pray to as many gods as there are flowers." She expresses her personal faith more clearly in her book of poetry. The book itself is dedicated to "the One in Whom we live and move and have our being" (Kilcher v). In the next-to-last poem in the collection, "God Exists Quietly," she closes, "Prayer is the greatest swiftest ship my heart could sail upon" (Kilcher 135). She has also remarked, "In silence the whispers of God are heard, and the answers to prayers are given" (Woodworth 219). The first single from Jewel's followup album *Spirit* (1998) is a track titled "Hands." The song also focuses on communion with God through prayer. Three times in a row the narrator repeats the line, "I will get down on my knees, and I will pray."

The most popular of the songs of 1996 that focus on the character of God is Joan Osborne's "One of Us" (no. 4) from her major-label debut album *Relish. Billboard* Editor-in-Chief Timothy White writes that *Relish* "manifests an almost mystical grasp of a culture in spiritual disarray" (269). In some respects, the God of "One of Us" is not unlike the disaffected God-commuter of the Dog's Eye View tune. Osborne's God also makes use of public transportation: he is "just a stranger on the bus trying to find his way home." Osborne sings of a lonely God who receives phone calls from no one "'cept for the Pope maybe in Rome." The chorus lines, "Yeah, yeah, God is great, yeah, yeah, God is good" borrow from a children's version of grace before a meal.

Though Osborne is a songwriter, and interested in the things of the spirit, she is not the composer of "One of Us." The song is the creation of Eric Bazilian, a member of the Hooters, the band from Philadelphia that rose to fame in the mid-1980s with "And We Danced," "Where Do the Children Go," and "All You Zombies," a song rife with Old Testament images of "Holy Moses" and Noah.

The main point of "One of Us" is not whether or not God's phone is ringing off the hook with supplications. More importantly, the song asks who God is: man, woman, child? Maybe God is like one of us, or is one of us. The narrator wonders. Maybe God is a "slob" like us. The narrator is not calling God a slob, but is labeling the crown of God's creation as such.

The video that accompanies the song clearly illustrates the lyric. Filmed on the boardwalk at Coney Island in Brooklyn, the focus is on a booth at an arcade. The attraction is a reproduction of the scene of God giving life to Adam as depicted by Michelangelo on the ceiling of the

Sistine Chapel. There is a hole where God's face would be in the painting. Anyone who pays can poke her or his head through the hole and have a photo taken. So, anyone can be God and maybe anyone, or everyone, is God. About the song, Osborne says, "I felt it was asking a question that could be answered any way the listener chose rather than trying to make a particular point. Despite the fact that the song didn't have an agenda, many people thought I was trying to push a secular way of thinking" (Woodworth 184). Those who labeled the song as secular were those who embraced the Biblical tradition. The lyric does not speak of a specifically Christian God. Eric Bazilian's lyrics suggest that God may be an anonymous and amorphous being. "If God had a name, what would it be?" are the opening words of the song. The second verse opens, "If God had a face, what would it look like?"

What these songs of the mid-1990s have in common is their lack of agreement regarding who God is. God may be a woman, or a man, a nameless, faceless being or any one of us. In a democratic theological environment, all have the opportunity to form opinions of who God is. The varied conceptions of God by individuals parallels the development of individual belief systems. Beliefs include the molding of the Godhead in a form that is meaningful to the individual. Do not be tied to the traditions of the past, the singer for Dishwalla seems to suggest in his comments about his group's hit single. He encourages the individual to decide who God is.

The most intriguing lines of Joan Osborne's "One of Us" occur in the second verse. If you had the opportunity to see the face of God, she asks, would you want to "if seeing meant that you would have to believe in things like heaven and in Jesus and the saints." Maybe the populace does not want to know who God is because then it would be responsible for some form of response or commitment. Without an image of God, people do not have to worry about answering to a higher authority. Individuals can create their own moral orders. Indeed, the culture may be in spiritual disarray.

From *Surfacing* (1997), the same album that contains "Building a Mystery," comes Sarah McLachlan's most heartfelt plea to find meaning. The song title "Witness" echoes the idea of congregants attesting to their faith during the testimony time at a worship service. The title of Marvin Gaye's "Can I Get a Witness" finds its basis in the same source. McLachlan's narrator desires to be removed from "darkness" and "doubt." She seeks a transformation from the present life, a change not unlike that which will come when there is a new heaven and a new earth according to Bible teaching. She asks, "Will a change come while we're waiting?" McLachlan does not direct the prayer specifically to the God of the Bible, though she does ask about heaven. In the chorus, she ponders whether heaven will be any different than the hell on earth. She muses about whether people will "burn" in heaven. Robert Detweiler, in his study of the intersection of religion and American fiction, found the narratives "reveal a reluctance of the characters to discard religious belief and practice" (205). McLachlan witnesses to this temperament in her lyrics.

Folksinger Dar Williams creates a fantasy in which the narrator has died and gone to heaven in "Alleluia" (1995). The lyric is one of a number in the mid-1990s that addresses and defines the character of God as one who may have more of the foibles of humanity than that which would be expected of an overwhelmingly other. God, who reminds the narrator of a "guidance counselor," is surprised that the narrator is in heaven. God, who is neither defined as male or female, suggests that a mistake may have been made and offers an excuse: "Silly me . . . I'm only God."

The theme of a romantic interest being the center of an individual's sacred order continues to exist in the 1980s and 1990s. John Hiatt's "Have a Little Faith in Me" from *Bring the Family* (no. 107, 1987) presents a narrator whose qualities parallel that of the Biblical God. His "love" will be a light "when the road gets dark." He will "catch [her] fall." Reflecting the sacredness of the narrator and his words of comfort, the musical arrangement has the backup singers mimic a church choir in the chorus. Hiatt mentions in the liner notes that many couples have told him that the composition was their wedding song. It is interesting that at the time of the sacrament of marriage, most likely held in a place of worship, couples choose to use words that identify a sacred order based on themselves rather than the sacred order that the house of worship represents. Michael W. Smith's "I Will Be Here for You" (no. 27, 1992) shares a similar sentiment about the individual being the meaning in his or her loved one's life. It is worth noting that Smith emerged from the contemporary Christian music scene and this song subverts the teachings of the Bible. Heavy metal band Judas Priest in their comeback *Painkiller* (no. 26, 1990) bend the type of song lyric that can be interpreted as either a love song to a romantic interest or to God to one that applies to a human love or to Satan. In the chorus of "A Touch of Evil," the narrator sings, "I'm still afraid but I feed the flame." He is enticed by a "dark angel of sin" who "prey[s] deep from within."

The inoffensive theological notion of a non-exclusionary heaven is still prevalent in the popular music of the 1990s. "One Sweet Day" (no. 1, 1995) by Mariah Carey and Boyz II Men is a conversation between the narrator and her love, who she "knows" is in "Heaven." She is just as sure that "one sweet day" she will be with him in heaven, too. She is also certain that her departed "Darling" listens when she prays. Tupac "2Pac" Shakur's "I Wonder if Heaven Got a Ghetto" also suggests that the afterlife is in a heaven, or at least a heaven for some. Snoop Dogg is sure that he will meet his friends in the afterlife though he does not identify the location as heaven in his recording "See Ya When I Get There."

In her multi-million selling debut album, *Jagged Little Pill* (no. 1, 1995), Canadian Alanis Morissette aims her diatribes not only at former boyfriends ("Are you thinking of me when you f*** her" from "You Oughta Know"), parents ("I'll live through you, I'll make you what I never was" from "Perfect") and record company moguls ("You took me out to wine dine 69 me but didn't hear a damn word I said" from "Right Through You"), but also at her Roman Catholic religious heritage and the priest in the confessional ("I confessed my darkest deeds to an envious man" from "Forgiven"). The theme of "Forgiven" reflects the need to find meaning in life and, if that meaning is found in an overwhelmingly other, to have the faith to accept the source of the meaning. The song presents an oscillation between belief and doubt.

In her play on the words of an important ritual of the Roman Catholic faith, the sign of the cross, Morissette's narrator expresses her insecurity about her faith. She sings, "In the name of the Father, the Skeptic and the Son," substituting herself for where the Son is named in the sign of the cross and omitting the Holy Spirit altogether. She sees herself as a martyr because of her perception of a double standard regarding gender in the church. Earlier in the same verse she notes that her brothers are not punished for participating in the same activities that she may be punished for.

Morissette underlines her wavering between belief and unbelief in the vocal arrangement of "Forgiven." The recording opens with a quiet electric guitar and percussion accompaniment. The first two lines are sung sotto voce. Then, the hard rock instrumentation kicks in and she shouts and screams the lyrics. Again, in the second verse, the same tension is presented. She makes reference to her experience in the church choir, softly ad libs, "Alleluia, Alleluia, Alleluia," and then turns and attacks the "envious" priest in the confessional. In the first chorus after the break, Morissette sings in a voice that sounds as if it is about to crack and break into tears as she confesses her need for something more. She returns to her hard rock voice as she moves into the second chorus.

There are things she resents about her religious heritage, but Morissette's narrator does not reject the Biblical sacred order. In the middle measures, she remarks that she "rejected" what she was taught, but she "believes"her questioning, her personal "inquisition" of the precepts of the church, will cause her to be punished. She then wonders if she will be "forgiven" (the one time she invokes the title of the song) if she immerses herself in her faith. Alluding to the baptismal font, she sings, "If I jump in this fountain." There can be no forgiveness unless there is someone or something that has the power to absolve. The narrator desires something she can "cling" to. She closes her song by singing, "We had to believe in something so we did." There is a need for meaning in life. Some of that meaning may be found in one's religious heritage.

Rap trio the Fugees scored a big hit with their remake of Roberta Flack's "Killing Me Softly" in 1996. Subsequent to the release of their album *The Score* (1996), each member of the band recorded solo albums. The cycle was completed with *The Miseducation of Lauryn Hill* (1998). Hill's recording, nominated for 10 Grammy Awards in 1999, won five categories including Record of the Year. The God of the Bible is the common thread among the collection's tracks. "To Zion," a love song to the artist's young son, speaks of her choice to keep her child: "I knew his life deserved a chance but everybody told me to be smart. Look at your career they said, 'Lauryn, baby, use your head.' But instead I chose to use my heart." Like the narrator of Madonna's "Papa, Don't Preach," Hill refuses to listen to advice to terminate her pregnancy. She states that a "gift so great" could only be God-given. The child's name "Zion" also refers to the promised land of the scriptures. Accompanied by a gospel choir, she repeats the phrase "the joy of my world is in Zion" referring both to her son and her ultimate destination. At the end of the song, Hill sings of "marching to Zion."

In the opening track "Lost Ones," the narrator proclaims she has found the path to truth: "I was hopeless now I'm on Hope Road." She declares that people need to "get down on [their] knees and repent." Hill uses meaningful language to unfold her faith. She states that God's people will be victorious because "the chain of Satan wasn't made that strong." In the title track, Hill confirms one last time where her hope and meaning in life lie. She sings, "Now I know His strength is within me."

Hill employs Jesus's words of forgiveness in his final hours on the cross (Luke 23:34) for the chorus of "Forgive Them Father." She petitions God to absolve those who attempted to seduce her bodily, monetarily and to "increase" their own well-being. The lyric opens with the words of the Lord's Prayer, "Forgive us our trespasses, as we forgive those who trespass against us." She immediately couples the words of the Christ with a statement that she will forgive the charmers, but she will "never, never trust" them again.

"I Used to Love Him" is a tale of a misdirected romance. It was an affair she "pray[s] the Father will forgive." As the Apostle Peter describes the day the Lord will return (2 Pet. 3:10), Hill's narrator explains that her paramour "stole [her] heart like a thief in the night." Looking back on the pairing she was rescued from, she announces at the end of the final verse, "I took back my soul and totally let my Creator control the life which was His to begin with." Hill warns the listener to be spiritually prepared in "Final Hour." Among the transgressions she observes are the injustices that challenged the "survival" of African-Americans and the seduction by "money" and "power." Her foundation is in the words of the Psalmist: "Whom have I in heaven but thee? and there is none upon earth that I desire beside thee" (Ps. 73:25). Hill underlines her trust as "Final Hour" draws to a close, "I remain calm readin' the 73 Psalm." Like the Psalmist, who also wrote in the same paean to his overwhelmingly other, "I have put my trust in the Lord God, that I may declare all thy works" (Ps. 73:28), Lauryn Hill expounds the place of her faith within the culture of hip hop.

Rita Coolidge, who released her debut album in 1971 and had two Top Ten hits in 1977 ("Higher and Higher" and "We're All Alone"), released a comeback album in 1998. The secular album, *Thinkin' About You*, includes a song based on 1 Corinthians 13, the "love" passage in the New Testament. "Without Love" is a gospel number that reveals Coolidge's influences. According to Clarke, she is the daughter of a Baptist minister and sang in church in her formative years (279). The instrumentation of "Without Love" is electric rhythm and blues and Southern gospel. It is an uptempo guitar-based recording with horn accompaniment.

The song lyrics are primarily derived from the first four verses of the scripture passage. The song's first verse is based on the first verse of the chapter: "If I speak with the tongues of men and of angels, but do not have love, I have become a noisy gong or a clanging cymbal" (2 Cor. 13:1, New American Standard). The second and third verses of the composition are derived from verse two of Paul's letter. In this verse, Paul writes that even if he has the gift of prophecy and the faith to move mountains, he is nothing if he does not have love (1 Cor. 13:2). The composer of "Without Love," Rhonda Gunn, translates the phrase to "ain't no big deal am I." The song varies from the New Testament text in the bridge. The lyrics add a mention and teaching of Jesus. The narrator sings, "Jesus said the world's gonna know you're mine by the love you show to one another." In the many mentions of "Jesus" in 1990s popular music, there are still some included in recordings that accept the Biblical sacred order. With background vocalists sounding as though they are in a church choir, "Without Love" is presented as a straightforward gospel workout.

Joni Mitchell also composed and recorded a song based on 1 Corinthians 13. The song, simply titled "Love," is the closing track on *Wild Things Run Fast* (no. 25, 1982). The musical arrangement, in contrast to Coolidge's recording, is a slow tempo jazz ballad. Lyricwise, the song has parallels to the Coolidge track. Mitchell also draws from the first four verses of Paul's letter in the opening of her song. Her focus, however, is not on the message of Jesus and, like the scripture passage, there is no mention of Jesus in her song. Mitchell's emphasis is more on the final verses of the chapter. She is drawn to the contrast of the child and the adult. The author of the scripture letter speaks of putting away "childish things" and of seeing "dimly" now until the spiritual transformation comes (1 Cor. 13: 11–12). Mitchell views things differently than the Apostle Paul. For her, the child understands the wonder of life. When woman or man matures, what she or he knew as a child has disappeared. She sings, "But when I became a woman, I put away childish things and began to see thru a glass darkly." Mitchell uses the scripture for her foundation but places her message on a secular plane. Tellingly, Mitchell misquotes the scripture reference in her liner notes as "Corinthians II:13."

The liner notes on Rita Coolidge's album reveal the reason she chose to record the song. Like other artists who share their spiritual biography in song, e.g., Noel Paul Stookey and Marvin Gaye, Coolidge's track reflects her faith in the God of the Bible. In her list of thanks in the liner notes, she writes, "The greatest thanks I offer is to God, My Heavenly Father for giving me the precious gift of music and choosing me as the messenger." Akin to Stookey, who suggested that he was a vessel through which "Wedding Song" flowed, Coolidge sees herself as one through whom the music becomes real and flows to the listener.

Jennifer Paige made her debut on the popular music charts in 1998 with the infectious dance pop hit "Crush" from her eponymously-titled debut album. On the second track, "Questions," a track placed where the artist, her management and the record company expect the song to be noticed by the listener, Paige uses the name "God" in the first line of the first verse. "Questions" makes a case for the recording artist as more than solely a dance pop "chick singer" (a reference Paige makes to herself in "Questions"). Unlike "Crush," which opens with a strong bass line settling into a dance groove, "Questions" opens quite differently with strumming acoustic guitars prominent in the mix.

As with many of the songs that deal with God or religion since the 1960s, Paige's midtempo ballad (she is a co-writer) is about searching for meaning in one's life. The performance opens with the narrator looking to God for answers. Paige starts the song with the words, "Stare into God's face trying to find my place." The chorus ends with the lines, "Who, what, where and why, questions of my life." The two chorus lines are the dominant motif in the song and are repeated a number of times before the song draws to a close. Though not a dance track of the "Crush" ilk, Paige's lyrical concerns in "Questions" are rare for an artist whose music is aimed at dancing feet. As she opened the song with an acknowledgment of an overwhelmingly other, in the last line of the last verse, Paige repeats this idea, noting, "I know there's something more." Though Paige does not define who God is, leaving open the question of whether or not she is singing of the God of the Biblical sacred order, there is the idea that she is not picking and choosing precepts from a number of alternative religious orders. She looks to God and has an "Angel on [her] shoulder." Though the mention of "God" is not rare in the late 1990s, it is rare in a song that appears to accept the Biblical sacred order.

A former dance pop singer, whose longevity in the recording industry has surpassed by far the expectations of any artist in the genre, continued to merge spiritual images with her dance grooves into the late 1990s. In *Bedtime Stories* (no. 3, 1994) Madonna opens the track "Sanctuary" with words spoken in a quiet whisper as though she is kneeling in a confessional booth. Her words are an offering. She says, "Surely whoever speaks to me in the right voice him or her I shall follow." The opening word "surely" matches the sentence structure of Christ's words in the Gospels. The narrator is seeking the right voice, perhaps one that can provide meaning or transcendence. After her opening proposition, she sings to the one who makes her forget that anything else matters. If it is a lover, he or she is the narrator's overwhelmingly other. She asks, "Who needs the sun?" or the "sky" or a "smile" or a "home," when she is in the "arms" or "heart" or "soul" of her sanctuary. In the midst of the song, Madonna speaks again, voicing her translation of the second verse of the Bible, Genesis 1:2. She draws forth the image of an "empty" and "dark" planet. And, again, she repeats her opening offering, except this time in a more assured voice and enhanced with reverb. She has found her sanctuary. The word sanctuary invokes a strong religious image, but there is no surety that her sanctuary is divine.

A number of lyrics incorporate the word "love" to connote the name of God in the 1980s and 1990s, including Amy Grant's "Love Has a Hold on Me" and U2's "When Love Comes to Town." Madonna's "Love Tried to Welcome Me" (from *Bedtime Stories*) employs a similar use of the word. The singer admits she is too deep in the darkness to allow herself to accept saving grace. In the chorus she confesses she was "guilty of lust and sin" and therefore can not accept a freely-offered agape love. Reflecting the Biblical image of sackcloth and ashes, she says she was "covered with dust and sin." The narrator is not willing to come to love unless it is on her own terms. Though the love offered is unconditional, she still believes she is not worthy. She is a member of the cult of personal religiosity and will be guided by her own theology and her own precepts.

Ray of Light (1998) opens with "Drowned World/Substitute for Love," a track that may be a slice of Madonna's autobiography. In a voice filled with resignation and regret, she discovers the emptiness of accomplishing all her goals. The narrator sings of loneliness and of "lovers who settled for the thrill of basking in [her] spotlight." At the end, after listing her achievements and her sorrows, she distills her life experience to one phrase. Half-singing, half-speaking, she states matter of factly, "this is my religion." Her career has become her surrogate for love, agape or erotic. Again, the individual molds the canon of the sacred order she or he will follow.

Madonna's spiritual exploration on *Ray of Light* ranges beyond the Catholicism of *Like A Prayer*. "Shanti/Ashtangi" is an Eastern prayer of worship. According to the liner notes, it is "adopted from text by Shankra Charyo taken from the Yoga Taravali." In another spiritual direction, Madonna reportedly attends the Kabbalah Learning Center in Beverly Hills. The center's teaching is founded in the cabala, a philosophy developed by Medieval rabbis from a mystical reading of the Scriptures. Cabala or Kabbalah teaches that "nothing in life happens by accident" (Yount).

"Sky Fits Heaven," which segues directly into the Eastern worship prayer, continues the theme of the individual constructing a personal sacred order. Madonna observes that this individual spiritual dynamic is de rigueur. She asks, "Isn't everyone just traveling down their own road?" So, as for her, she will "follow [her] heart," and, perhaps, create Madonnaism.

In the 1990s, the vagueness of spiritual images in popular music has come full circle. Artists (e.g., Michael W. Smith) who established their careers in the CCM industry, an outlet for meaningful, offensive references to the things of the spirit, retreat to vague, contentless phrases to develop their market potential with the mainstream audience. Mainstream releases that embrace the Biblical sacred order veil their messages to obtain airplay, while songs that deny the Biblical sacred order or employ strands of the order in the creation of personal sacred orders can refer to "God" and "Jesus" and employ other meaningful terminology.

The analysis of popular music contributes to an understanding of how secular constructions of religion are developed. Since these constructions pervade subcultures of a society, it can also be established that secular constructions have a role in the development of the religious subculture's construction of itself. Communication between the subculture and the society as a whole is hindered when the artist speaks in a way that does not fit comfortably with the myth or construction. Ivan Neville, part of the second generation of the famous New Orleans music family, told White, "It pisses me off sometimes that there's prejudice and typecasting, even among black people, about the kind of music we're supposed to be playing and who we're supposed to do it with" (237). Neville, a self-identified "black man who's into rock'n'roll," plays music that the mainstream can not identify with African-American musicians.

Along the same lines, Dionne Farris, who began her recording career with the rap group Arrested Development and then went solo and produced the modern rock hit "I Know" (no. 4, 1995), complains, "When black artists want to try something very different or just be ourselves, genuine and real, apart from a preconceived image of who we are, people look at us in disbelief because they can't place us" (Woodworth 261). Similarly, when artists who are not expected to sing gospel do so, it is difficult for the audience to hurdle the bar of acceptance. The mainstream audience can not "place" a rock song that praises Jesus.

The emergence of lyrics of civility is related to the dichotomy between the sacred and the secular in mainstream American culture. The mainstream market compartmentalizes faith. It is not part of everyday life. Therefore, lyrics that embrace the Biblical tradition require inoffensive terminology to prevent them from breaching day-to-day life, since faith is not integrated with daily activities. The integration of faith with the daily earthly walk is central to African-American culture and the corresponding music tradition. In recorded music history, this integration is found back to the rural blues of the early decades of the twentieth century. The seamless integration of the sacred and the profane, Sunday morning and Saturday night, is uncovered in the artistry of Marvin Gaye and Al Green. Stevie Wonder was most successful in establishing the possibilities of the merger of faith with earthly reality in his four albums that culminated with *Songs in the Key of Life* (1976). The controversy that found Bob Dylan after his conversion to Christianity was not present in the reaction to the bestselling work of Stevie Wonder because the mainstream read Wonder's artistry through a filter of civility due to his African-American heritage.

In the mainstream market, the late 1960s and early 1970s presented the integration of nature and grace in the songs of the revival rock era. Spirituality was married to life concerns. The lyrics presented the view that a theistic focus could be part and parcel of life experiences and the words used were not civil or connotation words. The segregation of nature and grace reappeared in the mid-1970s in the contemporary Christian music genre. CCM artists only sang about the deity. There was no sense (in the early years of CCM) that anything else in life mattered but one's relationship with Jesus Christ.

The substitution of a romantic love for a deity is an offshoot from the segregation of nature and grace. Rather than a romantic or sexual relationship being under the cover of a deity, the deity is replaced and transcendence is found alone in the earthly relationship. There is a dynamic of either/or. The longing for a transcendent romance is a result of a worldview that does not allow for spiritual activity within the natural.

In the late 1970s and early 1980s, Donna Summer and Teena Marie echoed earlier artists who combined not only the spiritual and the secular, but the spiritual and the sensual, too. In the liner notes of Summer and Marie, and the lyrics of Marie, this commingling is present. Madonna follows along these lines, though her employment of the spiritual and the sensual is not as much an integration of the two, but the placement of the two in close proximity. One or the other, particularly the spiritual, may be removed and the other is not affected. There is not the synergy uncovered in Al Green or Teena Marie. Tori Amos and Sarah McLachlan, who has commented that she finds the exploration of the mix of the spiritual and the sensual intriguing, continue to develop the integration of the sacred and the profane, particularly the sensual, in their work.

Beginning with *Slow Train Coming* (1979), Bob Dylan re-introduced the sacred to the mainstream. Though this first Christian album of his and its followup *Saved* focus more heavily on the spiritual, the two collections provided a groundwork for his later work that integrated the sacred with the garden. Dylan did not focus on the mix of the sensual with the spiritual, but the presence of the deity within the fabric of ordinary life. Contemporaries of Dylan, such as Arlo Guthrie, Van Morrison and Bruce Cockburn, continued in the same vein. In the 1980s and 1990s, Amy Grant, Lauryn Hill and U2 explore the marriage of worldly existence with the heavenly in their music.

The present study is a way of understanding how a subculture loses its uniqueness and attractiveness through the dilution of the meaning of its elemental thought. Displaced adherents are drawn to alternative cultures or orders that offer meaning to fill a void in the individual. In Stephen L. Carter's observation of Christianity in the United States, he writes:

> It is both tragic and paradoxical that now, just as the nation is beginning to invite people into the public square for the different points of view that they have to offer, people whose contribution to the nation's diversity comes from their religious traditions are not valued unless their voices are somehow esoteric. (57)

Individuals perceive the esoterica of alternative orders as attractive because of the promise of meaningful content, i.e., the language of the order has not been diluted. Content and meaning stand in opposition to the worn-out cliches that have resulted from the translation of meaningful precepts of the Biblical tradition to vague terminology. Carter cites a case in a Colorado school district where the Bible and other Christian books had to be removed from schools, whereas books on native American religions and the occult stayed on the shelves.

Silk points out a *Time* magazine article from the late 1980s that suggested the decline in membership in mainline Protestant denominations in the prior twenty years was due to "spiritual fecklessness" (134). *Time* religion writer Richard Ostling pinpointed "lo-cal theology" as one of the reasons for the movement from established churches (Silk 134). Similarly, lyrics without meaning will turn adherents away from traditional orders to alternative orders that fill the void of meaning in the individual. On the other side of the coin, Silk quotes from a *Life* article on rapidly growing churches. The reason for their growth, according to Henry P. Van Dusen, is that they "preach a direct biblical message readily understood" (Silk 135). The content provides meaning that attracts the disenfranchised mainline adherent.

By identifying how the dynamic of civility works, we can know better the time to sound an alarm when the language of a subculture is watered down in the interest of negotiation. There are times when negotiation is not in the best interest of a subculture, or even in the interests (though it may not be realized by the majority) of the larger, encompassing culture. The continued study of the intersection of religion and popular culture will provide fruitful conclusions about how religion works in American society.

Bibliography

BOOKS AND ARTICLES

Andersen, Christopher. *Madonna Unauthorized*. New York: Simon & Schuster, 1991.

Barnes, Ken. *The Beach Boys: A Biography in Words and Pictures*. New York: Sire-Chappell Music, 1976.

Bauder, David. "Patti LaBelle Versus Other Singers—Just No Contest." *Sentinel-Tribune* [Bowling Green, OH] 6 Sep. 1994: 10.

Berry, Venise. "Redeeming the Rap Music Experience." Epstein 165–187.

Berger, Peter L. *The Heretical Imperative: Contemporary Possibilities of Religious Affirmation*. Garden City: Anchor-Doubleday, 1980.

Boehlert, Eric. "Holy Rock and Rollers." *Rolling Stone* 3 Oct. 1996: 23–24.

Bolettieri, Stephen. "Donna Summer: Prodigal Daughter." *Contemporary Christian Magazine* July, 1983: 34.

Bronson, Fred. *The Billboard Book of Number One Hits*. New York: Billboard, 1985.

Bruce, Steve. *Religion in Modern Britain*. New York: Oxford UP, 1995.

Carter, Paul A. *Another Part of the Fifties*. New York: Columbia UP, 1983.

Carter, Stephen L. *The Culture of Unbelief: How American Law and Politics Trivialize Religious Devotion*. New York: Basic, 1993.

Cash, Rosanne. "Part Girl." *Bodies of Water*. New York: Hyperion, 1996.

Christgau, Robert. *Rock Albums of the '70s: A Critical Guide*. New York: Da Capo, 1990.

Clarke, Donald, ed. *The Penguin Encyclopedia of Popular Music*. New York: Viking Penguin, 1989.

Coleman, Mark. "XTC." *The Rolling Stone Album Guide: Completely New Reviews: Every Essential Album, Every Essential Artist*. Ed. Anthony

DeCurtis and James Henke with Holly George-Warren. New York: Random, 1992.

Coleman, Ray. *Lennon*. New York: McGraw-Hill, 1985.

Curtis, Jim. *Rock Eras: Interpretations of Music and Society, 1954-1984*. Bowling Green: Popular, 1987.

Cusic, Don. "Moving Music Through a Double Pipeline." *Billboard* 27 September 1980: G-16.

Denisoff, R. Serge and William D. Romanowski. *Risky Business: Rock in Film*. New Brunswick: Transaction, 1991.

DeSantis, Carla. "Performance: Manson/Hole, KeyArena, Seattle, March 3, 1999." *Rolling Stone* 15 April 1999: 46.

Detweiler, Robert. *Uncivil Rites: American Fiction, Religion, and the Public Sphere*. Urbana: U of Illinois P, 1996.

Dunphy, Eamon. *Unforgettable Fire: The Definitive Biography of U2*. New York: Warner, 1987.

Edgar, William. *Taking Note of Music*. London: SPCK-Third Way, 1986.

Epstein, Jonathon S. *Adolescents and Their Music: If Its Too Loud, You're Too Old*. New York: Garland, 1994.

Evans, Paul. "Santana." *The Rolling Stone Album Guide: Completely New Reviews: Every Essential Album, Every Essential Artist*.

Fishwick, Marshall W. *Great Awakenings: Popular Religion and Popular Culture*. Binghamton, NY: Haworth, 1995.

Frith, Simon. *Music for Pleasure: Essays in the Sociology of Pop*. New York: Routledge, 1988.

Gaines, Steven. *Heroes and Villains: The True Story of the Beach Boys*. New York: NAL, 1986.

Greeley, Andrew M. *Religion as Poetry*. New Brunswick: Transaction, 1995.

Gillett, Charlie. *The Sound of the City: The Rise of Rock and Roll*. New York: Outerbridge and Dientsfrey, 1970.

Gilmore, Mikal. *Night Beat: A Shadow History of Rock and Roll*. New York: Doubleday, 1998.

Goldberg, Michael. "Amy Grant Wants to Put God on the Charts." *Rolling Stone* 6 June 1985: 9-10.

Hansen, Barry. "Rhythm and Gospel." Miller 15-18.

Kelly, Christina. "Singles File: Dishwalla and Styx Fuse Their Illusions." *Rolling Stone* 22 Aug. 1996: 39.

Kilcher, Jewel. *A Night Without Armor: Poems*. New York: HarperCollins, 1998.

Lippy, Charles H. *Modern American Popular Religion: A Critical Assessment and Annotated Bibliography*. Westport, CT: Greenwood, 1996.

Marcus, Greil. *Mystery Train: Images of America in Rock 'n' Roll Music.* New York: Dutton, 1976.

Marsh, Dave. "Bob Dylan." *The New Rolling Stone Record Guide.* Ed. Dave Marsh and John Swenson. New York: Random House/Rolling Stone, 1983.

———. *The Heart of Rock and Soul: The 1,001 Greatest Singles Ever Made.* New York: NAL, 1989.

McCourt, Frank. "When You Think of God, What Do You See?" *Life* December 1998: 63–64.

McGee, David. "Elvis Presley." *The Rolling Stone Album Guide: Completely New Reviews: Every Essential Album, Every Essential Artist.*

Middleton, Richard. *Studying Popular Music.* Buckingham, Eng.: Open UP, 1990.

Miles, Barry, comp. *Beatles in Their Own Words.* New York: Delilah-Putnam, 1978.

Miller, Jim, ed. *The Rolling Stone Illustrated History of Rock and Roll, 1950–1980.* New York: Random-Rolling Stone, 1980.

Mohan, Amy B. and Jean Malone. "Popular Music as a 'Social Cement': A Content Analysis of Social Criticism and Alienation in Alternative-Music Song Titles." Epstein 283–300.

Motley, Isolde. Editor's Note. *Life* December 1998: 14.

Nathanson, Paul. *Over the Rainbow: 'The Wizard of Oz' As a Secular Myth of America.* Albany: State U of New York P, 1991.

Negus, Keith. *Popular Music in Theory: An Introduction.* Hanover, NH: Wesleyan UP, 1997.

Phy, Allene Stuart, ed. *The Bible and Popular Culture in America.* Philadelphia: Fortress, 1985.

Popovich, Ljubica D. "Popular American Biblical Imagery: Sources and Manifestations." Phy 193–233.

Reagon, Bernice Johnson. "When Trouble Comes: Some Songs Stay with You All Your Life." *Highlights for Children* Jan. 1993: 1.

Schaeffer, Francis A. *The God Who is There. A Christian View of Philosophy and Culture.* Vol. 1 of *The Complete Works of Francis A. Schaeffer: A Christian Worldview.* Westchester, IL: Crossway, 1982. 5 vols.

Schubert, Frank D. *A Sociological Study of Secularization Trends in the American Catholic University: Decatholicizing the Catholic Religious Curriculum.* Lewiston, NY: Mellen, 1990.

Schumacher, Michael. *Crossroads: The Life and Music of Eric Clapton.* New York: Hyperion, 1995.

Schwichtenberg, Cathy, ed. *The Madonna Connection: Representational Politics, Subcultural Identities, and Cultural Theory.* Boulder: Westview, 1993.

Scoppa, Bud. *The Byrds.* Scholastic, 1971.

Shaw, Greg. "The Teen Idols." Miller 96–100.

Sidey, Ken. "Once in Love with Amy." Editorial. *Christianity Today* 7 Oct. 1991: 17.

Silk, Mark. *Unsecular Media: Making News of Religion in America.* Urbana and Chicago: U of Illinois P, 1995.

Spencer, Jon Michael. *Blues and Evil.* Knoxville: U of Tennessee P, 1993.

Stambler, Irwin. *Encyclopedia of Pop, Rock and Soul.* New York: St. Martin's, 1977.

Tipton, Steven M. *Getting Saved From the Sixties: Moral Meaning in Conversion and Cultural Change.* Berkeley: U of California P, 1982.

Wenner, Jann. *Lennon Remembers: The Rolling Stone Interviews.* San Francisco: Straight Arrow, 1971.

Wenner, Jann S. "Bob Dylan and Our Times: The Slow Train Is Coming." *Rolling Stone* 20 Sept. 1979: 94–95.

Whitburn, Joel. *Joel Whitburn's Pop Memories, 1890–1954: The History of Popular Music.* Menomonee Falls, WI: Record Research, 1986.

———. *Joel Whitburn's Top Pop Albums, 1955–1996.* Menomonee Falls, WI: Record Research, 1996.

———. *Joel Whitburn's Top Pop Singles, 1955–1996.* Menomonee Falls, WI: Record Research, 1997.

White, Timothy. *Music to My Ears: The Billboard Essays: Profiles of Popular Music in the '90s.* New York: Henry Holt, 1996.

Williams, Paul. *The Map, Rediscovering Rock and Roll (A Journey).* South Bend, IN: and books, 1988.

Wilson, Brian with Todd Gold. *Wouldn't It Be Nice: My Own Story.* New York: HarperCollins, 1991.

Wilson, John F. *Public Religion in American Culture.* Philadelphia: Temple UP, 1979.

Woodard, Josef. "The Pop Wizardry of Sam Phillips." *Rolling Stone* 17 Oct. 1991: 24.

Woodworth, Marc, ed. *Solo: Women Singer-Songwriters in Their Own Words.* Photography by Emma Dodge Hanson. New York: Delta, 1998.

Yount, David. "Religion with a Price Tag on It." *Sentinel-Tribune* [Bowling Green, OH] 7 Feb. 1999: 7.

RECORDINGS AND SHEET MUSIC

AC/DC. "Hell Ain't a Bad Place to Be." *Let There Be Rock.* Atco 36–142, 1977.

———. "Hell's Bells." *Back in Black.* Atlantic 16018, 1980.

———. "Highway to Hell." *Highway to Hell.* Atlantic 19244, 1979.

Ames Brothers. "Stars Are the Windows of Heaven." Rec. 1950. *Sentimental Me: A Collection of Sentimental Songs.* Coral CRL-56024, n.d.

Amos, Tori. "God." *Under the Pink.* Atlantic 82567, 1994.

Annette. "O Dio Mio." Buena Vista F-354, 1960.

Arden, Jann. "Could I Be Your Girl." *Living Under June.* A&M 31454–0336–2, 1993.

———. "Looking for It (Finding Heaven)."

Arden, Toni. "Padre." Decca 30628, 1958.

Armstrong, Louis and His Orchestra. "Lawd, You Made the Night Too Long." Rec. 11 Mar. 1932. Columbia G-30416, n.d.

Arrested Development. "Tennessee." *3 Years, 5 Months & 2 Days in the Life of . . .* Chrysalis 21929, 1992.

Arrington, Steve. "Dancin' in the Key of Life." *Dancin' in the Key of Life.* Atlantic 81245-1, 1985.

———. "Feel So Real."

Arrington, Steve's Hall of Fame. Liner Notes. *Positive Power.* Atlantic 80127-1, 1984.

Baez, Joan. "The Dangling Conversation." *Joan.* Vanguard VSD-79240, 1967.

Baker, LaVern. "Saved." Atlantic 2099, 1961.

Beach Boys. "All This Is That." *Carl and the Passions-So Tough.* Brother/Warner Bros. 2MS- 2083, 1972.

———. "Anna Lee, The Healer." *Friends.* Capitol ST-2895, 1968.

———. "God Only Knows." *Pet Sounds.* Rec. 9 Mar.-11 Apr. 1966. Capitol CDP-7-48421-2, 1990.

———. "He Came Down." *Carl and the Passions-So Tough.*

———. "In My Room." Capitol 5069, 1963.

———. "TM Song." *15 Big Ones.* Brother/Warner Bros. MS-2251, 1976.

———. "Transcendental Meditation." *Friends.*

———. "Winds of Change." *M.I.U. Album.* Brother/Warner Bros. MSK-2268, 1978.

Beatles. "Ballad of John and Yoko." Apple 2531, 1969.

———. "Eleanor Rigby." Capitol 5715, 1966.

———. "Girl." *Rubber Soul.* Capitol SW-2442, 1965.

————. "Sexy Sadie." *The Beatles [White Album]*. Apple/Capitol CDP-7–46443-2, 1968.

————. "Tomorrow Never Knows." *Revolver*. Capitol CDP-7–46441-2, 1966.

————. "Within You Without You." *Sgt. Pepper's Lonely Hearts Club Band*. Capitol SMAS-2653, 1967.

Berlin, Irving. "God Bless America." New York: Irving Berlin, 1939.

Berry, Chuck. "Promised Land." Chess 1916, 1965.

Black Sabbath. "After Forever." *Master of Reality*. Warner Bros. B-2562, 1971.

————. "Black Sabbath." *Black Sabbath*. Warner Bros. 1871, 1970.

————. "Lord of This World." *Master of Reality*.

————. "N.I.B." *Black Sabbath*.

————. "Who Are You." *Sabbath Bloody Sabbath*. Warner Bros. B-2695, 1973.

Blind Faith. "Presence of the Lord." *Blind Faith*. RSO 1–3016, 1969.

Blood, Sweat and Tears. "And When I Die." Columbia 45008, 1969.

Boone, Debby. "You Light Up My Life." Warner Bros. 8455, 1977.

Boone, Pat. "There's a Gold Mine in the Sky." Dot 15602, 1957.

————. "A Wonderful Time Up There." Dot 15690, 1958.

Boulanger, Georges and Jimmy Kennedy. "My Prayer." New York: Skidmore Music, 1939.

Bowie, David. "Modern Love." *Let's Dance*. EMI America SO-17093, 1983.

Bread. "Everything I Own." Elektra 45765, 1972.

Brooks, Donnie. "Mission Bell." Era 3018, 1960.

Browns. "The Three Bells." RCA Victor 7555, 1959.

Burdon, Eric and the Animals. "Sky Pilot (Part One)." MGM 13939, 1968.

Burnette, Dorsey. "(There Was A) Tall Oak Tree." Era 3012, 1960.

Byrds. "Glory Glory Hallelujah." *Byrdmaniax*. Columbia 30640, 1971.

————. "Jesus Is Just Alright." *Ballad of Easy Rider*. Columbia 9942, 1970.

Carey, Mariah. "Make It Happen." *VH1 Divas Live*. Epic EK-69600, 1998.

Carey, Mariah and Boyz II Men. "One Sweet Day." Columbia 44–78075, 1995.

Carpenters. "I Won't Last a Day Without You." A&M 1521, 1974.

Caruso, Enrico and Marcel Journet. "The Crucifix." *The Complete Caruso, Vol. 9, 1911–1912*. RCA Red Seal ARM-1357, 1980.

Cash, Rosanne. "Change Partners." *The Wheel*. Columbia CK-5279, 1993.

————. "I Don't Have to Crawl." *King's Record Shop*. Columbia CK-40777, 1987.

————. "If I Were a Man." *10 Song Demo*. Capitol CDP-7243–8–32390, 1996.

————. "If There's a God on My Side." *The Wheel*.

————. "On the Inside." *Interiors*. Columbia CK-46079, 1990.

————. "Price of Temptation." *10 Song Demo*.

——. "Real Woman." *Interiors.*

——. "Rosie Strike Back." *King's Record Shop.*

——. "This World." *Interiors.*

——. "Western Wall." *10 Song Demo.*

Channels. "Altar of Love." *Alter (sic) of Hits.* XXXCH-1001, 1969?

Chantels. "Every Night (I Pray)." End 1015, 1958.

——. "Maybe." End 1005, 1958.

Charles, Ray. "Hallelujah I Love Her So." *A 25th Anniversary Salute to Ray Charles—His All- Time Greatest Performances.* ABC-Paramount ABCH-731, 1973.

——. "Hit the Road, Jack." ABC-Paramount 10244, 1961.

——. "The Night Time Is the Right Time." *A 25th Anniversary Salute to Ray Charles—His All- Time Greatest Performances.*

——. "What'd I Say." Atlantic 2031, 1959.

Christie, Lou. "Lightnin' Strikes." MGM 13412, 1966.

Cockburn, Bruce. "All the Diamonds in the World." *Salt, Sun and Time.* True North, 1974.

——. "Arrows of Light." *Joy Will Find a Way.* True North, 1975.

——. "Broken Wheel." *Inner City Front.* Columbia, 1981.

——. "Cry of a Tiny Babe." *Nothing But a Burning Light.* Columbia, 1991.

——. "Dweller by a Dark Stream." *Mummy Dust.* True North, 1981.

——. "He Came from the Mountain." *Sunwheel Dance.* Columbia, 1972.

——. "Justice." *Inner City Front.*

——. "A Life Story." *Joy Will Find a Way.*

——. "Lord of the Starfields." *In the Falling Dark.* True North, 9463, 1977.

——. "Man of a Thousand Faces." *Bruce Cockburn.* True North, 1970.

——. "Shipwrecked at the Stable Door." *Big Circumstance.* Columbia, 1989.

——. "Thoughts on a Rainy Afternoon." *Bruce Cockburn.*

——. "Up on a Hillside." *Sunwheel Dance.*

Cohen, Leonard. "Suzanne." *The Songs of Leonard Cohen.* Columbia CS-9533, 1968.

Cohn, Marc. "Walking in Memphis." *Marc Cohn.* Atlantic 7–82178–2, 1991.

Cole, Nat "King." "Faith Can Move Mountains." *Nat "King" Cole's 8 Top Pops.* Capitol H- 9110, 1952.

——. "My One Sin (In Life)." Capitol 3136, 1955.

Collective Soul. "All." *Hints, Allegations and Things Left Unsaid.* Atlantic 82596–2, 1993.

——. "Heaven's Already Here."

——. "Shine."

Collins, Judy. "Suzanne." *In My Life.* Elektra EKS-74027, 1966.

Coltrane, Chi. "Go Like Elijah." *Chi Coltrane*. Columbia KC-31275, 1972.

———. "Hallelujah." *Let It Ride*. Columbia KC-32463, 1973.

———. "Let It Ride."

———. "Thunder and Lightning." *Chi Coltrane*.

———. "The Tree."

———. "Turn Me Around."

Como, Perry. "Ave Maria." Rec. 1949. *I Believe*. RCA Victor LPM-1172, n.d.

———. "The Lord's Prayer."

———. "Somebody Up There Likes Me." RCA Victor 47-6590, 1956.

Cooke, Sam. "A Change Is Gonna Come." RCA Victor 8486, 1964.

Coolidge, Rita. "Without Love." *Thinkin' About You*. Innerworks FOF-2100-2, 1998.

Coolio. "Gangsta's Paradise." *Gangsta's Paradise*. Tommy Boy 1141, 1995.

Cornell, Don. "The Bible Tells Me So." Coral 61467, 1955.

Crests. "The Angels Listened In." Coed 515, 1959.

Crew-Cuts. "Angels in the Sky." Mercury 70741, 1955.

Crosby, Bing. "Just a Prayer Away." Rec. 1945. *Way Back Home*. Decca DL-5310, 1951.

Crouch, Andrae and the Disciples. "Jesus Is the Answer." *Live at Carnegie Hall*. Light LS-5602, 1973.

Cymbal, Johnny. "Teenage Heaven." Kapp 6853, 1963.

Dana, Vic. "Little Altar Boy." Dolton 48, 1961.

Dee, Tommy with Carol Kay and the Teen-Aires. "Three Stars." Crest 1057, 1959.

Del Riego, Teresa. "Thank God for a Garden." New York: Chappell, 1915.

DeShannon, Jackie. "What the World Needs Now Is Love." Imperial 66110, 1965.

Diamonds. "The Church Bells May Ring." Mercury 70835, 1956.

Dinning, Mark. "Teen Angel." MGM 12845, 1960.

Dishwalla. "Counting Blue Cars." *Pet Your Friends*. A&M 31454-0319-2, 1995.

Divas. "Testimony." *VH1 Divas Live*. Epic EK-69600, 1998.

Dixie Cups. "Chapel of Love." Red Bird 001, 1964.

Dog's Eye View. "Everything Falls Apart." *Happy Nowhere*. Columbia CK-66882, 1995.

Donovan. "Wear Your Love Like Heaven." *A Gift from a Flower to a Garden*. Epic B2N-171, 1967.

Doors. "The Soft Parade." *The Soft Parade*. Elektra 75005, 1969.

———. "When the Music's Over." *Strange Days*. Elektra 74014, 1967.

Drifters. "Vaya con Dios." Atlantic 2216, 1964.

Dylan, Bob. "Are You Ready." *Saved.* Columbia FC-36553, 1980.

———. "Covenant Woman."

———. "Death Is Not the End." *Down in the Groove.* Columbia 40957, 1988.

———. "Do Right to Me Baby." *Slow Train Coming.* Columbia FC-36120, 1979.

———. "Every Grain of Sand." *Shot of Love.* Columbia TC-37496, 1981.

———. "Father of Night." *New Morning.* Columbia KC-30290, 1970.

———. "God Knows." *Under the Red Sky.* Columbia 46794, 1990.

———. "Gonna Change My Way of Thinking." *Slow Train Coming.*

———. "Gospel Plow." *Bob Dylan.* Columbia CL-1779, 1962.

———. "Gotta Serve Somebody." *Slow Train Coming.*

———. *Highway 61 Revisited.* Columbia JC-9189, 1965.

———. "Idiot Wind." *Blood on the Tracks.* Columbia PC-33235, 1975.

———. "In the Garden." *Saved.*

———. "Joey." *Desire.* Columbia JC-33893, 1975.

———. "Leopard-Skin Pill-Box Hat." *Blonde on Blonde.* Columbia C2S-841, 1966.

———. "Man of Peace." *Infidels.* Columbia 38819, 1983.

———. "Masters of War." *The Freewheelin' Bob Dylan.* Columbia CK-8786, 1963.

———. "New Pony." *Street-Legal.* Columbia JC-35453, 1978.

———. "No Time to Think."

———. "Oh, Sister." *Desire.*

———. "Precious Angel." *Slow Train Coming.*

———. "Pressing On." *Saved.*

———. "Property of Jesus." *Shot of Love.*

———. "Saved." *Saved.*

———. "Saving Grace."

———. "Senor." *Street-Legal.*

———. "Shelter from the Storm." *Blood on the Tracks.*

———. "Solid Rock." *Saved.*

———. "Slow Train." *Slow Train Coming.*

———. "Standing in the Doorway." *Time Out of Mind.* Columbia, 1997.

———. "Til I Fell in Love with You."

———. "Trying to Get to Heaven."

———. "Watered-Down Love." *Shot of Love.*

———. "When He Returns." *Slow Train Coming.*

———. "When You Gonna Wake Up."

———. "With God on Our Side." *The Times They Are A-Changin'.* Columbia PC-8786, 1964.

Electric Prunes. *Mass in F Minor*. Reprise, 1967.

Elegants. "Little Star." Apt 25005, 1958.

Elliman, Yvonne. "I Don't Know How to Love Him." Decca 32785, 1971.

Everly Brothers. "Ebony Eyes." Warner Bros. 5199, 1961.

Five Man Electrical Band. "Signs." Lionel 3213, 1971.

Franklin, Aretha. "Amazing Grace." *Amazing Grace*. Atlantic 2–906, 1972.

————. "Respect." Atlantic 2403, 1967.

Gaye, Marvin. "Can I Get a Witness." Tamla 54087, 1963.

————. "God Is Love." *What's Going On*. Tamla TS-310, 1971.

————. Liner Notes. *Midnight Love*. Columbia 38197, 1982.

————. Liner Notes. *What's Going On*.

————. "Right On."

————. "Wholy Holy."

Genesis. "Jesus He Knows Me." *We Can't Dance*. Atlantic (CD) 82452–2, 1993.

Grant, Amy. "Angels." *Straight Ahead*. Myrrh SPCN-7–01–675706–4, 1984.

————. "Ask Me." *Heart in Motion*. Myrrh 7–01–690761–9, 1991.

————. "El-Shaddai." *Age to Age*. Myrrh MSB-6697, 1982.

————. "Everywhere I Go." *Unguarded*. Myrrh 7–01–680606–5, 1985.

————. "Find a Way."

————. "Fight."

————. "Hope Set High." *Heart in Motion*.

————. "I Will Remember You."

————. "Lead Me On." *Lead Me On*. A&M 5199, 1988.

————. "Love Has a Hold on Me." *House of Love*. A&M 31454–0230–2, 1994.

————. "Love of Another Kind." *Unguarded*.

————. "My Father's Eyes." *My Father's Eyes*. Myrrh MSB-6625, 1979.

————. "1974." *Lead Me On*.

————. "Never Alone." *Never Alone*. Myrrh, 1980.

————. "The Power." *House of Love*.

————. "Saved By Love." *Lead Me On*.

————. "Sharayah." *Unguarded*.

————. "Stepping in Your Shoes."

————. "What About the Love." *Lead Me On*.

————. "Where Do You Hide Your Heart." *Straight Ahead*.

————. "You're Not Alone." *Heart in Motion*.

Grant, Gogi. "Suddenly There's a Valley." Era 1003, 1955.

Green, Al. "Belle." *The Belle Album*. Hi 6004, 1977.

Greenbaum, Norman. "Spirit in the Sky." Reprise 885, 1970.

Greene, Jeanie. "Peter, Put Away Your Sword." *Mary Called Jeanie Greene.* Elektra EKS- 74103, 1971.

Greene, Marlin. "Tiptoe Past the Dragon." *Tiptoe Past the Dragon.* Elektra 75028, 1972.

Grossman, Bernie and Alex Marr. "Say a Prayer for the Boys Out There." New York: Joe Morris Music, 1917.

Guthrie, Arlo. "Gabriel's Mother's Hiway Ballad #16 Blues." *Washington County.* Reprise RS- 6411, 1970.

———. "Power of Love." *Power of Love.* Warner Bros. BSK-3558, 1981.

Guthrie, Arlo with Shenandoah. "Drowning Man." *Outlasting the Blues.* Warner Bros. BSK- 3336, 1979.

———. "Prologue."

———. "Which Side."

Harrison, George. "Hear Me, Lord." *All Things Must Pass.* Apple STCH-639, 1970.

———. "My Sweet Lord."

Hawkins, Edwin Singers. "Oh, Happy Day." Pavilion 20001, 1969.

Head, Murray and the Trinidad Singers. "Superstar." Decca 32603, 1971.

Hendrix, Jimi. "Are You Experienced?" *Are You Experienced?* Reprise RS- 6261, 1967.

———. "Have You Ever Been?" *Electric Ladyland.* Reprise RS-6307, 1968.

———. "Spanish Castle Magic." *Axis: Bold as Love.* Reprise RS-6281, 1967.

———. "Voodoo Chile." *Electric Ladyland.*

Hiatt, John. "Have a Little Faith in Me." *The Best of John Hiatt.* Capitol CDP-7243-8-59179- 29, 1998.

Hibbler, Al. "He." Decca 29660, 1955.

Hill, Faith. "Somebody Stand By Me." *Faith.* Warner Bros. 9362-46790-2, 1998.

Hill, Lauryn. "Final Hour." *The Miseducation of Lauryn Hill.* Ruffhouse CK 69035, 1998.

———. "Forgive Them Father."

———. "I Used to Love Him."

———. "Lost Ones."

———. "The Miseducation of Lauryn Hill."

———. "To Zion."

Highwaymen. "Michael." United Artists 258, 1961.

Hooters. "All You Zombies." *Nervous Night.* Columbia BFC-39912, 1985.

Hunter, Ian. "God (Take 1)." *All-American Alien Boy.* Columbia PC-34142, 1976.

Husky, Ferlin. "Wings of a Dove." Capitol 4406, 1960.

Impressions. "Amen." ABC-Paramount 10602, 1964.

——. "Keep on Pushing." ABC-Paramount 10554, 1964.

——. "Meeting Over Yonder." ABC-Paramount 10670, 1965.

——. "People Get Ready." ABC-Paramount 10622, 1965.

Ink Spots. "My Prayer." Rec. 1939. *The Best of the Ink Spots.* Decca DXB-182, n.d.

Iron Maiden. "Number of the Beast." *The Number of the Beast.* Harvest, 1982.

Jackson, Mahalia. "Move on Up a Little Higher." Rec. 1948. *Mahalia Jackson's Greatest Hits.* Columbia CL-2004, n.d.

James, Tommy and the Shondells. "Crystal Blue Persuasion." Roulette 7050, 1969.

——. "Sweet Cherry Wine." Roulette 7039, 1969.

Jars of Clay. "Flood." *Jars of Clay.* Essential 5573, 1995.

Jewel. "Hands." *Spirit.* Atlantic 82950–2, 1998.

——. "Who Will Save Your Soul." *Pieces of You.* Atlantic 82700–2, 1994.

John, Elton. "Tiny Dancer." *Madman Across the Water.* UNI 93120, 1971.

Judas Priest. "Burn in Hell." *Jugulator.* BMG/CMC International, 1997.

——. "A Touch of Evil." *Painkiller.* Columbia 46891, 1990.

Keaggy, Phil. "Little Ones." *Ph'lip Side.* Sparrow SP-9908, 1980.

——. *Love Broke Thru.* New Song NS-002, 1976.

——. *What a Day.* New Song NS-001, 1973.

——. "What a Wonder You Are." *Town to Town.* Sparrow SPR-1053, 1981.

Kenny, Charles and Nick Kenny. "Cathedral in the Pines." New York: Irving Berlin, 1938.

——. "There's a Gold Mine in the Sky." New York: Irving Berlin, 1937.

King, Jonathan. "Everyone's Gone to the Moon." Parrot 9774, 1965.

Kool Moe Dee. "I Go to Work." *Knowledge Is King.* Jive/RCA 1182–1–J, 1989.

——. "Knowledge Is King."

KRS-One. "Fourth Quarter-Free Throws." *I Got Next.*

——. "Higher Level." *Return of the Boom Bap.* Jive 41517, 1993.

——. "The Truth." *KRS-One.* Jive 41570, 1995.

Laine, Frankie. "Answer Me, O Lord." *I Believe.* Capitol ST-2277, n.d.

——. "I Believe."

Led Zeppelin. "The Battle of Evermore." *Led Zeppelin IV (Zoso).* Atlantic SD-7208, 1971.

——. "Houses of the Holy." *Physical Graffiti.* Swan Song SS-2–200, 1975.

——. "Immigrant Song." *Led Zeppelin III.* Atlantic 7201, 1970.

——. "In My Time of Dying." *Physical Graffiti.*

Lennon, John. "Serve Yourself." *Wonsaponatime*. Rec. 1980. Capitol CDP 724349763920, 1998.

Lennon, John and Plastic Ono Band. "God." *John Lennon-Plastic Ono Band*. Apple SW-3372, 1970.

———. "Imagine." Apple 1840, 1971.

Lewis, Sam M, Pete Wendling, and Geo. W. Meyer. "I Believe in Miracles." New York: Leo Feist, 1934.

Lewis, Sam M., Joe Young, and M.K. Jerome. "Just a Baby's Prayer at Twilight (For Her Daddy Over There)." New York: Waterson, Berlin & Snyder, 1918.

Lewis, Sam M. and Victor Young. "Lawd, You Made the Night Too Long." New York: Shapiro, Bernstein, 1932.

Live. "Selling the Drama." *Throwing Copper*. Radioactive RARD-10997, 1994.

Lloyd, Charles. "TM." *Waves*. A&M SP-3044, 1972.

Loesser, Frank. "Praise the Lord and Pass the Ammunition!" New York: Famous Music, 1942.

London, Laurie. "He's Got the Whole World (In His Hands)." Capitol 3891, 1958.

Lone Justice. "I Found Love." *Shelter*. Geffen GHS-24122, 1986.

———. "Shelter."

———. "You Are the Light." *Lone Justice*. Geffen GHS-24060, 1985.

Loveless, Patty. "When Fallen Angels Fly." *When Fallen Angels Fly*. Epic EK-64188, 1994.

Madonna. "Act of Contrition." *Like a Prayer*. Sire W2-25844, 1989.

———. "Drowned World/Substitute For Love." *Ray of Light*. Maverick/Warner Bros. 9-46847-2, 1998.

———. "Like a Prayer." *Like a Prayer*.

———. "Like a Virgin." *Like a Virgin*. Sire 25157-1, 1984.

———. "Love Tried to Welcome Me." *Bedtime Stories*. Maverick/Sire 9-45767-2, 1994.

———. "Papa Don't Preach." *True Blue*. Sire 9-25442-2, 1986.

———. "Sanctuary." *Bedtime Stories*.

———. "Shanti/Ashtangi." *Ray of Light*.

———. "Sky Fits Heaven."

———. "Spanish Eyes." *Like a Prayer*.

Mamas and the Papas. "California Dreamin'." Dunhill 4020, 1966.

———. "Dedicated to the One I Love." Dunhill 4077, 1967.

Mann, Gloria. "Teenage Prayer." Sound 126, 1955.

Marie, Teena. "Help Youngblood Get to the Freaky Party." *Starchild*. Epic FE-39528, 1984.

———. "Irons in the Fire." *Irons in the Fire.* Gordy G8–997M1, 1980.

———. Liner Notes. *It Must Be Magic.* Gordy G8–1004M1, 1981.

———. Liner Notes. *Lady T.* Gordy G7–992R1, 1980.

———. Liner Notes. *Robbery.* Epic FE-38882, 1983.

———. Liner Notes. *Starchild.*

———. Liner Notes. *Wild and Peaceful.* Gordy G7–986R1, 1979.

———. "My Dear Mr. Gaye." *Starchild.*

———. "Opus III (Does Anybody Care)." *It Must Be Magic.*

———. "Opus III-The Second Movement." *Naked to the World.* Epic FE-40872, 1988.

———. "Portuguese Love." *It Must Be Magic.*

———. "Starchild." Poem. *Starchild.*

———. Untitled Poem. *Lady T.*

———. Untitled Poem. *Naked to the World.*

Marley, Bob and the Wailers. "Chant Down Babylon." *Confrontation.* Island 90085, 1983.

———. "Duppy Conqueror." *Burnin'.* Island 9256, 1973.

———. "Exodus." *Exodus.* Island 9498, 1977.

———. "Get Up Stand Up." *Burnin'.*

———. "Give Thanks and Praises." *Songs of Freedom.* Tuff Gong 512280, 1992.

———. "Jamming." *Exodus.*

———. "Jump Nyabinghi." *Confrontation.*

———. "Positive Vibration." *Rastaman Vibration.* Island 9383, 1976.

———. "Rastaman Chant." *Burnin'.*

———. "Small Axe."

———. "Stiff-Necked Fools." *Confrontation.*

———. "Zion Train." *Uprising.* Island 9596, 1980.

Martindale, Wink. "Deck of Cards." Dot 15968, 1959.

Mattea, Kathy. "Sending Me Angels." *Love Travels.* Mercury 314–532–99–2, 1997.

———. "You're the Power." *Walk the Way the Wind Blows.* Polygram 830405–2–M-1, 1986.

Mayfield, Curtis. "(Don't Worry) If There's a Hell Below, We're All Gonna Go." Curtom 1955, 1971.

Mayfield, Percy. "Please Send Me Someone to Love." Rec. 16 Aug. 1950. *Percy Mayfield: For Collectors Only.* Specialty SP-7000, 1990.

McCormack, John. "God Be with Our Boys Tonight." Victor 64773, 1918.

McDaniels, Gene. "A Hundred Pounds of Clay." Liberty 55308, 1961.

McLachlan, Sarah. "Back Door Man." *Solace.* Arista 18631, 1991.

———. "Building a Mystery." *Surfacing.* Arista 07822–18970–2, 1997.

———. "Drawn to the Rhythm." *Solace.*

———. "Hold On." *Fumbling Towards Ecstasy.* Arista 18725–2, 1993.

———. "Into the Fire." *Solace.*

———. "Witness." *Surfacing.*

McKee, Maria. "Breathe." *Maria McKee.* Geffen 9–24229–2, 1989.

McKee, Maria and Tim White. "Cover Me." *Come As You Are.* Maranatha!, n.d.

McTell, Blind Willie. "Don't You See How This World Made a Change." Rec. 18 Sept. 1933. *The Definitive Blind Willie McTell.* Columbia/Legacy C2K-53234, 1994.

———. "Lord Have Mercy if You Please."

Metallica. "Creeping Death." *Ride the Lightning.* Elektra 60396, 1984.

———. "Devil's Dance." *ReLoad.* Elektra, 1997.

———. "The God That Failed." *Metallica.* Elektra 61113, 1991.

———. "Jump in the Fire." *Kill 'Em All.* Megaforce 069, 1983.

———. "Master of Puppets." *Master of Puppets.* Elektra 60439, 1986.

———. "Thorn Within." *Load.* Elektra 61923, 1996.

———. "To Live Is to Die." *. . . And Justice for All.* Elektra 60812, 1988.

Mr. Mister. "Kyrie." *Welcome to the Real World.* RCA NFL1–8045, 1985.

Mitchell, Joni. "Banquet." *For the Roses.* Asylum SD-5057, 1972.

———. "Blue." *Blue.* Reprise MS-2038, 1971.

———. "Lesson in Survival." *For the Roses.*

———. "Love." *Wild Things Run Fast.* Geffen GHS-2019, 1982.

———. "Roses Blue." *Clouds.* Reprise RS-6341, 1969.

———. "The Same Situation." *Court and Spark.* Asylum 7E-1001, 1974.

———. "The Sire of Sorrow (Job's Sad Song)." *Turbulent Indigo.* Reprise 9–45786–2, 1994.

Morissette, Alanis. "Forgiven." *Jagged Little Pill.* Maverick 9–45901–2, 1995.

Morrison, Van. "Ancient of Days." *A Sense of Wonder.* Mercury 822895, 1985.

———. "Astral Weeks." *Astral Weeks.* Warner Bros. WS-1768, 1968.

———. "Be Thou My Vision." *Hymns to the Silence.* Polydor 849026, 1991.

———. "Full Force Gale." *Into the Music.* Warner Bros. HS-3390, 1979.

———. "Give Me My Rapture." *No Guru, No Method, No Teacher.* Mercury 830077, 1986.

———. "If I Ever Needed Someone." *His Band and Street Choir.* Warner Bros. WS-1884, 1970.

———. "In the Garden." *No Guru, No Method, No Teacher.*

———. "A New Kind of Man." *A Sense of Wonder.*

———. "No Religion." *Days Like This.* Polydor 527307, 1995.

———. "On Hyndford Street." *Hymns to the Silence.*

———. "Rolling Hills." *Into the Music.*

———. "See Me Through Part II (Just a Closer Walk with Thee)." *Hymns to the Silence.*

———. "Take Me Back."

———. "Whenever God Shines His Light on Me." *Avalon Sunset.* Polydor 839262, 1989.

———. "Youth of 1,000 Summers." *Enlightenment.* Mercury 847100, 1990.

Norman, Larry. "The Rock That Doesn't Roll." *In Another Land.* Solid Rock SRA-2001, 1976.

Nyro, Laura. "Stoney End." Rec. 1966. *The First Songs.* Columbia C-31410, 1973.

———. "And When I Die."

Ocean. "Put Your Hand in the Hand." Kama Sutra 519, 1971.

Orioles. "Crying in the Chapel." Jubilee 5122, 1953.

Osborne, Joan. "One of Us." *Relish.* Blue Gorilla/Mercury 314–526–699–2, 1995.

Pacific Gas and Electric. "Are You Ready?" Columbia 45158, 1970.

Page, Patti. "Croce di Oro (Cross of Gold)." Mercury 70713, 1955.

Paige, Jennifer. "Questions." *Jennifer Paige.* Edel America/Hollywood HE-62171-2, 1998.

Paul, Les and Mary Ford. "Vaya con Dios." *Hits of Les and Mary.* Capitol T-1476, n.d.

Pease, Harry, Ed G. Nelson, and Duke Leonard. "Light a Candle in the Chapel." New York: Mills Music, 1942.

Peter, Paul and Mary. "Hymn." *Late Again.* Warner Bros. 1751, 1968.

———. "Tell It on the Mountain." Warner Bros. 5418, 1964.

Peterson, Ray. "Tell Laura I Love Her." RCA Victor 7745, 1960.

Phillips, Leslie. "Black and White in a Grey World." *Black and White in a Grey World.* Myrrh SPCN 7–01–682606–6, 1985.

———. "By My Spirit." *Dancing with Danger.* Myrrh SPCN 7–01–680206–X, 1984.

———. "Down." *The Turning.* Myrrh LA/A&M Horizon SP-0757, 1987.

———. "Expectations." *The Turning.*

———. "Gina." *Beyond Saturday Night.* Myrrh MSB-6743, 1983.

———. "God Is Watching You." *The Turning.*

———. "Hiding in the Shadows." *Dancing with Danger.*

———. "I Won't Let It Come Between Us."

———. "Light of Love."

———. Liner Notes. *Beyond Saturday Night.*

———. "Psalm 55." *Black and White in a Grey World.*

———. "River of Love." *The Turning.*

———. "Walls of Silence." *Black and White in a Grey World.*

Phillips, Sam. "Flame." *The Incredible Wow.* Virgin 7–90919–1, 1988.

———. "I Need Love." *Martinis and Bikinis.* Virgin 7243–8–39438–2–1, 1994.

———. "Signposts."

Polland, Pamela. "Lighthouse." *Pamela Polland.* Columbia KC-31116, 1972.

———. "The Rescuer."

———. "Sing-a-Song Man."

Polnareff, Michel. "If You Only Believe (Jesus for Tonite)." Atlantic 3314, 1975.

Presley, Elvis. "Crying in the Chapel." Rec. 31 Oct. 1960. RCA Victor 447–0643, 1965.

———. "(There'll Be) Peace in the Valley (for Me)." *Peace in the Valley.* RCA Victor EPA-4054, 1957.

———. "Where Did They Go, Lord." RCA Victor 47–9980, 1971.

Prince. "1999." *1999.* Warner Bros. 23720–1F, 1984.

Prince and the Revolution. "I Would Die 4 U." *Purple Rain.* Warner Bros. 1–25110, 1984.

Puckett, Gary and the Union Gap. "Let's Give Adam and Eve Another Chance." Columbia 45097, 1970.

Rascals. "Heaven." Atlantic 2599, 1969.

———. "People Got to Be Free." Atlantic 2537, 1968.

———. "A Ray of Hope." Atlantic 2584, 1968.

Ray, Johnnie. "I'm Gonna Walk and Talk with My Lord." *Johnnie Ray in Las Vegas.* Columbia CL-1093, 1953.

———. "A Sinner Am I." Columbia 4–39788, 1952.

Redding, Otis. "Respect." Volt 128, 1965.

Reynolds, Lawrence. "Jesus Is a Soul Man." Warner Bros. 7322, 1969.

Ritter, Tex. "I Dreamed of a Hill-Billy Heaven." Capitol 4567, 1961.

Robin, Leo and Richard Meyers. "Jericho." New York: Harms, 1929.

Rodgers, Jimmie. "Make Me a Miracle." Roulette 4070, 1958.

Rodgers, Richard and Oscar Hammerstein 2nd. "You'll Never Walk Alone." New York: Williamson, 1945.

Ronstadt, Linda. "He Dark the Sun." *Silk Purse.* Capitol ST-407, 1970.

———. "Rock Me on the Water." *Linda Ronstadt.* Capitol SMAS-635, 1971.

———. "We Need a Whole Lot More of Jesus (And a Lot Less Rock and Roll)." *Hand Sown . . . Home Grown.* Capitol ST-208, 1969.

Russell, Larry, Inez James and Buddy Pepper. "Vaya con Dios (May God Be with You)." New York: Ardmore Music, 1953.

Santana. *Abraxas.* Columbia JC-30130, 1970.

————. *Amigos.* Columbia PC-33576, 1976.

————. *Caravanserai.* Columbia PC-31610, 1972.

————. "Meditation." Lotus. CBS 66-325 (81047/48/49), 1975.

————. *Santana III.* Columbia KC-30595, 1971.

————. *Shango.* Columbia FC-38122, 1982.

————. *Welcome.* Columbia PC-32445, 1973.

Santana, Carlos and Mahavishnu John McLaughlin. *Love Devotion Surrender.* Columbia C- 32034, 1973.

Santana, Devadip Carlos. *The Swing of Delight.* Columbia C2–36590, 1980.

Seay, Davin. Liner Notes. Phillips *Beyond Saturday Night.*

2nd Chapter of Acts. "Hey Whatcha' Say." *In the Volume of the Book.* Myrrh MSA-6542, 1975.

————. *With Footnotes.* Myrrh MSA-6526, 1974.

2nd Chapter of Acts, Phil Keaggy and 'A Band Called David.' "Dance with You." *How the West Was One.* Myrrh MSY-6598, 1977.

————. "My Life."

————. "Now That I Belong to You."

Shakur, Tupac. "I Wonder if Heaven Got a Ghetto." *R U Still Down (Remember Me).* BMG/Jive, 1997.

Shangri-Las. "Long Live Our Love." Red Bird 048, 1966.

Shirelles. "Dedicated to the One I Love." Scepter 1203, 1961.

Shull, Chester R. and George Hoven. "(It's No) Sin." New York: Algonquin Music, 1951.

Sill, Judee. *Heart Food.* Asylum SD-5063, 1973.

————. "The Lamb Ran Away with the Crown." *Judee Sill.* Asylum SD-5050, 1971.

Simon, Paul and Art Garfunkel. "Blessed." *The Sounds of Silence.* Columbia PC-9269, 1965.

————. "Bridge Over Troubled Water." Columbia 45079, 1970.

————. "Flowers Never Bend with the Rainfall." *Parsley, Sage, Rosemary and Thyme.* Columbia PC-9363, 1966.

————. "Go Tell It on the Mountain." *Wednesday Morning, 3 A.M.* Columbia, KCS-9049, 1964.

————. "A Hazy Shade of Winter." Columbia 43873, 1966.

————. "Kathy's Song." *The Sounds of Silence.*

————. "Mrs. Robinson." Columbia 44511, 1968.

————. "7 O'Clock News/Silent Night." *Parsley, Sage, Rosemary and Thyme.*

———. "Sounds of Silence." Columbia 43396, 1965.

———. "You Can Tell the World." *Wednesday Morning, 3 A.M.*

Smith, Michael W. "I Will Be Here for You." Reunion 19139, 1992.

Snider, Todd. "I Believe You." *Step Right Up.* UNI/MCA, 1996.

Snoop Dogg. "See Ya When I Get There." *Da Game Is to Be Sold, Not to Be Told.* Priority, 1998.

Springfield, Rick. "Speak to the Sky." Capitol 3340, 1972.

Springsteen, Bruce. "Adam Raised a Cain." *Darkness on the Edge of Town.* Columbia JC- 35318, 1978.

———. "Mansion on the Hill." *Nebraska.* Columbia TC-38358, 1982.

———. "My Father's House."

———. "Open All Night."

———. "Pink Cadillac." *Tracks.* Columbia CXK-69475, 1998.

———. "Promised Land." *Darkness on the Edge of Town.*

Staple Singers. "I'll Take You There." *Be Attitude: Respect Yourself.* Stax 3002, 1972.

Sting. "All This Time." *The Soul Cages.* A&M CD-6405, 1991.

———. "If Ever I Lose My Faith in You." *Ten Summoners Tales.* A&M (CD)-31454–0070-2, 1993.

Stookey, Noel Paul. "Building Block." *Real to Reel.* Neworld NWS-090477, 1977.

———. "Hymn." *One Night Stand.* Warner Bros. BS-2674, 1973.

———. "Where Do Songs Come From."

Stookey, Paul. "Wedding Song (There Is Love)." Warner Bros. 7511, 1971.

Storm, Gale. "Teenage Prayer." Dot 15436, 1955.

Streisand, Barbra. "Stoney End." Columbia 45236, 1970.

Summer, Donna. "Forgive Me." *Cats Without Claws.* Geffen GHS-24040, 1984.

———. "I Believe in Jesus." *The Wanderer.* Geffen GHS-2000, 1980.

———. Liner Notes. *Bad Girls.* Casablanca NBLP-2-7150, 1979.

———. Liner Notes. *Cats Without Claws.*

———. Liner Notes. *Donna Summer.* Geffen GHS-2005, 1982

———. Liner Notes. *She Works Hard For the Money.* Mercury 812–265–1–M-1, 1983.

———. Liner Notes. *The Wanderer.*

———. "Love Has a Mind of Its Own." *She Works Hard For the Money.*

———. "Unconditional Love."

Sweathog. "Hallelujah." Columbia 45492, 1971.

Taylor, James. "Country Road." Warner Bros. 7460, 1971.

———. "Fire and Rain." Warner Bros. 7423, 1970.

———. "Lo and Behold." *Sweet Baby James.* Warner Bros. 1843, 1970.

Teegarden and Van Winkle. "God, Love and Rock and Roll (We Believe)." Westbound 170, 1970.

Temptations. "Just My Imagination (Running Away with Me)." Gordy 7105, 1971.

Tobias, Charles and David Kapp. "Just a Prayer Away." New York: Shapiro, Bernstein, 1944.

Townshend, Peter. "Content." *Who Came First.* Decca DL 7–9189, 1972.

———. "Nothing Is Everything (Let's See Action)."

———. "Parvardigar."

———. "Pure and Easy."

U2. "Bullet the Blue Sky." *The Joshua Tree.* Island 90581, 1987.

———. "Bullet the Blue Sky." *Rattle and Hum.* Island 91003, 1988.

———. "40." *Live/Under a Blood Red Sky.* Island 7–90127-2, 1983.

———. "Gloria." *October.* Island 9680, 1981.

———. "God Part II." *Rattle and Hum.* Island 91003, 1998.

———. "I Still Haven't Found What I'm Looking For." Island 99430, 1987.

———. "I Will Follow." *Boy.* Island 7–90040-1, 1980.

———. "If God Will Send His Angels." *Pop.* Island, 1997.

———. "Last Night on Earth."

———. "Love Rescue Me." *Rattle and Hum.*

———. "Mofo." *Pop.*

———. "October." *October.*

———. "One." *Achtung Baby.* Island 10347, 1991.

———. "Scarlet." *October.*

———. "Staring at the Sun." *Pop.*

———. "Sunday Bloody Sunday." *War.* Island 90067, 1983.

———. "Tomorrow." *October.*

———. "Wake Up Dead Man." *Pop.*

———. "When Love Comes to Town." *Rattle and Hum.*

———. "Where the Streets Have No Name." Island 99408, 1987.

———. "With a Shout." *October.*

Waller, "Fats." "I Believe in Miracles." 1935. Rec. 5 Jan. 1935. *Swingin' the Organ with "Fats" Waller.* RCA Victor LPT-3040, n.d.

Ward, Billy and the Dominoes. "St. Therese of the Roses." Decca 29933, 1956.

Warwick, Dionne. "I Say a Little Prayer." Scepter 12203, 1967.

We Five. "Let's Get Together." A&M 784, 1965.

Weil, Brucie. "God Bless Us All." Barbour 451, 1953.

Who. "Christmas." *Tommy.* MCA 2–10005, 1969.

Who. "Heaven and Hell." Rec. May 1970. *Thirty Years of Maximum R&B.* MCA MCAD4– 11020, 1994.

Williams, Dar. "Alleluia." *The Honesty Room.* Razor & Tie RT-2816, 1995.

———. "The Christians and the Pagans." *Mortal City.* Razor & Tie RT-2821– 2, 1996.

Williams, Harry and Egbert Van Alstyne. "The Tale the Church Bells Tolled." New York: Jerome H. Remick, 1907.

Willows. "Church Bells May Ring." Melba 102, 1956.

Wilson, J. Frank and the Cavaliers. "Last Kiss." Josie 923, 1964.

Wilson, Jackie. "(Your Love Keeps Lifting Me) Higher and Higher." Brunswick 55336, 1967.

Winwood, Steve. "Higher Love." *Back in the High Life.* Island 9–25448–1, 1986.

Withers, Bill. "Lean on Me." Sussex 235, 1972.

Wonder, Stevie. "As." *Songs in the Key of Life.* Tamla T13–340C2, 1976.

———. "Have a Talk with God."

———. "Heaven Help Us All." Tamla 54200, 1970.

———. "Heaven Is 10 Zillion Light Years Away." *Fulfillingness' First Finale.* Tamla T6–332S1, 1974.

———. "Higher Ground." *Innervisions.* Tamla T6–326S1, 1973.

———. "I Believe (When I Fall in Love It Will Be Forever)." *Talking Book.* T7–3197, 1972.

———. "Jesus Children of America." *Innervisions.*

———. Liner Notes. *Songs in the Key of Life.*

XTC. "Dear God." *Skylarking.* Geffen 24117, 1986.

Youngbloods. "Get Together." RCA Victor 9752, 1967.

Index

www.ingramcontent.com/pod-product-compliance
Ingram Content Group UK Ltd.
Pitfield, Milton Keynes, MK11 3LW, UK
UKHW020412010325
455677UK00029B/860